CONFRONTATION AT GETTYSBURG

CONFRONTATION AT GETTYSBURG

A NATION SAVED, A CAUSE LOST

JOHN DAVID HOPTAK

Series Editor Doug Bostick

Charleston   London

THE
History
PRESS

Published by The History Press
Charleston, SC 29403
www.historypress.net

Cover image: *Charge of the Pennsylvania Reserves at Plum Run (as seen from the Union side)*, by Peter Frederick Rothermel. *Courtesy of the State Museum of Pennsylvania, Pennsylvania Historical and Museum Commission.*

Featuring original, illustrated maps by Mannie Gentile, with additional maps by Hal Jespersen.

First published 2012

Manufactured in the United States

ISBN 978.1.60949.426.1

Library of Congress CIP data applied for.

Dedicated to my family…

my mom and dad, Colleen and David Hoptak; my sister, Dr. Angela Hoptak-Solga; and my beautiful wife, Laura

…for everything.

Contents

A Note on Sources

B ecause the sources utilized in the preparation of this volume were so many, it was decided that instead of flooding the narrative with foot or endnotes, the author would present a bibliographical synthesis at the end of each chapter documenting and summarizing those sources that were relied on most heavily. As will be noticed, this book is a synthesis, based largely on the most recent studies of the battle—published, for the most part, within the past twenty to thirty years—with all quotes garnered from these works. The hope is that anyone seeking to learn more about the battle, or looking to gain further understanding of any particular aspect of it, will next turn to any or all of the sources provided in each of the chapter notes. Full bibliographic citations for all of these works can be found in the bibliography.

Three works laid the foundation for this entire book. They were Edwin Coddington's 1968 classic, *The Gettysburg Campaign: A Study in Command*, which has since gone into many printings and which is still widely regarded as the best single-volume history of the battle; Stephen Sears's masterfully written *Gettysburg* (2003); and Noah Andre Trudeau's equally impressive *Gettysburg: A Testing of Courage* (2002). Steven Woodworth's *Beneath a Northern Sky* and Craig Symonds's *American Heritage History of the Battle of Gettysburg*—two smaller but still richly informative volumes that, like this book, sought to synthesize the battle—were also frequently consulted, as were *Gettysburg: The Confederate High Tide* and *Voices of the Civil War: Gettysburg*, both published by Time-Life Books in 1985 and 1995, respectively.

A Note on Sources

A number of guidebooks and atlases were also heavily used, including *Gettysburg: A Battlefield Guide* by Mark Grimsley and Brooks Simpson (1999), *The Complete Gettysburg Guide* by J.D. Petruzzi and Steve Stanley (2009) and Brad Gottfried's *The Maps of Gettysburg* (2007). Larry Tagg's *The Generals of Gettysburg* provided concise biographical sketches of each of the Union and Confederate brigade, division, corps and army commanders who led troops at Gettysburg and analyses of their roles and actions there, while Brad Gottfried's companion piece, *The Brigades at Gettysburg*, was helpful in providing unit histories and the placements of each of the two armies' brigades on the battlefield.

Introduction

Addressing Gettysburg

Gettysburg is America's most famous battle, and for the past 150 years, it has dominated both the history and the memory of the nation's greatest tragedy, the Civil War. Indeed, it was not long after the cessation of hostilities that Gettysburg came to assume a central place in how Americans remembered their four-year fratricidal struggle. During the postwar years, with the history of the conflict already fast becoming obscured by hindsight and clouded by nostalgia, the Battle of Gettysburg and its larger campaign became in much popular thought the "high-water mark" of the Confederacy—both literally, as it was the battle fought farthest north during the course of the war, and figuratively, as many believed that it was there, at Gettysburg, where the Confederacy came closest to achieving victory. And though this thought has tempered some in recent decades, still today many believe that the Battle of Gettysburg was the "turning point" of the war, when the fortunes of the Confederacy reached their zenith before they began receding.

Fought during the first three days of July 1863, Gettysburg would prove, in terms of numbers engaged, to be one of the largest and, in terms of numbers lost, to be by far the bloodiest battle of the American Civil War. During those three sultry summer days, some 165,000 Americans—90,000 in Union blue and 75,000 in Confederate gray—slaughtered one another on the gently rolling farm fields and rocky hillsides surrounding the southern Pennsylvania town, and when the smoke cleared over the scarred and bloodied landscape and as the thunderous din of battle drifted away, the results were simply horrific. More than 50,000 men—nearly 1 of out of every 3 engaged—had been killed, wounded or captured or went listed as missing in action.

Yet the importance of this great conflagration cannot be measured simply by numbers alone, for the battle's significance extended far beyond its grim and ghastly toll. And while the case can certainly be made, convincingly, that Gettysburg was neither the true "high-water mark" of the Confederacy nor the most important "turning point" moment of the conflict, there can be no denying that the battle was a critical one, for there was much at stake and a lot riding on its outcome.

In the spring of 1863, in the wake of his most recent victory at Chancellorsville, General Robert E. Lee had led his highly vaunted Army of Northern Virginia on an invasion of the North. He sought to draw the Union Army of the Potomac after him and score yet another victory, only this time on Union soil—a victory, he hoped, with results more decisive than what had attended his previous battlefield wins in Virginia. The two armies collided at Gettysburg, where for three days the action raged with a hellish intensity, and when it was over, it was instead the Union army that had emerged triumphant and the Confederate army that was soundly defeated. Lee was turned back, his bold gamble having failed. And although the war would continue on for two more long and devastating years following this unimaginable bloodletting, never again would a Confederate army make it that far north, and it may well be argued that the Army of Northern Virginia would never truly recover from the blow it sustained at Gettysburg. As Private Alexander McNeil of the 12th South Carolina wrote just a few days after the battle, "We came here the best army the Confederacy ever carried into the field, but thousands of our brave boys are left upon the enemys soil and in my opinion our Army will never be made up such material again."

But perhaps it was Abraham Lincoln who, in just 272 words in a speech that lasted fewer than three minutes, best explained the true importance of the sanguinary struggle at Gettysburg and the purpose of the conflict that had divided the nation and pitted Americans against one another in murderous combat. Four months after the battle—on November 19, 1863—President Lincoln traveled to Gettysburg to deliver "a few appropriate remarks" at the dedication of a national soldiers' cemetery that had been established there. Before a vast crowd of some fifteen to twenty thousand people, Lincoln began his address with a history lesson, reminding those in attendance that it had been just "four score and seven years" since the United States—a "new nation," one "conceived in liberty and dedicated to the proposition that all men are created equal"—was first founded. Yet, just a few generations later, that nation now found itself engaged in a "great civil war"—a war, explained Lincoln, being waged to determine whether such a nation "so conceived and so dedicated can long endure."

Lincoln, of course, paid tribute to the fallen—those who gave their lives so that "that nation might live." But their work was finished, said Lincoln, and it was now up to "the living" to commit themselves "to the great task remaining" before them, that from "these honored dead" they were to take "increased devotion to the cause for which they gave their last full measure of devotion." By doing so, they will ensure that the dead "shall not have died in vain," that the nation can and finally will live up to its founding ideals and experience "a new birth of freedom" and "that government of the people, by the people, for the people, shall not perish from the earth."

Lincoln's words have long since become woven into the fabric of America, while the battle itself remains indelibly etched into the national consciousness.

More attention has been paid to Gettysburg than any other battle in American history. The number of books written on this three-day fight extends well into the hundreds, while the number of articles, essays and dissertations documenting certain aspects of the fighting is simply too many to count. Scores of books document in great and minute detail particular portions of the battle, such as at Devil's Den or in the Wheatfield, while others focus on the specific actions of certain individuals or particular units during the fight. Indeed, so substantial is the historiography of Gettysburg that a comprehensive bibliography of the battle could itself fill volumes. Add to this vast historiography the nearly 2 million visitors drawn annually to the Gettysburg National Military Park, and it is clear that Lincoln was certainly correct when in his famous address he further declared that the world would never forget what the soldiers did there.

This book is in no way intended to be an exhaustive account of the battle and its larger campaign. The intention, instead, is to present a concise narrative of the three-day battle, documenting why it was fought, explaining how it unfolded and summarizing its consequences, geared especially toward those who are seeking, perhaps for the first time, a solid understanding of this monumental fight. I set out neither to mine new sources nor to pave new ground; indeed, from the start, my approach has been to be more storyteller than historian. When first asked if I would be interested in writing this title as part of The History Press's Civil War Sesquicentennial Series, I was a bit hesitant to accept since the literature is so vast and the history of the battle and campaign so shrouded in legend, myth and, especially, controversy that it is sometimes difficult to separate fact from fiction. But having previously worked with The History Press in the publication of my 2011 study of the Battle of South Mountain and having been presented with this opportunity, I concluded that this was something I could not pass up.

This work would not have been possible if not for the great support and assistance from a number of friends and fellow Civil War historians and enthusiasts, beginning with Doug Bostick, Adam Ferrell and everyone else at The History Press. As a park ranger at both the Antietam National Battlefield and the Gettysburg National Military Park, I am blessed to work alongside the best rangers and volunteers the National Park Service has to offer. For everything they are and for everything they do, I thank them. My thanks go out especially to Brian Baracz, Dave Maher, Holly Moran and Allan Schmidt, each good friends and colleagues who very early on encouraged me to proceed with this work. For taking the time to read portions of the manuscript, offer helpful suggestions and make critical corrections, I thank Rangers Christopher Gwinn, Daniel Vermilya and Scott Hartwig, chief of interpretation and supervisory historian at Gettysburg National Military Park. For bringing his masterful talents to bear in the development of the hand-drawn illustrated maps used in this book, I thank my friend and colleague Mannie Gentile, while my thanks also go out to Hal Jespersen (www.cwmaps.com) for the use of many of his exceptional Gettysburg battle maps.

Mostly, though, I wish to thank my family—my mom and dad, Colleen and David Hoptak; my sister, Dr. Angela Hoptak-Solga; and my amazing wife, Laura, for their lifetime of support. Indeed, it was a family trip to Gettysburg when I was but five or six years old that first inspired my passion for the study of the American Civil War, and their support has not relented since. It has only grown stronger. None of this would have been possible without them and without their lasting love and unfailing encouragement. Although it is impossible to express my true appreciation, it is nevertheless to them that this book is lovingly and gratefully dedicated.

Chapter 1

Roads North to Gettysburg

M arcellus Ephraim Jones, a thirty-three-year-old lieutenant in Company E, 8th Illinois Cavalry, fired the first shot of the Battle of Gettysburg. It was sometime around 7:30 a.m. on the morning of July 1, 1863, a Wednesday. Jones and several of his men were positioned on the advanced Union picket line several miles northwest of the south-central Pennsylvania town, on a gently rising piece of high ground then known as Wisler's Ridge and today known as Knoxlyn Ridge. Noticing a column of approaching gray- and butternut-clad Confederate soldiers, the lieutenant borrowed a carbine from one of his soldiers, rested it on a fence rail to steady his aim and pulled the trigger. Although the bullet missed its mark, this opening shot pierced the morning silence and initiated the culminating battle of Confederate general Robert E. Lee's second invasion of Union soil—sparking what would prove to be one of the largest clashes and by far the bloodiest battle of the American Civil War.

Or at least so goes the story accepted by most students of the battle. In the postwar years, there would be some debate over who actually fired the first shot of the Battle of Gettysburg, as several other veterans would claim that distinction. But Jones's account has become the one most widely accepted. Still, it is a testament to the momentous nature of the battle that followed that others would make similar claims. For no other battle of the Civil War—excepting, perhaps, the war's opening salvo fired on Fort Sumter—would there be such clamor made to identify the soldier who fired the first shot. One would, for example, be hard-pressed to name the soldier who fired the first shot at Shiloh, Antietam, Spotsylvania, Chickamauga or at any of the other great battles of

Postwar photograph of
Marcellus E. Jones. As
a lieutenant in the 8th
Illinois Cavalry, Jones is
credited as having fired
the first shot of the Battle
of Gettysburg. *Wheaton
Center for History*.

the war. And on no other battlefield of the war—again excepting in Charleston Harbor, South Carolina, where a marker stands commemorating the first shot fired at Sumter—would a monument stand marking the spot where the battle's first shot was fired, as there stands today on Knoxlyn Ridge a few miles northwest of Gettysburg. More than two decades after the battle, in an effort to further his claim and to forever note his place in the history books, Jones in 1886 helped to place a small granite marker near the spot where twenty-three years earlier he had leveled the carbine on that fence rail and fired that first fateful shot at Gettysburg.

The events leading up to this much remembered first shot of the Battle of Gettysburg were set in motion four weeks earlier—on June 3, 1863—and more than one hundred miles away, when the soldiers of Robert E. Lee's Confederate Army of Northern Virginia began marching away from their campsites along the Rappahannock River, near Fredericksburg, Virginia, setting off first westward to Culpeper before turning north, passing down through the Shenandoah Valley and ultimately into Pennsylvania.

When the Gettysburg Campaign thus commenced, Americans had already been at war with one another for twenty-six months, the divided nation having witnessed more than two years of unimaginable loss and bloodshed. Tens of thousands of men in both blue and gray had already fallen, shedding their lifeblood on fields of battle across the war-torn nation. No one at its outset could have imagined what this war would become. And what no one could then know was that this awful struggle—this fratricidal conflict—would continue long after Gettysburg, for yet another two years, with all its remorseless devastation and heartache and with the casualty lists growing ever longer until, by war's end, at least 620,000 soldiers (and thousands of civilians) were dead.

The Confederate States of America had suffered a number of critical reverses during the first two years of the conflict, and by the spring of 1863—even though history would later reveal that the war was just then *only* at its halfway point—there was a growing sense of urgency felt by many in the South, a sense that time was fast running out in their struggle to break away from the Union and establish their own independent nation. The number of U.S. warships and gunboats patrolling the Southern coastline continued to grow, ever-strengthening the blockade and slowly but surely strangling the Confederacy. Inflation ran rampant, while the very social and economic foundation of the Confederacy— slavery—continued to crumble, having received another heavy blow with the recently enacted Emancipation Proclamation. With this, not only had Lincoln redefined the purpose of the war from solely a political struggle to restore a divided nation to a crusade to erase the blight of slavery from the American landscape, but he had also helped to dash Confederate hopes for European recognition of their would-be nation.

Militarily, Confederate forces had also suffered a number of stinging battlefield defeats, particularly in the war's Western Theater, where Union forces had emerged triumphant at such places as Forts Henry and Donelson and at Shiloh. Federal land and naval forces had gained control of the Tennessee and Cumberland Rivers and much of the Mississippi. Nashville and Memphis had fallen, as had New Orleans, the Confederacy's largest city and principal port. And although in the spring of 1863 one Union army in the west, under General William Rosecrans, was seemingly neutralized in Tennessee, another one, much more menacing, under General Ulysses S. Grant, continued to tighten the noose around Vicksburg, the loss of which would cut the Confederacy in two and give the Union unfettered control of the vital Mississippi River. Much of the Confederacy's attention that third spring of the war was thus naturally focused on this deteriorating situation in the west and especially on Grant and his blue columns as they continued to close in on the critical river port.

The situation for the Confederacy was considerably brighter in the war's Eastern Theater, and with affairs looking poor elsewhere, it is little wonder why so many looked to the east, placing much of their hopes for victory on General Lee and the soldiers of his Army of Northern Virginia. Lee had assumed army command the previous year—on June 1, 1862—taking the place of Joseph Johnston, who had fallen seriously wounded at the Battle of Seven Pines, and during the next twelve months, with Lee at its helm, the Army of Northern Virginia compiled an impressive record of battlefield successes: during the Seven Days' battles, at Second Manassas, Fredericksburg and, most recently, at Chancellorsville. Its only major setback had occurred late the previous summer in Maryland, where it had suffered defeats at the Battles of South Mountain and Antietam during Lee's first invasion of Union territory. But despite this reverse in Maryland, Lee had triumphed more than he had failed, oftentimes against seemingly impossible odds, and had by that third year of the war emerged as the Confederacy's greatest chieftain. It was thus

By the spring of 1863, fifty-six-year-old Robert E. Lee had emerged as the Confederacy's greatest military commander, having achieved a sting of stunning battlefield victories, often against great odds. *Library of Congress.*

on his shoulders—and those of his men—where the hopes of the Confederate nation increasingly rested.

Yet even with his stellar record of battlefield victories, Robert E. Lee was one of those who sensed the clock ticking. He was winning battles, to be sure, but the Confederacy was simply not winning the war, and Lee was perfectly aware that the longer the war dragged on, the lesser the chances became for ultimate victory. Lee's own battlefield victories, spectacular though they might have been, had been costly, and any gains had proven temporary. At Chancellorsville, for example, a battle many students of the war regard as Lee's most masterful triumph, the cost of victory was exceptionally high. There, Lee lost more than 20 percent of his army, while casualties in the Union army equaled only 13 percent. Lee had also lost his most trusted subordinate and the Confederacy one of its greatest warriors when General Thomas "Stonewall" Jackson was accidentally shot down by his own troops, mortally wounded. With such a high price paid, Lee was hoping that Chancellorsville's results would have been greater. Instead, the Union army was able to slip away and was soon holding the same positions it had occupied before the battle. One can sense Lee's frustration when he reported that at Chancellorsville, "our loss was severe, and again we had gained not an inch of ground and the enemy could not be pursued." Echoing this growing frustration was Lee's second in command, General James Longstreet, who declared that such victories "were consuming us and would eventually destroy us."

Thus, in the wake of Chancellorsville, Lee set out to achieve more. Instead of remaining on the defensive, awaiting the next Federal offensive, he would seize the initiative and lead his army north a second time. Such a movement had much to offer. It would disrupt Federal plans for the upcoming season and take the conflict away from war-ravaged Virginia, relieving the land and its people from the burdens of war. His men could also gather much-needed provisions from the lush agricultural countryside of the North, and an invasion north would trigger widespread alarm.

More than this, though, Lee went north seeking to achieve yet another battlefield victory, one with greater results. Lee realized that a victory on Union soil would capture the headlines, as all his previous victories had, and though Lee doubted that this movement would compel the Union to shift troops from the west, thereby loosening its grip on Vicksburg, it would, he reasoned, at the very least help to offset the probable loss of the Mississippi port city. A victory on Union soil would also further bolster the cries of the ever-growing number of antiwar activists in the North, clamoring for peace, and would serve to further discredit Lincoln, creating even greater opposition to his efforts at prosecuting the war. Lee thus went north not just hoping to crush the Federal army; he was also hoping to crush the North's willingness to fight, to wear down its resolve and convince the people that this war was a contest they could not win.

In mid-May, a week and a half after the Battle of Chancellorsville and even as the remains of Stonewall Jackson were being laid to rest, Lee traveled to Richmond to plead his case directly to President Jefferson Davis and his cabinet. He found some opposition to his plan; there were those, for example, who wanted to strip troops away from Lee and send them west to help with their beleaguered forces there, while others expressed concern for the safety of Richmond should Lee go north. Still, Lee prevailed in convincing Davis of the soundness of his plan. Having received approval to undertake the invasion, the fifty-six-year-old army commander returned to his army's campsites near Fredericksburg and prepared for the invasion. It was a bold gamble, but the payout—if successful—would be great.

Spirits were high as Lee's gray columns began slipping away from their campsites along the Rappahannock, the men having great confidence both in themselves and in their commander. Colonel E.P. Alexander, one of Lee's finest artillerists, echoed the sentiment of most when he wrote that "there can never have been an army with more supreme confidence in its commander than that army had in Gen. Lee. We looked forward to victory under him as confidently as to successive sunrises." Lee, too, held great faith in his men, the recent victory at Chancellorsville again demonstrating the superb fighting qualities of his soldiers and again showing that they could triumph in the face of tremendous odds. But along with this supreme confidence there developed among the rank and file of the Army of Northern Virginia a false sense of invincibility, a sense that no matter the odds or the circumstances they could—and would—prevail. Lee felt it, too, and the very thought that his men could be defeated was one that seemed to never enter his mind in the campaign ahead.

Lee marched north with an army of seventy-five thousand men, recently reorganized into three corps. Since October 1862, his army had consisted of two corps—commanded by Lieutenant Generals James Longstreet and Thomas J. Jackson—with each numbering about thirty thousand men. Believing these organizations too large and unwieldy, Lee did some restructuring following Chancellorsville, breaking the two corps into three, with each now averaging about twenty thousand soldiers. Longstreet, a reliable soldier and a tough, determined fighter whom Lee once referred to as his "old war horse," maintained command of the First Corps. To replace the lamented Jackson at the helm of the Second Corps, Lee selected the brave if just a bit eccentric Richard Stoddert Ewell, one of Jackson's most trusted subordinates and a hard fighter, who was just then returning to the army after recovering from a severe wound suffered during the Second Manassas Campaign, a wound that had cost him his left leg. To lead the newly organized Third Corps, Lee chose the fiery, combative Ambrose Powell Hill, commander of the famed Light Division, whose heroics at Antietam may have saved the army from possible destruction. In recommending Hill to take the helm of the Third Corps, Lee stated that he was "the best soldier of his grade with me."

Each of the army's three corps was composed of three divisions of infantry, each with its own battalion of artillery, while each of the corps themselves had an artillery reserve. Rounding out the army was a "grand" division of cavalry, totaling nearly ten thousand horsemen, led by the thirty-year-old James Ewell Brown (Jeb) Stuart, who, despite his young age, had proven himself the most capable of cavaliers. All of these officers were West Point graduates, and all were hard-fighting, seasoned soldiers. Yet some questions remained, especially regarding Ewell and Hill, who were superb in divisional command but entirely untested at the higher corps level.

Lafayette McLaws's Division of Longstreet's First Corps led the army's march away from Fredericksburg, setting off on June 3 for Culpeper, some thirty miles to the west. Over the next few days, most of the army's First and Second Corps assembled there, as did Jeb Stuart's horsemen. In addition to providing intelligence on the whereabouts of the Union army, Stuart's task in the campaign ahead would be to provide a screen for the infantry as it moved north from Culpeper, down the Shenandoah Valley and into Pennsylvania. As the infantry prepared to move out, Stuart took advantage of the opportunity to stage two grand reviews, demonstrating the grandeur of the army's mounted arm. "It was a brilliant day," said one of Stuart's aides of the first of these two reviews, "and the thirst for the 'pomp and circumstance' of war was fully satisfied." Lee was equally impressed while observing the second of these reviews, declaring it a "splendid sight." Stuart, said the army commander, "was in all his glory."

Meanwhile, as Stuart orchestrated his mounted spectacles and as Longstreet and Ewell continued to marshal their forces near Culpeper, A.P. Hill and the soldiers of his Third Corps remained behind at Fredericksburg, occupying the attention of Union general Joseph Hooker and his Army of the Potomac, camped out on the opposite side of the Rappahannock.

As Lee's men prepared for the invasion north, their blue-coated foes licked their wounds and took stock of the recent slugfest at Chancellorsville, assessing the performance of the army and its most recent commander. Since he had assumed command of the Army of the Potomac just a few months earlier—in the midst of what was truly a winter of despair for the Union war effort—Joe Hooker had done much to revitalize the spirit of the men, taking a number of steps to instill pride in the ranks and bolster morale. It could thus be a tribute to his efforts, then, that in the aftermath of Chancellorsville, after yet another resounding defeat, there was no real widespread demoralization in the army. Many of the boys in blue could not imagine how they were bested, and many simply could not believe that Hooker had ordered a retreat; blame for the defeat at Chancellorsville, they reasoned, rested on Hooker's shoulders, not on theirs. Confidence remained high, and the men were still full of fight. Captain Stephen Weld may have said it best when he wrote, "This Army of the Potomac is a truly wonderful army. They had something of the English bull-dog in them. You can whip them time and again, but the next fight they go into, they are in good spirits, and as full of pluck as ever." Concluded the Union captain, "Some day or [the] other, we shall have our turn."

The Army of the Potomac suffered 17,000 casualties at Chancellorsville and lost thousands more in the weeks that followed as enlistments expired for those two-year volunteers who had signed up in the spring of 1861 and for those who had volunteered the summer before for a nine-month stint. But as the army marched north in pursuit of Lee, it would be reinforced by troops sent from Washington and other departments so that on the eve of the battle of Gettysburg, its total strength, at least on paper, exceeded 100,000 men. Despite its recent string of defeats, the Army of the Potomac still remained a formidable force and a truly resilient one, capably led by some of the finest brigade, division and corps commanders produced in the entire war. By the onset of the Gettysburg campaign, the cream of the Army of the Potomac was rising near the top.

Of course, at the very top was forty-eight-year-old Joseph Hooker, who, like most of his troops, was still full of fight after the drubbing at Chancellorsville. The problem, however, was developing a sound new strategy. At one point during the unfolding campaign, the ever-critical Marsena Patrick, the army's provost marshal, confided in his diary that Hooker "is entirely at a loss what to do, or how to match the enemy, or counteract his movements." While Patrick was admittedly no admirer of Hooker, in the wake of Chancellorsville there was considerable grumbling among many of the army's highest-ranking officers,

Major General Joseph Hooker had done much to restore morale and inspire confidence within the ranks of the Army of the Potomac, but following the drubbing at Chancellorsville, there were many who wished to see him replaced as army commander. *Library of Congress.*

many having lost all faith in the capabilities of the man dubbed "Fighting Joe." There was some cry in Washington for Hooker's removal, but Lincoln, who appreciated Hooker's aggressiveness, stuck with him, allegedly commenting that he "was not disposed to throw away a gun because it misfired once." He would, instead, "pick the lock and try again."

Hooker did seek out ways to strike a blow but was unsuccessful in devising a strategy that won Lincoln's approval. Well aware of the Confederate movement away from the Rappahannock, Hooker's first inclination was to cross river and strike at Hill's still-entrenched Third Corps, but Lincoln quickly dismissed this idea. Lincoln was more concerned with the Confederate columns that were moving north instead of Hill's inactive men south of the Rappahannock at Fredericksburg. "If [Lee] should leave a rear guard at Fredericksburg, tempting you to fall upon it," Lincoln counseled Hooker, "it would fight in intrenchments, and have you at [the] disadvantage, and so, man for man, worst you at that point, while his main force would in some way be getting an advantage of you northward. In one word, I would not take any risk of being entangled upon the river, like an ox jumped half over a fence, and liable to be torn by dogs, front and rear, with out a fair chance to gore one way or kick another." Thus advised against striking after Hill's lone force at Fredericksburg, Hooker next flirted with the idea of moving his army south and attacking what he reasoned must have been the lightly defended Confederate capital, but Lincoln again turned this down, telling the general that "Lee's army and not Richmond is your sure objective point."

Hooker did have his sights set on at least a portion of Lee's army. Learning of the build-up of Stuart's gray-coated cavalrymen near Culpeper, Hooker ordered his own chief of cavalry, Major General Alfred Pleasonton, to "disperse and destroy" them. The vainglorious Pleasonton, with eight thousand horsemen and three thousand infantry, set out on June 8, the very same day the equally vain but far more capable Stuart was staging the second of his grand reviews. The following morning, near a stopping point along the Orange and Alexandria Railroad named Brandy Station, north of Culpeper, the Union horsemen caught Stuart entirely unawares. What followed was a tremendous clash of sabers, involving nearly twenty thousand troops. The action raged back and forth all day. Stuart was rattled at the unexpected attack, but he recovered quickly and managed to thwart each of

Artist Edwin Forbes captured some of the intensity of the fierce cavalry struggle at Brandy Station, the largest cavalry battle of the American Civil War, fought on June 9, 1863. *Library of Congress*.

the Union thrusts while holding on to the critical high ground and battling the Union troopers to a standstill. Late that afternoon, convinced that he was heavily outnumbered and content with what his men had been able to achieve, Pleasonton ordered a withdrawal across the Rappahannock.

This cavalry battle at Brandy Station was the first engagement of the Gettysburg Campaign and is notable since it proved to be the largest cavalry battle of the entire war. Union forces suffered nearly nine hundred casualties and the Confederates about five hundred. Although Pleasonton's Union troopers withdrew, the battle was tactically inconclusive, and it is difficult to discern any strategic gains for either side. Stuart, although he rebounded nicely and though his men ultimately held the field, was roundly criticized both within the army and among the Southern press for being caught napping; for the prideful Stuart, these criticisms must have stung. On the Union side, Brandy Station was a statement battle, proving that the Federal cavalry was now fully the equal of its once seemingly superior foes. Thus, when Pleasonton's troopers galloped away from the field, they did so with much greater confidence.

The dust had hardly settled on the Brandy Station battlefield when on the following morning June 10—Lee, undeterred by Pleasonton's unexpected attack, directed his men north. The soldiers of Ewell's Second Corps marched away from Culpeper and headed for the Shenandoah Valley, spearheading the campaign. Accustomed to hard marches, Ewell's men covered more than fifty miles within just three days and, by June 13, had arrived south of Winchester, a town garrisoned by a sizable division of Union soldiers under General Robert Milroy. A smaller detachment of U.S. troops was stationed at nearby Berryville. Tasked with clearing the valley of all enemy troops, Ewell prepared to attack. Over the next two days, Ewell's men smashed the hapless and outnumbered Union force at Winchester, inflicting more than 400 casualties and capturing 4,000 of the bluecoats—a full half of Milroy's command—while the breathless Union survivors scattered in all directions. In their victory, Ewell's men also bagged three hundred wagons, fully loaded, as many horses and more than twenty cannons, all at a cost of 270 casualties. For Ewell, it was a brilliant start to his tenure in corps command, appearing to many that he was, indeed, the rightful heir of the mighty Stonewall.

Having cleared the Shenandoah Valley of Union forces and thereby paving the way for the invasion, Ewell's men pressed on all the way to the Potomac River, the dividing line, in the East, between the Union and the Confederacy. On the afternoon of June 15, exactly one month after Lee first

Nicknamed "Old Bald Head," General Richard Ewell was the grandson of the United States' first secretary of the navy, a West Point graduate and Mexican-American War veteran. He was one of Stonewall Jackson's most capable subordinates, and his victory at Winchester convinced many that he was the rightful heir of Jackson's Second Corps. *Library of Congress.*

pitched his invasion scheme to President Davis in Richmond, the soldiers of Robert Rodes's division, along with a brigade of cavalry under General Albert Jenkins, splashed across the river near Williamsport and made their way onto Maryland soil. Edward "Allegheny" Johnson's division crossed the Potomac farther south at Shepherdstown, while Ewell's final division, under Jubal Early, crossed the Potomac at Boteler's Ford, the same crossing point Lee's shattered army had used late the previous summer in its retreat from the blood-soaked battlefield at Antietam. Now, nine months later, they were back again on Union soil.

Ewell's men paused in Maryland a few days, catching their breath and waiting for the rest of the army to catch up, Lee having by this time ordered both Longstreet and A.P. Hill to march north with their commands. Meanwhile, as Ewell's men waited, Albert Jenkins led his cavalry brigade across the Mason-Dixon Line and into Pennsylvania, galloping as far north as Chambersburg, fifteen miles away, striking fear into the hearts of the citizens and wreaking some havoc by cutting telegraph wires and

A.C. Redwood's depiction of Confederate soldiers preparing to cross the Potomac River in mid-June 1863 in what would be Lee's second invasion of Union soil. *From* Battles and Leaders of the Civil War.

burning train depots. They also rounded up scores of African Americans, sending them south under armed guard to be sold into slavery. This ugly practice would only continue in the weeks ahead as all of Lee's army moved into Pennsylvania, though most of the black residents of south-central Pennsylvania, including the nearly two hundred who made Gettysburg their home, fled in advance of Lee's columns, seeking safe haven and hoping to keep their families intact.

At this same time but well over one hundred miles away, General Joseph Hooker, urged by Lincoln to go after Lee, ordered his men north. The Army of the Potomac began moving out on June 13, and since the head of Lee's army under Ewell had a considerable head start, the Union soldiers were forced to endure some hard marching in the sweltering heat in order to catch up.

The Army of the Potomac advanced north on the "inside track," keeping between Lee's columns and Washington. Within a few days and after some

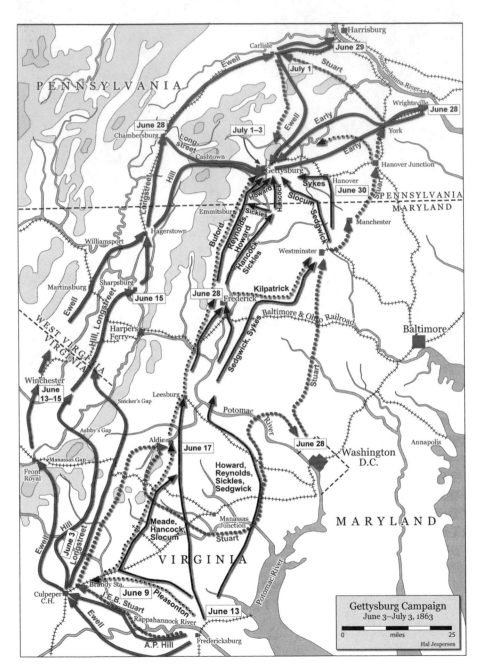

The roads north to Gettysburg. Map by *Hal Jespersen*.

exhaustive marches, the advance of the army arrived on the southern banks of the river that lent it its name, near Leesburg, while its tail stretched south to the familiar battlegrounds near Manassas. The army would remain south of the river for several days while Hooker tried to get a better handle on the precise whereabouts of his foes and better discern Lee's intentions.

Hooker had been kept almost entirely in the dark about the locations of his gray- and butternut-coated foes because of the masterful work done by Jeb Stuart and his horsemen in screening the Confederate drive north and in guarding the gaps in the Blue Ridge Mountains. Hooker's own cavalry under Pleasonton, reinforced at times by some infantry, made a number of determined attacks to pierce the Stuart's screen, such as at Aldie (June 17),

Thirty-nine-year-old Alfred Pleasonton, commander of the Cavalry Corps of the Army of the Potomac, tried several times to break through Jeb Stuart's tight screen in the gaps of the Blue Ridge Mountains but was each time unsuccessful. *Library of Congress.*

Artist Alfred Waud's sketch of the Battle of Upperville, June 21, 1863, a battle that resulted in an estimated four hundred casualties. *Library of Congress.*

Middleburg (June 18–19) and Upperville (June 21), but all to no avail. The only result of these spirited clashes was the death, injury or capture of nearly nine hundred Union cavalrymen, while casualties in Stuart's command over this five-day span numbered just over five hundred.

With Stuart ably defending the mountain gaps and as Longstreet's and Hill's soldiers continued their trudge up the valley, Lee ordered Ewell to move north into Pennsylvania. Should the state capital of Harrisburg "come within your means," Lee straightforwardly told his Second Corps commander, "capture it." Crossing the Mason-Dixon Line, Ewell's Second Corps cast a wide net as it spread out across much of south-central Pennsylvania. Rodes's and Johnson's Divisions marched north up the Valley Turnpike, heading toward Harrisburg by way of Shippensburg and Carlisle, while Early's brigades followed a more easterly route before turning right and heading toward York and the Susquehanna River at Wrightsville beyond. As Ewell spread out across Pennsylvania, A.P. Hill and James Longstreet led their corps, in turn, across the Potomac, through Maryland and onward into the Keystone State. Last across the river was General George Pickett's division, at the rear of Longstreet's First Corps, which crossed on June 25.

Spirits soared as Lee's rank and file made their way deeper into Union territory than ever before, many of them jibing the Pennsylvania residents they encountered along the way that they had at last returned to the Union. British officer Arthur Fremantle, who traveled with the Army of Northern Virginia, captured the spirit of Lee's troops as they marched across southern Pennsylvania, recording that "[a]t no other time…have the men been so well equipped, so well clothed, so eager for a fight, or so confident of success." Yet, along with this supreme confidence, there was also a detectable desire for vengeance, a yearning to make the Northern people feel the proverbial hard hand of war as the people of the South had so long endured at the hands of their contemptuous Yankee foes. To help prevent against any willful destruction of private property, Robert E. Lee issued General Orders No. 72, which forbade his soldiers from pillaging and required that all requisitioned goods be paid for. In this, Lee sought to curb the level of plunder and to at least give the impression that his men were much better behaved and more respectful of private property than Union troops operating in the South.

Despite his best efforts, many of Lee's men paid little heed to these instructions. "The officers in command issued some stringent orders with reference to private property," said one of Lee's men, "but the soldiers paid no more attention to them than they would the cries of a screech owl." Officers turned a blind eye as their men raided pantries, ransacked barns and merchants' stores, stole livestock or confiscated horses from Pennsylvania farmers. A soldier in Longstreet's corps bragged that the men "lived on the very fat of the land—milk, butter, eggs, chickens, turkeys, apple butter, pear butter, cheese, honey, fresh pork, mutton & every other imaginable thing that was good to eat." Many Pennsylvanians fled at the approach of the gray columns, taking with them their money, livestock and other valuables, while many others, having no real choice in the matter, accepted with grim resignation the receipts or the worthless Confederate scrip offered in return for their goods.

Ewell's soldiers had the greatest opportunity for plunder and for the gathering of good food and provisions from the lush Pennsylvania countryside. As they made their way into each of the towns in their path, a list of demands was presented to the citizens. At York, for example, which surrendered to Early's men on June 27, General Early demanded nearly thirty thousand pounds of baked bread, thirty-two thousand pounds of beef, two thousand pairs of shoes and $100,000 in cash. As in most other towns, the people of York could not meet all of these demands. Satisfied that they had at least made an honest effort, however, Early accepted the $28,000 that had been quickly raised. That same day, Richard Ewell presented a similar list of demands to the people of Carlisle, though he was only looking for twenty-three thousand pounds of bacon, one hundred sacks of salt, 1,500 barrels of flour and three thousand pounds each of coffee and sugar.

If these sometime preposterous demands for shoes, flour and other such goods were not met, as was true with Ewell's list of demands in Carlisle, the Confederates simply took what they could gather, searching through homes and businesses. In the end, Ewell's men carried out a tremendously successful foraging expedition, gathering much-needed foodstuffs, thousands of horses and heads of cattle and hundreds of wagons laden with other provisions. There was very little real wanton destruction of property. One of Lee's officers later concluded, "There was, in short, a good deal of lawlessness, but not so much as might have been expected under the circumstances." Still, the Pennsylvanians were none too pleased. "The people look as sour as vinegar," wrote Second Corps commander Richard Ewell, "and I have no doubt would gladly send us all to Kingdom come if they could."

The Caledonia Iron Works at the western base of South Mountain was not spared the torch. Marching east on their way to York on June 26, the soldiers of Early's Division burned the ironworks to the ground, largely to send a message to its owner, the abolitionist congressman Thaddeus Stevens. After setting fire to the ironworks, Early's men continued their march east. Crossing over South Mountain at the Cashtown Pass, these veteran troops encountered the 26th Pennsylvania Emergency Militia, a hastily organized regiment composed largely of eager men from the surrounding area, but it did not take long for Early's men to send these rookie soldiers running.

After dispersing this small band of eager but entirely untrained troops, Early directed General John Gordon to take his brigade to the nearby market town of Gettysburg, the seat of Adams County. Riding in advance of Gordon's Georgians was a battalion of Virginia cavalry nicknamed the "Comanches." Professor Michael Jacobs, a resident of town, remembered that the Comanches galloped into Gettysburg at 3:15 p.m., "shouting and yelling like so many savages from the wilds of the Rocky Mountains; firing their pistols, not caring whether they killed or maimed man, woman, or child." Gordon's men marched into town behind the pistol-wielding Virginians, as did division commander Early, who then presented a list of demands. He was told that the town could provide neither the requested food nor the money he demanded but that the town's storeowners would open their shops and provide whatever they could. Early did not make an issue of it, later stating that "[t]he authorities of Gettysburg declared their inability to furnish any supplies, and a search of the stores resulted in securing only a very small quantity of commissary supplies, and about two thousand rations were found in a train of cars."

Gordon's men spent the night in Gettysburg, and the following morning, June 27, they set off for York. Believing the worst of the Confederate invasion to be over, the people of Gettysburg breathed a collective sigh of relief as Gordon's men marched away from town. No one could have then predicted that the war would return to Gettysburg with a fury just four days later.

Roads North to Gettysburg

General Jeb Stuart was one of the war's greatest cavalry commanders, but his otherwise stellar record would be tarnished after the Gettysburg Campaign, first for being caught off-guard at Brandy Station and then for his "ride" around the Army of the Potomac, during which he was out of touch with Lee. *From Miller's Photographic History of the Civil War.*

Notably absent from the Army of Northern Virginia as it maneuvered throughout Pennsylvania during this last week of June was Jeb Stuart and much of the army's mounted arm. In one of the Gettysburg Campaign's most enduring controversies, Stuart, on June 25, had galloped *away* from the army with three of his five brigades—more than half of the army's cavalry force in a ride around the Army of the Potomac.

Having fended off the Union's efforts at breaking through his cavalry screen in the Blue Ridge Mountains, Stuart met with Lee and proposed this operation, having successfully undertaken two such rides the previous year—during the Peninsula Campaign in June and then again in October following the Maryland Campaign. Lee liked the idea, and on June 22 23, with Hooker still idle south of the Potomac, he issued the necessary instructions to Stuart. Lee reminded his cavalry chief that his primary task was to screen the right flank of the army as it moved into Pennsylvania, but if he believed he could accomplish this by passing around Hooker and then linking back up with the army in Pennsylvania, then he was permitted to do so, "doing all the damage you can," but with Lee cautioning him to be "watchful and circumspect" in all his movements.

The purpose of such a bold undertaking was to garner intelligence, gather provisions and disrupt Federal communications, essentially to cause headaches both within the Union army and in Washington. Stuart might also have viewed this as an opportunity to regain some of the glory lost by being caught off guard at Brandy Station. Whatever the motivation, Stuart received Lee's largely discretionary orders—all too often the case with Lee—and prepared for the operation. As per Lee's instructions, Stuart directed that two of his brigades—under Generals William "Grumble" Jones and Beverley Robertson, with a total of 2,700 men—remain with the army's main body, continuing to screen its advance north and protect its supply lines south. Then, with his three remaining brigades—arguably the finest horsemen in the Army of Northern Virginia, led by Stuart's most capable subordinates in the form of Fitzhugh Lee, Wade Hampton and John Chambliss—Stuart set out on what would prove his most famous (or infamous) ride. As events showed, these three brigades would be away from the army and Stuart himself would be out of contact with Lee for the next seven days—much longer than both he and Lee had ever anticipated—and would not link back up with the army until July 2, after the two sides had already come to blows at Gettysburg.

During the week they were away from the army, Stuart's troopers succeeded admirably in gathering provisions and disrupting Federal communications. However, Stuart's absence from Lee would be deeply felt. Critics of Stuart later claimed that he left Lee blind, causing the Confederate army commander to stumble into battle at Gettysburg without any clear idea of either the lay of the land or even the whereabouts of the Union army. Stuart's defenders counter by arguing that he had carried out—or at least attempted to carry out—all Lee had instructed of him and pointing out that the two brigades Stuart had left behind should have been enough to provide sound intelligence. Whether things might have turned out differently had Stuart not undertaken this ride cannot be known, but the controversy surrounding it remains one of Gettysburg's most enduring.

Setting out early on the morning of June 25, Stuart very quickly ran into an unexpected problem: the road he planned to take was clogged by Union infantry. Hooker was again on the move, leading his army across the Potomac and pushing toward Frederick, Maryland. Stuart dispatched a message to Lee, informing him that the Union army was in motion, heading north across the river. However, Stuart did not believe that Hooker's drive north of the Potomac necessitated his return to the army, and so he turned his horsemen farther south, forced now to take a different and longer route in getting around the Army of the Potomac. What Stuart did not know was that as his columns moved farther away from their own army, the message he had sent to Lee informing him of Hooker's advance north of the Potomac never reached the army commander. Further, much more inexplicably and through no fault of Stuart's, the two brigades he had left behind with Lee, under Jones and Robertson, remained south of the Potomac, defending the mountain gaps, while the rest of the army trudged north, where it was of little, if any value. Additionally, neither Jones nor Robertson provided any intelligence to Lee on the whereabouts of Hooker and his Union army. Because of this and Stuart's undelivered dispatch, it would not be until very late on the night of June 28—a full three days after Stuart began his ride—that Lee would finally learn that the Army of the Potomac was north of the Potomac and gathered near Frederick, just a hard day's march from his divided forces in southern Pennsylvania.

As soon as his own intelligence sources confirmed that the Army of Northern Virginia was in Pennsylvania, Hooker, on June 25, put his army in motion. Lincoln had been urging Hooker to attack. Earlier in the campaign, when reports reached Washington that the head of Lee's army was at Winchester and its tail near Fredericksburg, the president told his army commander that "the animal must be slim somewhere," suggesting that he find where that was and strike it.

After putting his army in motion toward Frederick, Hooker's attention next turned to what he believed was the more urgent matter of reinforcements. Believing himself outnumbered, Hooker hounded General in Chief Henry Halleck for more men. He was able to secure a few brigades, but Hooker's main focus was on the large, ten-thousand-man force at Harpers Ferry, where Hooker believed they were "of no earthly account." He wanted these troops to bolster his own army, but Halleck turned down all of Hooker's requests, which compelled Hooker to appeal directly to Lincoln, claiming that he simply could not work with Halleck. More concerned with prosecuting the war than with getting in between personal feuds, Lincoln forcefully reminded Hooker of the chain of command, telling him in no uncertain terms that he was to report directly to Halleck and that he was to obey all of Halleck's orders. But Hooker would not be outdone. On June 27, from his headquarters near Frederick, he decided to force the issue by again demanding the Harpers Ferry garrison; if denied this time, he wished to be relieved of his command.

Lincoln's patience with Hooker had been wearing thin. Despite avowing to stick with him in the immediate aftermath of Chancellorsville, Lincoln had, for the past several weeks, been considering replacing Hooker and had even sounded out a few generals about army command—men such as John Reynolds, John Sedgwick and Darius Couch, who each expressed no real desire for the job. Hooker's most recent spat with Halleck finally pushed Lincoln over the edge, and when he received Hooker's ultimatum, Lincoln obliged, relieving Hooker and appointing forty-seven-year-old Major General George Gordon Meade, commander of the army's Fifth Corps, in his place. For the Army of the Potomac, it was the third change of commanders within the past eight months.

George Meade was a soldier's soldier. Born on December 31, 1815, in Cadiz, Spain, Meade was an 1835 graduate of West Point. As a lieutenant in the army's elite Corps of Topographical Engineers, he turned in a creditable performance in Mexico and, shortly after the commencement of the Civil War in 1861, was commissioned a brigadier general of volunteers. Strict and no-nonsense, Meade cared little for appearances and, like Lee, possessed a fiery, sometimes explosive temper. Personally brave, Meade was always one to lead from the front. At the Battle of Glendale in late June 1862, he was shot through the lungs and severely wounded. Meade rose steadily in rank, commanding first a brigade, then a division and finally a corps, earning the respect of his men if not their love.

Meade's peers thought highly of him, so much so that when Lincoln began sounding out potential candidates to replace Hooker, they all recommended Meade for the post. What might have made Meade particularly appealing to Lincoln was that in an army so heavily influenced by politics, he had neither political ambition nor any ties to politicians in Washington. While most famously described by one Union soldier as that "old goggle-eyed snapping turtle," to a captain in the 20th Massachusetts, Meade had more the look of "a good sort of a family doctor." But perhaps it was James Rusling, a quartermaster in the army's Third Corps, who best described the Army of the Potomac's newest—and as it turned out, last—commander. Meade, said Rusling, was "tall and slender, gaunt and sad of visage, with iron-gray hair and beard, ensconced behind a pair of spectacles, and with popular traits about him, but with a keen and well-disciplined intellect, and cool and sound judgment." Concluded the observant Rusling, "[B]y both education and temperament, he was every inch a soldier."

Meade was awoken from his slumber at 3:00 a.m. on Sunday morning, June 28. His first thought was that, for some reason, he was being placed under arrest. When told instead that he was replacing Hooker at the helm of the army, Meade protested, but there was to be no appeal—these were orders. As Meade later wrote to his wife, "[A]s a soldier, I had nothing to do but accept and exert my utmost abilities to command success."

Meade's first task upon assuming army command was to ascertain the locations of his army's various corps, which he learned during what must have been an awkward meeting with the displaced Hooker. Then, from both his cavalry and from the army's intelligence bureau, Meade was brought up to speed with the latest information on the whereabouts of Lee. Taking over army command in the very midst of a campaign, Meade inherited a momentous task. Indeed, in his orders appointing Meade to army command, Halleck summed it up nicely, telling him that "[n]o one ever received a more important command."

Meade had to be careful. Like they were for his predecessor, George McClellan, during Lee's first invasion north the previous September, Meade's instructions were to both go after and drive Lee back while

Forty-seven-year-old George Meade, a career soldier and gifted engineer, learned of his appointment to army command early on the morning of June 28, 1863. Just three days later, his army would come to blows with Lee's at Gettysburg. *Library of Congress.*

at the same time keeping between the Confederate army and Washington in order to protect the capital. In addition, following the twin disasters at Fredericksburg and Chancellorsville, the Army of the Potomac could ill afford to lose another fight, especially one waged on Northern soil. But Meade rose quickly to the great challenge, displaying an eagerness to bring Lee to battle. As he later explained, "My object being at all hazards to compel [Lee] to loose his hold on the Susquehanna and meet me in battle at some point. It was my firm determination, never for an instant deviated from, to give battle wherever and as soon as I could possibly find the enemy." In a letter to his wife, he declared, "I am going straight at them and will settle this thing one way or the other. The men are in good spirits...and with God's blessing I hope to be successful."

Meade issued orders for his army to continue advancing north from Frederick. General John Reynolds, a close friend of Meade's, commanded the army's left wing, consisting of his own First Corps, plus the Third and Eleventh under Generals Daniel Sickles and Oliver Howard, respectively. Reynolds led his three corps toward Emmitsburg, near the Pennsylvania border and just a few miles south of Gettysburg, while the army's other corps moved toward Taneytown and Westminster.

Temperatures soared during these final days of June, and hundreds of soldiers collapsed from the heat. Exhausting marches were the order of the day as the men covered great distances. Winfield Scott Hancock's Second Corps, for example, marched more than thirty miles on June 29. But despite the heat and the relentless marching, overall the Union soldiers were, as Meade noted, in good spirits, their confidence buoyed by the grateful citizens of Maryland and later Pennsylvania, who lined the roadways, cheering on the troops, waving flags and handing out fresh bread and water. Sergeant James Wright of the 1st Minnesota Infantry remembered the kind reception the Union troops received on their march through Maryland and on into Pennsylvania:

> *Flags, handkerchiefs, aprons and sun-bonnets were waved from windows, door-steps and front yard fences as we tramped hurriedly on. These things had a soothing effect on our disturbed feelings, and a little later, when we made a short halt, women and children came with baskets of buttered bread and real doughnuts, pails of water and jugs of buttermilk, the boys cheered them with hearty goodwill.*

There was a growing sense in the ranks that they were heading toward a showdown with Lee. Meade, too, believed that battle was imminent. On June 30, he issued orders for his men to carry three days' rations and sixty rounds of ammunition—a sure sign that battle was in the offing.

Meade's strategy was to seek out good ground and fight a defensive battle. As his forces continued northward and continued to close up with Lee, Meade sent out his engineers to find favorable ground, the intention being to place his army in a position that would compel Lee to attack *him*. That position, or so he believed, was soon located—a few miles south of the Mason-Dixon Line, near Taneytown, on high ground overlooking Pipe Creek, a tributary of the Monocacy River. Thinking this to be an ideal defensive position, Meade instructed the army's chief engineer, Gouverneur K. Warren, to lay out a defensive line there, while his headquarters staff prepared what came to be known as the Pipe Creek Circular. Sent out early on the morning of July 1, this circular instructed his subordinates that should they encounter Lee and should Lee attack, they were to fall back to this position, drawing Lee toward it. Later, critics of Meade would claim that this Pipe Creek Circular was proof positive that he did not want to fight at Gettysburg, but this was simply not the case. Meade was certainly not wedded to this Pipe Creek position should other defensible ground be found—as it would be at Gettysburg—and the circular was intended only as a contingency measure.

Meade was greatly aided in his efforts by the very good intelligence he was receiving both on the size of Lee's army and on the locations of each of the Confederate corps. He knew that most of the Confederate army—Longstreet's and A.P. Hill's corps—was concentrated near Chambersburg, while Ewell's men were scattered farther to the north and east. Reports also arrived that Stuart's errant column was across the Potomac and on Maryland soil. Stuart's column crossed the Potomac at Great Falls, twelve miles upriver from Washington, early on the morning of June 28—indeed, at the very same time Meade, in Frederick, was being stirred awake with news of his elevation to army command. Later that same day, Stuart's men captured 125 wagons at Rockville, fully loaded with grains and provisions; tore up some railroad tracks; and cut, temporarily it turned out, the telegraph link between Washington and the army charged with defending it. Stuart then trotted off toward Westminster. Meade sent some of his own cavalry chasing after Stuart, but he did not pay too much attention to Stuart's galloping columns, believing that Lee was his true objective and as such he would have to "submit to the cavalry raids around me in some measure."

Stuart, by this point, had fallen seriously behind schedule, and not only had he lost contact entirely with Lee, but also now the Union army moving north out of Frederick—was squarely between his force and the Army of Northern Virginia. Still attempting to link up with Ewell and now being harassed by Union cavalry nipping at his column's heels, Stuart continued north and crossed into Pennsylvania early on morning of June 30.

Robert E. Lee had not heard a single word from Stuart since June 25. It came as something of a surprise, then, when late on the night of June 28, the Confederate army commander learned from a spy named Henry Harrison that the Army of the Potomac was fully across the Potomac and as far north as Frederick, only a hard day's march south of the Mason-Dixon Line. The previous year in Maryland, during Lee's first invasion north, the Union army, then under McClellan, had caught up to him rather unexpectedly while his army was widely scattered, forcing him to give battle at South Mountain. He would now ensure that this would not happen again. With his three corps widely separated across southern Pennsylvania, Lee immediately set out to corral them back together, issuing orders for his army to converge east of South Mountain and gather either at Cashtown, a small hamlet at the mountain's eastern base, or at nearby Gettysburg, eight miles southeast of Cashtown, where a vast network of roads entering town from all points of the compass would easily allow his forces to gather.

On June 29, following Lee's orders, A.P. Hill's and Longstreet's men set out from Chambersburg, marching east toward South Mountain. They were later followed by Edward Johnson's division of Ewell's Second Corps, which had been at Shippensburg. Ewell, for his part, was just then with Rodes's men at Carlisle, planning to move on to Harrisburg. The orders recalling Ewell to move south to either Cashtown or Gettysburg, "as circumstances might dictate," came as a disappointment to the Second Corps commander, who had envisioned great laurels for capturing the Pennsylvania capital. Robert Rodes said as much when he wrote that seizing Harrisburg was a prospect "contemplated with eagerness" by every man in his division. Meanwhile, Ewell's final division, under Early, received orders to march west from his present locations north of York in order to link up with Rodes as his men tramped south from Carlisle. Lee was neither panicked nor greatly alarmed by the report he had received from Harrison late on June 28; after all, he had come north to draw the Union army to battle. What did trouble him, though, was that he learned of the Union army's locations—and of its new commander, Meade—not from his trusted cavalry chief Stuart, whose absence was now starting to weigh heavily on him, but from a spy instead.

As opposed to Lee, Meade was very well served by his own mounted arm as it screened his army's advances north through Maryland and into Pennsylvania. General Judson Kilpatrick's division screened the Army of the Potomac's right flank as it made its way to Taneytown and beyond. Screening the army's left flank was the hard-fighting John Buford, described by a member of Meade's staff as a "compactly built man of middle height with a tawny mustache and a little triangular, gray eye, whose expression is determined, not to say sinister… he is a soldierly-looking man…of good disposition but not to be trifled with."

Buford's task was to cover the army's left wing under Reynolds that, on June 30, was reaching its destinations at both Marsh Creek and Emmitsburg.

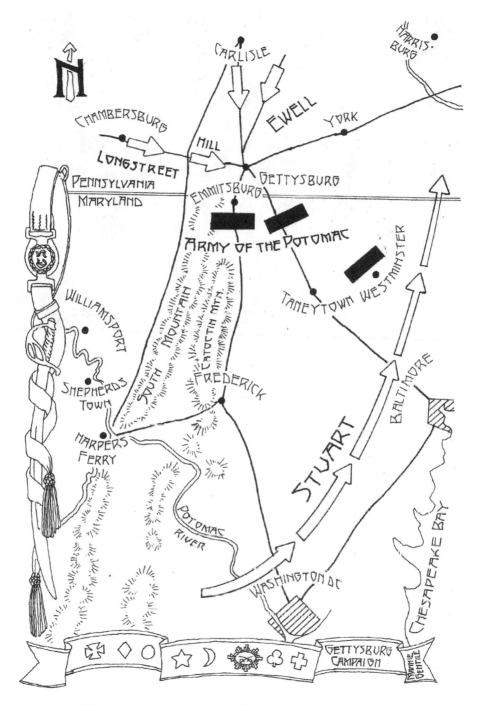

By June 30, 1863, the armies were set on a collision course toward Gettysburg. *Map by Mannie Gentile.*

General John Buford (seated) and his staff. A gifted horseman, Buford's shining moment would come at Gettysburg. Just five months later, Buford was dead, having succumbed to typhoid fever at the age of thirty-seven. *Library of Congress*.

Buford was to push farther north, to Gettysburg, where he would continue to gather information and better fix Lee's locations. With two of his three brigades—under Colonels William Gamble and Thomas Devin—Buford set off for the town, arriving there to a hero's welcome at about 11:00 a.m. on Tuesday, June 30. The people of Gettysburg, whom Buford described as being in a "terrible state of excitement," turned out to greet the dusty horsemen, offering up bread, baked goods and water, while children sang out patriotic songs. No doubt pleased by this very welcoming reception, Buford still had a job to do.

A seasoned campaigner, Buford liked what he saw when examining the terrain around Gettysburg, for not only were the roads of vital importance, but the town itself was also surrounded by high ground, particularly to the south. It was ground, Buford realized, that was well suited and even ideal for defense. Buford was aware that Lee's army was close; the main body, under Hill and Longstreet, he knew to be just to the west, with its lead elements already at Cashtown, just eight miles away, while other reports placed another column—under Rodes—advancing from the north. Buford reported all of this to both Reynolds and Meade, who was just then establishing army headquarters near Taneytown.

Determining to hold Gettysburg, Buford began establishing a line of defense west and north of town, on a series of high ridgelines, in an attempt to cover as many of the roads leading into town as possible. Buford's decision was a bold one. Although he had fewer than three thousand men, he sought to put up a fight should the Confederate infantry advance toward town. His plan was to delay any Confederate advance long enough for Reynolds and his infantry to arrive. He would then leave it to Reynolds to decide whether Gettysburg would be a good place to fight a defensive battle. The grizzled cavalryman later explained his thoughts to his brigade commanders. Colonel Devin boasted that they would be able to hold back any Confederate force Lee threw their way. "No you won't," Buford snapped back, "They will attack you in the morning and they will come booming—skirmishers three deep. You will have to fight like the devil to hold your own until supports arrive."

That Tuesday night, Buford's nearest supports lay just five miles south of Gettysburg, near Marsh Creek, where the First Corps went into bivouac. Oliver Howard's Eleventh Corps and Dan Sickles's Third Corps were a few miles farther south near Emmitsburg. The rest of the Union army was spread out across some twenty-five miles farther to the east and just south of the Mason-Dixon Line, stretching from Emmitsburg, through Taneytown and toward Manchester. Receiving Buford's reports, Meade ordered Reynolds late on June 30 to march to Gettysburg the following morning to Buford's aid. Reynolds would receive these instructions early the following morning, on Wednesday, July 1.

On June 30, as Buford's cavalrymen were getting acquainted with the lay of the land around Gettysburg and setting up a defensive line north and west of town, A.P. Hill's Third Corps, Army of Northern Virginia, continued to gather at Cashtown. Henry Heth's division had arrived there the previous day. Heth was brand new to divisional command but had earned the esteem of both his immediate superior, A.P. Hill—one of his West Point classmates—and of army commander Lee. From Cashtown, Heth ordered Brigadier General J. Johnston Pettigrew, one of his brigade commanders, to push on to Gettysburg on a foraging expedition, with instructions "to search the town for army supplies (shoes especially) and return the same day." Presumably, Heth was either unaware that Gordon's

Ambrose Powell Hill was never one to back away from a fight. When asked by Henry Heth if he had any objections to him returning to Gettysburg on the morning of July 1, Hill allegedly replied, "None in the world." *Library of Congress.*

Brigade had passed through town just a few days earlier, or he may have simply sought to round up what may have been hidden from Gordon's men.

With three of his North Carolina regiments, plus a regiment of Virginians borrowed from John Brockenbrough's brigade, Pettigrew set off on his expedition. Pettigrew was under strict orders not to engage any enemy force he might encounter. Thus, when he spotted Union horsemen (Buford's men, as it turned out) galloping toward Gettysburg from the south, kicking up clouds of dust as they rode along the Emmitsburg Road, Pettigrew wisely turned around and marched back to Cashtown, where he reported what he believed to be a sizable Union force just down the road at Gettysburg—trained horsemen, he said, and not untrained militia.

Heth and Hill listened carefully to Pettigrew's report but thought that surely he was mistaken. Neither believed that the advance of the Army of the Potomac was that close; the troops Pettigrew detected were most likely only a local home guard. Even so, the sickly Hill resolved to head back toward Gettysburg the following morning to find out exactly what kind of troops

Pettigrew had seen just eight miles from his corps' campsites at Cashtown. This time, though, he would order a much larger force to march toward Gettysburg: Heth's entire division, backed up by Dorsey Pender's—fifteen thousand men in all. Hill, never one to back away from a fight, later reported that he simply "intended to advance the next morning and discover what was in my front." When he notified Lee that he would be moving on toward Gettysburg on the morning of July 1, the army commander approved but repeated his standing orders not to precipitate battle—at least not until his army was fully concentrated.

And so it was that with A.P. Hill deciding to head back toward Gettysburg on the morning of July 1 and with General John Buford determining to resist any Confederate advance toward town, the stage was set for what would prove to the bloodiest battle of the Civil War.

CHAPTER NOTES

For further study of the campaign leading up to the battle and its many incidents, see Coddington, chapters 1–10 (pages 3–241); Sears, chapters 1–6 (pages 1–153); Trudeau, prologue and chapters 1–11 (pages 1–143); and Woodworth, chapters 1–3 (pages 1–46). See also John Schildt's 1978 publication *Roads to Gettysburg*. For in-depth and detailed studies on each of the various battles and skirmishes fought on the way to Gettysburg, see *The Battle of Brandy Station* by Eric Wittenberg; *The Cavalry Battles of Aldie, Middleburg, and Upperville: June 10–27, 1863* by Robert O'Neill Jr.; *Gateway to Gettysburg: The Second Battle of Winchester* by Larry Maier; and *The Second Battle of Winchester* by Charles Grunder and Brandon Beck. Stuart's controversial role in the campaign has captured much attention over the years. For the single best account of his famous or infamous "ride," see *Plenty of Blame to Go Around: Jeb Stuart's Controversial Ride to Gettysburg* by Eric Wittenberg and J.D. Petruzzi. For additional study on the cavalry of both armies during the drive north, see *Cavalry on the Roads to Gettysburg: Kilpatrick at Hanover and Hunterstown* by George Rummel. Accounts and incidents of the Confederate invasion of Pennsylvania and its impact on the people there can be found in W.P. Conrad and Ted Alexander's *When War Passed This Way*, as well as in Scott Mingus's *Flames Beyond Gettysburg*, an excellent account Confederate general John Gordon's late June expedition to Wrightsville along the Susquehanna River.

Chapter 2

"Hard Times at Gettysburg"

The First Day, July 1, 1863

DAY ONE OVERVIEW

Military parlance defines the first day's battle at Gettysburg as a "meeting engagement," with units of both armies arriving on the field at different times throughout the day and, for the most part, entering the action either division by division or brigade by brigade. Neither army commander had intended to fight there. Robert E. Lee had even instructed his subordinates to avoid a general engagement. With the continued absence of his cavalry chief Jeb Stuart with most of the army's mounted arm, Lee was entirely ignorant of the whereabouts of the various Union corps and of the nature of the ground around Gettysburg, and he was seeking to avoid battle until his forces were fully joined. Yet once the battle commenced, Lee would ultimately commit to fighting there. So, too, would George Meade. Even though two of his corps would meet with a tactical defeat—and sustain heavy losses—on July 1, Meade would nevertheless resolve to concentrate his army at Gettysburg after being assured that it was an ideal place to wage a defensive battle.

The contest began on a series of ridgelines west of town as two brigades of Federal cavalry led by the gruff John Buford stubbornly resisted the advance of Confederate infantry under Henry Heth. Just as Buford's men were reaching their limit, Union infantry arrived to thwart Heth's advance and send the Confederates reeling. But this was just the start of what proved to be a bitter, daylong fight. As the hours passed that Wednesday, additional forces arrived on the fields north and west of town so that by day's end, the soldiers of four

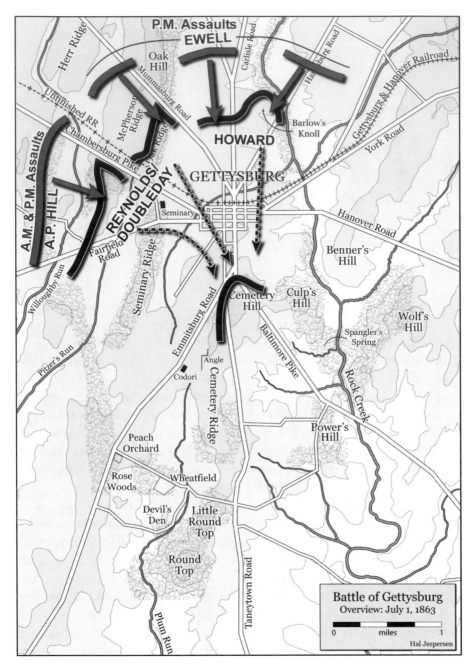

Overview of the First Day's Battle at Gettysburg. *Map by Hal Jespersen.*

"Hard Times at Gettysburg"

Confederate divisions (two from A.P. Hill's Third Corps and two from Richard Ewell's Second) had slugged it out with the soldiers of two Federal corps (the First and Eleventh). It was one of the few instances in the war in which the Confederates enjoyed a substantial numerical advantage—almost two to one— although both sides would pay a heavy price. Lee lost more than 6,100 men that day. Union losses were much higher. Of the 16,500 Federals engaged, about 9,000 were listed among the casualties, whether killed, wounded or captured. The First and Eleventh Corps were simply torn to shreds.

By late afternoon, Confederate forces would at last prevail. After a determined stand, the Union lines north and west of Gettysburg finally collapsed, and the blue-coated soldiers were driven back in some disorder through the labyrinthine streets of town. They rallied south of Gettysburg on a prominent piece of high ground known as Cemetery Hill, which a number of Union officers had earlier recognized as *the* key position and which Eleventh Corps commander Oliver Howard had designated and prepared as a rallying point. The hilltop bristled with artillery, while Union officers worked feverishly to rally the men. But there would be no Confederate attack that evening against this important position, and the day's action would come to an end with the battered, though still determined, Union forces holding this good, high ground.

History often records the first day's battle at Gettysburg as a Confederate victory. If so, then it must be considered an incomplete one, or at least a victory in a purely tactical sense. Although Lee's forces inflicted heavy losses on two Union corps and forced them off the fields in disarray, they succeeded in only driving the Union troops back to a much better defensible position. Union officers informed Meade of the value of the ground south of Gettysburg, ultimately convincing the army commander to gather his forces there. And as Meade issued orders for his remaining corps to make their way to Gettysburg, Robert E. Lee, desirous of more decisive results, determined that it would be there, at Gettysburg, where he would seek that crowning victory he came north hoping to achieve.

* * *

Soldiers in both blue and gray were stirring in their camps early on Wednesday morning, July 1, 1863. By 5:00 a.m., half an hour after sunrise, Henry Heth had his division of 7,500 men on the march, setting off from

Despite orders to avoid triggering an engagement, Henry Heth precipitated the Battle of Gettysburg on the morning of July 1 when his two leading brigades, under Archer and Davis, encountered Buford's horsemen west of town. *Library of Congress.*

Cashtown and heading toward Gettysburg along the Chambersburg Pike. There was no haste in the Confederate advance that morning, and few expected battle. If anything, Heth anticipated to encounter only local home guard troops, which his division, he thought, could easily brush aside. Of the advance toward Gettysburg that morning, one Confederate artillerist wrote, "We moved forward leisurely smoking and chatting as we rode along, not dreaming of the proximity of the enemy."

Like Heth, A.P. Hill did not expect much trouble that day either. Nevertheless, he backed up Heth with the soldiers of Dorsey Pender's division, adding another 7,500 men to the mix. Two of Hill's three divisions—a total of 15,000 men— were now approaching Gettysburg by way of the Chambersburg Pike. Hill had notified Lee the night before that he would be pushing on to Gettysburg with Heth and Pender. The army commander, who awoke that morning west of South Mountain, raised no objections to Hill's advance but had reminded his Third Corps commander that he was not to bring on a general engagement should the enemy be found.

"Hard Times at Gettysburg"

With his men in motion, Hill also notified Second Corps commander Richard Ewell on the morning of July 1 that he was moving on toward Gettysburg. Ewell was just then traveling with Robert Rodes's division as it marched south from Carlisle, trying to make sense of Lee's orders of June 29 that instructed him to march his corps to either Cashtown or Gettysburg, "as circumstances dictated." On June 30, he had met with Rodes and Jubal Early to discuss what Ewell deemed Lee's "indefinite phraseology" and to decide just where to go. Not accustomed to Lee's oftentimes discretionary orders, Ewell wondered aloud, "Why can't a commanding general have someone on his staff who can write an intelligible order?"

Having learned that Hill's corps was that day massing at Cashtown, Ewell and his subordinates decided that they should go there. However, when Hill's courier found Ewell sometime around 9:00 a.m. on the morning of July 1 and told him that Heth and Pender were now moving on to Gettysburg, Ewell decided to change course and swing Rodes and Early south, the "circumstances" now dictating that he should also move on to Gettysburg. Rodes's 8,000-man division tramped south along the Carlisle Pike, while Early's 5,500 men followed a parallel route several miles farther east, marching south along the Harrisburg Road. Ewell then sent his stepson, Major J. Campbell Brown, who served on his staff, to let Lee know that he, too, was moving toward Gettysburg.

And so that Wednesday morning, four Confederate divisions—two from Hill's Third Corps and two from Ewell's Second, a total of 28,500 Confederate soldiers—were making their way toward the crossroads town, advancing from points west and north. At this same time, but drawing toward Gettysburg from the south, marched the soldiers of two Union corps—the First and Eleventh, some 16,500 men strong.

Major General John Reynolds, commanding the left wing of the Army of the Potomac, was awakened well before dawn with instructions from army commander Meade to march to Gettysburg. Through Buford's reports, Meade and Reynolds were both aware that the Confederates were close, with most of them stacked up between Chambersburg and Cashtown to the west and with other forces further off to the north, but neither necessarily expected a battle that day. Reynolds's instructions were to simply move on to Gettysburg, thus enabling Buford to push out farther from there, and like Heth, Reynolds displayed little haste in his advance. The skies began to lighten a little after 4:30 a.m., but it was already 8:00 a.m. when the soldiers of the First Corps set out from their campsites near Marsh Creek, roughly five miles south of town. Half an hour later, the three divisions of Oliver

Howard's Eleventh Corps got underway. Since Howard's men began the day at Emmitsburg, south of the Mason-Dixon Line and several miles from Marsh Creek, they would have more ground to cover than the First Corps in reaching Gettysburg.

The blue and gray columns were thus set in motion, advancing on a collision course as they converged inexorably on Gettysburg, a thriving market town at the center of the gathering storm. Gettysburg was not quite eighty years old, having been laid out in 1786 by town founder James Gettys, who, after purchasing several hundred acres of land, divided it into 210 lots, all emanating from a central square, or "diamond," as it would later be called. The town grew quickly, so much so that by 1860 there were some 450 buildings in town and some 2,400 people who called Gettysburg their home.

In 1863, Gettysburg was a prosperous and growing community, the seat of government for Adams County and a town that boasted two institutions of higher education: Pennsylvania (later Gettysburg) College and the Lutheran Theological Seminary. The telegraph had arrived in town in 1862 and a railroad a few years earlier. Gettysburg was also home to three weekly newspapers, seven churches and a respectable number of hotels and inns. The economy was based primarily on agriculture, but there was a sizable carriage- and wagon-making industry. There was also a good number of blacksmiths and merchants; twenty-two residents listed "shoemaker" as their trade. No fewer than ten roads entered Gettysburg from all points of the compass. From above, Gettysburg would have thus resembled the hub of a large wagon wheel. These roads made the town an ideal place for scattered armies to gather. But it was not just the roads that seemingly fated Gettysburg as a place for battle; it was also surrounded by ground well suited for defense, particularly south of town.

Cavalryman John Buford recognized the potential value of this terrain as he and his 2,700 men galloped into town late on the morning of June 30. Expecting Confederate infantry to come "booming" toward Gettysburg the following day, Buford determined to delay their advance, or "entertain" them, as he later phrased it, until the infantry arrived. As night thus fell on June 30, Buford and his dusty horsemen may have been the only soldiers in either blue or gray who were both expecting and prepared for action on the morning of July 1.

A well-trained and seasoned cavalryman, Buford had a good eye for terrain, and that morning, he would make the most of it. Like waves approaching the shore, the ground west of Gettysburg rose and fell to form a succession of roughly parallel ridgelines, each running generally north–south and each bisected by both the northwest-southeast running

Chambersburg Pike and by an unfinished railroad cut, which ran parallel to the pike two hundred yards to its north and which, in places, was some twenty feet deep. Nearest to Gettysburg—three-quarters of a mile west from the town square—was Seminary Ridge, topped by the buildings of Lutheran Seminary.

The ground sloped downward from there, bottoming out into a broad swale before it rose again to form McPherson's Ridge, named for a family whose large farmstead cut into the western arm of the ridgeline. A seventeen-acre woodlot, known as Herbst's Woods, stood atop this ridgeline south of the McPherson house and barn. Continuing westward from McPherson's Ridge, the ground again sloped down to Willoughby Run, a meandering stream that ran along the western base of the ridgeline. Three-quarters of a mile farther west, the ground rose up once more to form Herr's Ridge, named for a tavern that crowned this ridge. To the north of the Chambersburg Pike and north of the Railroad Cut, Seminary Ridge became known as Oak Ridge, topped by Sheads's Woods, and then rose to form Oak Hill, the highest point north of Gettysburg and a dominating military position.

It was ground well suited for Buford's designs. He planned a defense in depth, with his troopers holding on for as long as possible to each of these successive ridgelines before falling back to McPherson's Ridge, where he established his main line of defense. Armed with single-shot, breech-loading carbines, Buford's men would fight dismounted. But any advantage they might have had with their weapons, which allowed for a more rapid rate of fire, was negated by the fact that every fourth man was removed from the firing line to hold horses. Plus, Buford's men would be heavily outnumbered; Heth's Division alone numbered 7,500. The greatest advantage Buford and his men had was not in their weapons nor even their defensive positions. Instead, it was in the fact that Heth, in the forefront of the Confederate advance, was neither expecting nor prepared for any serious resistance as he marched his division to Gettysburg. And once he did come into contact with Buford's men, he would commit just half his force—two brigades—to battle.

Buford's men slept on their arms on the night of June 30 and awoke on July 1 prepared for a fight. Observers noted that the normally stoic Buford appeared more anxious than usual. He received a message from Meade early that morning, informing him that Reynolds would be making his way to Gettysburg. But would Reynolds get there in time? It was a question that weighed heavily on Buford's mind that morning as he braced for the Confederate advance.

Colonel William Gamble's brigade was posted on McPherson's Ridge, covering the Chambersburg Pike, while the horsemen of Colonel Thomas

Devin's brigade stretched northward in a lengthy semicircular formation, covering the roads that led to Gettysburg from the north and east. Advanced vedettes, or pickets, were stationed well to the front of the main cavalry line, keeping alert for any Confederate activity.

Stationed on Whisler's Ridge, some three miles northwest of Gettysburg and beyond Herr's Ridge, almost halfway to Cashtown, was a small detachment of troopers from Company E, 8th Illinois Cavalry, commanded by Lieutenant Marcellus Jones. At about 7:30 a.m., Jones's men caught sight of Heth's men marching toward them. As the gray column neared Marsh Creek, seven hundred yards to his front, Private George Sager raised his carbine to fire, but Jones stopped him. "Hold on, George," said Jones, coolly, "give me the honor of opening this ball." The thirty-three-year-old lieutenant then rested Sergeant Shafer's borrowed carbine on a fence rail and pulled the trigger.

With that shot, the ball had opened; the Battle of Gettysburg had commenced.

Jones's salvo triggered a flurry of others from the widely dispersed dismounted cavalrymen atop the ridgeline. General James Archer, whose brigade led Heth's column, responded by sending forward several hundred of his men as skirmishers, while a cannon belonging to Willie Pegram's battalion of artillery unlimbered in the middle of the roadway and fired off a few rounds. Archer's skirmishers, fanning out on either side of the Chambersburg Pike, pushed ahead through brush and briar, across Marsh Creek and the swampy ground surrounding it and up the gentle slope of the

Fighting dismounted, with every fourth man assigned to hold horses, Buford's cavalrymen delayed Heth's advance long enough to allow Reynolds to arrive with his First Army Corps. *From* Battles and Leaders of the Civil War.

ridgeline. The Union horsemen gave ground slowly, the troopers falling back on foot, loading as they retired, turning every now and then to deliver a well-aimed shot. By 8:00 a.m., the Confederates had swept up and over Whisler's Ridge and were now advancing steadily toward Herr's Ridge, where they would encounter a more formidable line of Yankee horsemen.

By now aware that the Confederates were advancing, Buford directed Gamble to send several hundred of his men to Herr's Ridge, where they were soon joined by their comrades falling back before Heth's skirmishers. Seeing this much stronger line spread out before him—roughly 700 dismounted Union cavalrymen—Heth concluded that skirmishers would no longer suffice and sent orders to both Archer and General Joseph Davis, following behind Archer, to deploy their brigades into lines of battle. With the Union horsemen feverishly plugging away, Archer fanned out his 1,200 men south of the Chambersburg Pike, while Davis, with more than 1,700 men, lined up three of his regiments north of the roadway. It took nearly one hour for Archer and Davis to fully deploy, but the action would quickly intensify as these two brigades then stepped forward to the attack, backed up as they were by some of Pegram's guns. Gamble's men—supported on their right by a number of Devin's troopers—put up a tough, determined stance, holding on as long as possible to Herr's Ridge, but after thirty minutes of combat, they could hold no longer and again retired, forced from their position in the face of heavy odds.

From the cupola of the Lutheran Seminary Building, John Buford watched nervously as his horsemen fell back. Thus far, his men had done all he had asked of them in delaying—already for nearly two hours—the Confederate advance. But as his men streamed westward, splashing across Willoughby Run and falling back to McPherson's Ridge, and as Heth's men were forming up for a continuation of the attack, Buford realized that his time was running short. He had earlier sent a desperate message to Reynolds, telling him that Confederate forces were advancing in strength and urging him to come forward quickly. Buford then watched as some twenty Confederate artillery pieces unlimbered on Herr's Ridge to support Heth's infantry. The Confederate cannons opened fire; their main target, it seemed, was Lieutenant John Calef's Battery A, 2nd U.S. Artillery, the lone battery Buford had on the field. Four of Calef's six guns were positioned astride the pike atop McPherson's Ridge; the other two were farther south, beyond Herbst's Woods, placed there to give the impression of greater strength. The heavily outgunned Union artillerists stood nobly to their pieces while the air around them filled with shot and shell. Buford gritted his teeth and prepared for another Confederate push, determined to hold McPherson's Ridge, even "if it costs every man in our command."

Then there came a most welcome sight to the harried Buford: Major General John Reynolds had arrived. Having set his First Corps in motion, Reynolds galloped ahead of his columns, spurring his horse even quicker when he received Buford's report of advancing Confederates. He could hear the distant thunder of the guns as he rode on toward Gettysburg. Along the way, he had caught sight of Cemetery Hill and the surrounding high ground south of town and liked what he saw. Reynolds met up with Buford near the Seminary sometime at about 9:30 a.m. "What's the matter, John?" asked the corps commander. "The Devil's to pay!" was Buford's famous reply.

The two scanned the battlefield and Heth's columns as they moved forward. Reynolds asked if Buford could hold on until his infantry arrived. "I reckon I can," said Buford, and with that, Reynolds galloped back to hurry along his troops. He also sent two staff officers racing off to locate Oliver Howard and Daniel Sickles with orders for them to march their Eleventh and Third Corps to Gettysburg as quickly as possible. He sent another staff officer to army headquarters, fourteen miles away at Taneytown, with a terse message for Meade. "The enemy is advancing in strong force," reported Reynolds, who feared that the Confederates would be able to reach the high ground "on the other side" of town. He promised that he would do all he could to prevent this. "I will fight him inch by inch," vowed Reynolds, "and if driven into town I will barricade the streets and hold him back as long as possible." Reynolds knew that the army commander was eager to find Lee and to bring him to battle. He believed that the ground around Gettysburg offered as good a position as any, and like Buford, he resolved to make a stand there.

The head of Reynolds's First Corps was just a mile away, marching north along the Emmitsburg Road, past Joseph Sherfy's Peach Orchard and on toward the Nicholas Codori house, where Reynolds, back from his meeting with Buford, met up with them. Reynolds turned the soldiers of General James Wadsworth's leading division left off the Emmitsburg Road, the men knocking down the fences that lined the roadway and then racing cross-lots toward Seminary Ridge. Lysander Cutler's brigade led the way, followed by the famed Wisconsin, Indiana and Michigan soldiers of the Iron Brigade. They moved at the double-quick, many of them with unloaded rifles. As they raced their way to Buford's support, these hard-fighting veteran troops could hear the ominous though familiar sound of battle again picking up.

Henry Heth would not be denied. By this time, he must have known that the enemy troops to his front were by no means mere local militia. Gazing

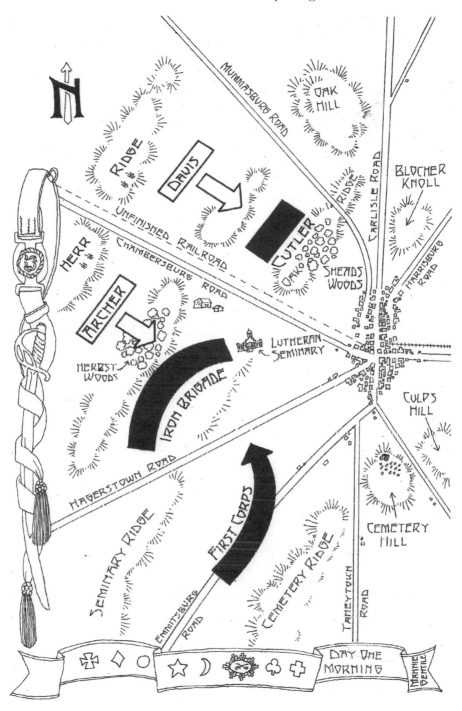

Pushing back Buford, Heth unexpectedly encountered Union infantry on McPherson's Ridge, and he, too, was soon driven back. *Map by Mannie Gentile.*

eastward at what one soldier described as a "blood red sun" that continued to climb higher in the morning sky, Heth saw yet another line of defense on McPherson's Ridge. Despite the Yankees' stubborn resistance—and despite Lee's orders not to bring on battle—Heth determined to push on. As he later wrote, "[B]lood now having been drawn, there seemed to be no calling off the battle." With Herr's Ridge alive with the thunder of the artillery, Heth ordered his brigades forward. Archer objected to the advance, fearful that his men would be marching into the unknown. But Heth insisted, and his men again swept forward.

It seemed a relentless tide as Archer's and Davis's lines swept down Herr's Ridge and toward Willoughby Run. Union carbines blazed away, as did Calef's guns. To young John Calef, a recent graduate of West Point, the approaching Confederate battle flags "looked redder and bloodier in the hot July sun than I had ever seen them before." Union casualties mounted as Buford's men gave their all to hold on, but their line on McPherson's Ridge was reaching its breaking point. One can only imagine the relief, then, when Buford's exhausted troopers looked back, just as it seemed they would be overwhelmed, and saw the arrival of the First Army Corps. It was sometime around 10:15 a.m.

Reynolds began placing his units as soon as they arrived on the field, first sending Captain James Hall's 2nd Maine Battery to take up Calef's position astride the pike as a relieved John Calef withdrew his pieces. Hall's task was to occupy the Confederates' attention and buy some time for the infantry to deploy on the ridgelines behind them. Cutler's 1,600 men were the first Union infantry on the field. Sweeping past the Seminary, Cutler divided his brigade, sending three of his regiments (the 76th New York, 56th Pennsylvania and 147th New York) north of the Chambersburg Pike and north of the Railroad Cut, with instructions to form up on the right of Hall's Battery, while his remaining two regiments (the 95th New York and 14th Brooklyn) took up positions around the McPherson farm buildings, south of the pike and to the left of Hall.

With Cutler's brigade going into position, Reynolds next rode back to the crest of McPherson's Ridge, behind Herbst's Woods, to hurry along the Iron Brigade, just then reaching the field. Commanded by Brigadier General Solomon Meredith, the men of the Iron Brigade were some of the hardest-fighting soldiers in the Army of the Potomac, having earned that reputation on the blood-soaked fields of Brawner's Farm, South Mountain and Antietam, where they suffered appalling losses. They were easily recognizable on any battlefield, for they wore not the standard sack coat and

Captain James Hall's Maine battery, positioned along the Chambersburg Pike, fires toward Heth's advancing infantry. *From* Battles and Leaders of the Civil War.

kepi but rather their dress frocks and black Hardee hats, pinned up on one side and topped with a black ostrich plume.

The Iron Brigade was fed into the fight, regiment by regiment, as each arrived on the field. In the lead was the 2nd Wisconsin Infantry, three hundred men strong. Sweeping forward from the Seminary in order to link up with the left flank of Cutler's men south of the pike, the soldiers of the 2nd deployed from column into line, loading their rifles as they advanced directly toward Herbst's Woods, a largely open woodlot free of underbrush, its towering oaks widely scattered. On that bloody Wednesday in July, this otherwise pleasant woodlot would be transformed into a horrific killing zone.

Pushing through the trees from the west were the soldiers of Archer's Brigade. The left of Archer's line had already made contact with the 95th New York and 14th Brooklyn near the McPherson property, but its center and right, having splashed across Willoughby Run, continued to move forward, chasing away the last of Buford's men positioned in the woods. John Reynolds, on the opposite edge of the woodlot, saw Archer's men approaching, and as the 2nd Wisconsin raced past, he yelled out, "Forward men, forward for God's sake, and drive those fellows out of those woods!" Archer's men let loose a devastating volley that reportedly struck down a full 30 percent of the Wisconsin regiment. The survivors of that opening blast pressed forward, and there quickly developed a savage firefight, the two lines just fifty paces apart in the scattered trees. For the moment, the men of the 2nd were alone, but advancing quickly to their assistance were their fellow Badger State men in the 7th Wisconsin.

It is likely that the last thing forty-two-year-old John Reynolds ever saw was the soldiers of the 7th Wisconsin Infantry sweeping forward from Seminary Ridge, fanning out into line of battle as the 2nd had done just

The Fall of Reynolds, by artist Alfred Waud. Highly respected, Reynolds would be the highest-ranking soldier to die at Gettysburg. *Library of Congress*.

minutes earlier. After the 2nd entered the woods, Reynolds turned in his saddle to see if the other regiments were moving forward. As he did so, a bullet slammed into the back of his head, and he fell dead from the saddle. "He never spoke a word, or moved a muscle after he was struck," said Charles Veil, one of Reynolds's staff officers, who further claimed that he "never saw a ball do its work so *instantly* as did the ball which struck General Reynolds." The death of Reynolds would be deeply felt. In paying tribute to the fallen officer, Veil wrote that Reynolds was "a man who knew not what fear or danger was, in a word, [he was] one of our very best Generals. Where ever the fight raged the fiercest, there the General was sure to be found, his undaunted courage always inspired the men with more energy & courage." Carried from the field, Reynolds's body was ultimately escorted back to his native Lancaster, where he was laid to rest on July 4. With Reynolds's death, Major General Abner Doubleday assumed command of the Federal forces on the field.

Word of Reynolds's demise spread quickly through the ranks of the Iron Brigade as they moved forward into the fight, but there was no time just then to mourn his loss. The 7th Wisconsin advanced to the left of the 2nd, soon joined on *its* left by the 19th Indiana and, finally, the 24th Michigan, a large regiment at five hundred men strong. (The Iron Brigade's remaining regiment, the 6th Wisconsin, was, for the moment, held in reserve near the Seminary.) Supported now on its left, the 2nd Wisconsin pushed forward through the trees, losing men "with terribly rapidity" but driving Archer's men back. The left of the Iron Brigade far overlapped the right of Archer's line, and it was not long before the Union soldiers got around and behind it.

Thus caught in a closing vise, Archer's men retreated, falling back across Willoughby Run in a desperate bid to escape. They had no support—the nearest troops were back on Herr's Ridge—and hundreds of Archer's men fell into Union hands, including Archer himself, the "Little Gamecock," who was captured after a brief struggle. In just half an hour, Archer lost more than 500 of his 1,200 men. As his battered brigade fled back to Herr's Ridge, the captured general was taken to the rear, where he was turned over to Doubleday. The two had known each other during the prewar days, but it had been a while since they had last met. "Good morning, Archer! How are you? I am glad to see you," said Doubleday, extending his hand. But Archer was in no mood for reminiscences. He refused to shake the hand of the portly Doubleday, telling him bluntly, "Well, I am *not* glad to see you by a damned sight!"

Even as the Iron Brigade was driving Archer's men from the field, the situation north of the Chambersburg Pike was not going quite as well for Federal arms. After pushing Gamble's and Devin's horsemen back, the three regiments of Joe Davis's Confederate brigade continued to push forward, descending like an avalanche on the three regiments of Cutler's brigade, just then deploying into lines of battle north of the Railroad Cut. In a reverse of the situation that was then unfolding between Archer and the Iron Brigade farther south, Davis's left flank extended well beyond the right of Cutler's line, manned by the 76th New York. The 55th North Carolina on the left of Davis's line swung south and headed directly toward the exposed Union flank. Major Ira Grover, commanding the 76th, turned his New Yorkers to face this threat, but there was little that could be done. Grover fell dead as Davis's men continued to close in.

Seeing their plight, division commander Wadsworth directed Cutler to fall back to the cover of Sheads's Woods. The 76th New York and 56th Pennsylvania withdrew in decent order, but the 147th New York, on the left of Cutler's line, never got the order to retreat; its commander was struck from the saddle and severely wounded before he could relay the order. This small band of New Yorkers—380 strong—thus stood alone and, said one man, "fell like autumn leaves" as Davis's Confederates closed in from the front, flank and rear. Wadsworth sent another order, and the New Yorkers finally retreated, but not before they had lost 76 men killed, 144 wounded and 70 captured, a 76 percent loss.

With the infantry to the right of his battery now gone and with Davis's regiments closing quickly on his pieces, Captain James Hall ordered his 2nd Maine Battery back, the men and horses running a gauntlet of bullets as they made a harrowing escape. The right flank of the First Corps line, north of the Chambersburg Pike, was collapsing. Seeing this, the 14th Brooklyn and 95th New York, which had been facing west, near the McPherson buildings, turned to their right, aligning along the pike and firing into the advancing Confederates. They were soon joined by the soldiers of the 6th Wisconsin, commanded by Colonel Rufus Dawes. The 6th had been kept behind at the Seminary while the rest of the Iron Brigade dealt with Archer. With that threat now gone, Doubleday ordered Dawes to advance north to contend with Davis. The man who delivered Doubleday's order told Dawes simply "to go like hell."

The 6th charged north and lined up behind the post-and-rail fence that lined the pike. In response, Davis's regiments wheeled to their right and advanced south. To help shelter themselves from the destructive fire poured into them from the two New York regiments and from the 6th Wisconsin, Davis's men took up positions in the Railroad Cut, where they soon began trading shots with the Union troops along the pike. His men falling rapidly under this fire, Dawes decided to break the stalemate by ordering a charge. He sought out Major Edward Pye of the 95th New York, yelling, "Let's go for them, major!" With that, the three First Corps regiments scrambled up and over the fences and, said Dawes, "moved forward upon a double-quick, well closed, in [the] face of terribly destructive fire from the enemy." Indeed, it was destructive. Dawes later reported that no less than 180 of his men fell during this deadly charge.

Despite the casualties, the Union line was soon on the lip of the cut, which, because of its depth, had now become a trap for many of Davis's Confederates. A couple dozen men of the 6th Wisconsin entered the cut at its eastern end and fired directly into the Confederate flank. Those who could retreated, but many of Davis's men, despairing of an escape, dropped their guns and raised their hands in surrender. The fighting in the cut ended after a short, desperate melee, complete with some hand-to-hand combat. Hundreds of Confederates tramped to the rear of the Union line as prisoners of war as the action subsided. The First Corps, having repulsed Archer and now Davis, held possession of the field.

"[T]he enemy had now been felt, and found to be in heavy force in and around Gettysburg," was how Henry Heth described the results of his morning advance, in pronounced understatement. His two brigades under

"Hard Times at Gettysburg"

Archer and Davis had been roughly handled, suffering heavy losses at the hands of the Union First Corps. As the shattered ranks of these two brigades streamed back to Herr's Ridge, Heth reorganized his division. He rallied Davis's survivors north of the Chambersburg Pike while lining up his two fresh brigades—under Brockenbrough and Pettigrew—to the south.

Archer's battered brigade, now commanded by Colonel Birkett Fry, formed up to the right of Pettigrew. Pegram's artillery continued to bang away from atop the ridgeline, where it was joined by several batteries from Lieutenant Colonel David McIntosh's Battalion of Pender's Division, bringing the total number of guns on Herr's Ridge to thirty-three. Pender had advanced his four brigades behind Heth, and now they, too, were settling into position astride the Chambersburg Pike, west of Herr's Ridge. Having reset his division, Henry Heth now did what perhaps he should have done earlier: he waited for further instructions. It was by now approaching noon, and the action around Gettysburg was abating. For the next several hours, a lull descended across the smoldering fields.

Abner Doubleday took advantage of this break in the action to sort out and strengthen his lines on McPherson's Ridge. He had inherited command of the field upon the death of Reynolds but had no idea of the slain general's plans or intentions. He only assumed that Reynolds must have intended to hold this position west of Gettysburg, and he thus determined that he would do all he could to hold on to it.

Doubleday reformed the Iron Brigade in Herbst's Woods while Cutler led his battered regiments back to a position north of the Railroad Cut. By now, and with the exception of a brigade of nine-month Vermont soldiers led by George Stannard, the rest of the First Corps had arrived on the field. Dividing his own division, commanded now by Brigadier General Thomas Rowley, Doubleday placed its two brigades on either side of the Iron Brigade, with Colonel Chapman Biddle's men forming to their left rear on the crest of McPherson's Ridge and Colonel Roy Stone's Pennsylvanians going into position around the McPherson farm buildings, their line stretching north from Herbst's Woods to the Chambersburg Pike. Brigadier General John Robinson's division was held in reserve, taking up positions near the Seminary, where some of his men began piling up earth and fence rails to form an improvised line of breastworks. Colonel Charles Wainwright, commanding the First Corps artillery, had arrived as well. Selecting good spots for the guns, Wainwright's artillerists began trading shots with Pegram's and McIntosh's pieces 1,300 yards away, on Herr's Ridge. For the moment, the First Corps stood alone at Gettysburg, but help would soon be arriving.

Widely and wrongly believed to be the man who invented baseball, Abner Doubleday, pictured here with his wife, was a career soldier and West Point graduate who in April 1861 found himself stationed inside Fort Sumter when the war's opening shots were fired. Indeed, it was Doubleday, reportedly, who fired the first shot from inside the fort in response to the Confederate guns. *Library of Congress.*

Oliver Howard's Eleventh Corps had set out from its campsites near Emmitsburg at about 8:30 a.m. with instructions to follow the First Corps to Gettysburg. To help alleviate congestion on the roadways and to expedite the march, Howard had one division (under Francis Barlow) move north in the footsteps of the First Corps along the Emmitsburg Road, while his other two divisions (under Generals Carl Schurz and Adolph von Steinwehr) approached town along the Taneytown Road.

At age thirty-three, Howard was the youngest corps commander in the Union army. He was a West Pointer (class of 1854), a deeply religious man and a fervent abolitionist. Howard's right arm had been shattered the previous year at the Battle of Fair Oaks, necessitating amputation. Rising from regimental to brigade and later divisional command, Howard was appointed commander of the Eleventh Corps in April 1863. About half of Howard's soldiers in the Eleventh Corps were either German by birth or by ancestry, and they had suffered much from the prejudices of the other army corps and were unfairly scapegoated for the disaster at Chancellorsville.

Howard galloped ahead of his men and rode on to Gettysburg. Along the way, he was intercepted by one of Reynolds's breathless aides with instructions to "come quite up to Gettysburg." Howard sent hurry-up orders back to his columns and then made his way toward the ever-growing sounds of battle. Approaching town from the south, Howard reined

Upon his arrival at Gettysburg late on the morning of July 1, Oliver Otis Howard assumed command of the Federal forces on the field. For his decision to prepare Cemetery Hill as a rallying point, the brave Howard would later receive the Thanks of Congress, as well as the Medal of Honor for his gallantry at the Battle of Fair Oaks. *Library of Congress.*

up on Cemetery Hill and liked what he saw. Turning to one of his staff officers, the one-armed warrior said, "This seems to be a good position, colonel," to which the officer replied, "It is the *only* position, general." While Buford and Reynolds might have also recognized the value of this high ground, it was Howard who would take steps to defend it, later posting Von Steinwehr's division and some of the corps artillery there while his other two divisions would hurry through town to the fields beyond.

Galloping off Cemetery Hill, Howard next rode into Gettysburg and climbed to the roof of the Fahnestock Building on Baltimore Street, where, along with several of the more curious of townspeople, he watched the battle unfolding to the west between the First Corps and the two brigades of

Heth's Division. While there, Howard learned that Reynolds had been killed and that he, as the ranking officer present, was now in command of all the Union forces on the field, taking over for Doubleday. "My heart was heavy and the situation was grave indeed," Howard later wrote, "but surely I did not hesitate a moment." He galloped quickly back to Cemetery Hill, where he set up headquarters.

Meanwhile, Howard's Eleventh Corps soldiers continued making their way toward town, double-quick most of the way. As they drew nearer to Gettysburg, the soldiers were met by a steady stream of civilians fleeing town. General Carl Schurz remembered one woman yelling out to him, "Hard times at Gettysburg! They are shooting and killing! What will become of us!"

There would be no rest for the much fatigued soldiers of the Eleventh Corps once they reached the southern limits of town. Receiving reports from both Buford and Doubleday that a large Confederate force was approaching Gettysburg from the north, Howard determined to send Barlow's and Schurz's divisions through town in an effort to link up with Doubleday's right, somewhere in the area of Oak Hill, in order to meet this new threat. Howard kept the two brigades of Von Steinwehr's division behind to defend Cemetery Hill, telling the division commander, "We must hold this hill!" Howard then rode ahead through town with Barlow, hoping to effect a junction with Doubleday's right flank, but he would be too late, for even as the Eleventh Corps raced its way north through Gettysburg, cheered along by some of the townspeople lining the streets, Major General Robert Rodes's division, of Richard Ewell's Confederate Second Corps, was just then arriving on Oak Hill.

Rodes's Division—the largest in Lee's army with eight thousand men in its five brigades—approached Gettysburg that morning along the Carlisle Pike, accompanied by Ewell. When his division was within several miles of town, Rodes heard the sounds of battle unfolding far off to his right. In response, Rodes veered off the Carlisle Pike with four of his five brigades, angling southwest along the crest of ridgeline that debouched onto Oak Hill. The Georgians of George Doles's brigade would continue moving south in order to cover the division's left until Jubal Early's division, advancing farther east along the Harrisburg Road, could catch up.

When they arrived on Oak Hill, Rodes and Ewell had a commanding view of the morning's battlefield. The fighting had recently ended, but they could clearly see Heth's men, backed up by Pender's Division, reforming on Herr's Ridge, while to their front they saw Union First Corps soldiers resetting themselves on McPherson's Ridge and north of the Railroad

Cut. It was immediately recognized that Rodes, on Oak Hill, had arrived squarely on the right flank of the First Corps line. Then, off to their left, the two Confederate generals saw another Union force racing north through Gettysburg and deploying into lines of battle on the broad, open fields south and east of Oak Hill—the Eleventh Corps was arriving. Ewell ordered up Rodes's artillery under Lieutenant Colonel Thomas Carter, and soon sixteen cannons were wheeled into position on Oak Hill, throwing shot and shell toward the exposed right of the First Corps line and toward the panting, exhausted soldiers of the Eleventh Corps.

Earlier that morning, Ewell had sent his stepson, Major Campbell Brown, to find Robert E. Lee and notify him that his corps was advancing toward Gettysburg. Brown located Lee just east of Cashtown and discovered the army commander to be greatly agitated. Lee had first heard the sounds of battle as he rode with Longstreet over South Mountain sometime around 11:00 a.m. He hurried on toward Cashtown to locate A.P. Hill and to find out exactly what was happening. Hill told Lee that he simply did not know but would gallop forward to find out. In addition to the violation of his standing orders *not* to bring on a battle, Lee's agitation was due more to the fact that he simply did not know what lay ahead of him, as the absence of any report from his cavalry chief Stuart weighed heavily on his mind.

After Hill galloped away to consult with Heth, Lee singled out General R.H. Anderson, commanding another of Hill's divisions, and asked whether he knew anything about the unfolding situation. Anderson shook his head no, and then Lee ("more to himself than to me," Anderson later recalled) stated, "I cannot think what has become of Stuart. In the absence of any reports from him, I am in ignorance of what we have in front of us here. It may be the whole Federal force, or it may be a detachment. If it is the whole Federal force, we must fight a battle here." But, stressed Lee, not before his army was fully joined.

It was just about this time that Ewell's man Brown arrived. The army commander asked Brown if Ewell had heard anything of Stuart. When Brown answered no, Lee sent him galloping back to Ewell with the same instructions he had issued earlier to Hill and Heth: he was to avoid a general engagement. With his staff in tow, Lee then rode on toward Gettysburg.

At this same time and much like Lee, Union army commander George Meade, at his headquarters some fourteen miles away in Taneytown, was also trying to make sense of things from the reports he had been receiving throughout the morning hours. Upon learning of Reynolds's death, Meade summoned one of his most trusted subordinates, Major General Winfield

Historian Douglas Southall Freeman famously described Robert Rodes as "a Norse God in Confederate gray," a warrior who looked as though he had "stepped from the pages of Beowulf." A graduate of the Virginia Military Institute, Rodes, under Ewell's orders, reopened the Battle of Gettysburg on the afternoon of July 1. *From* Miller's Photographic History of the Civil War.

Scott Hancock, whose Second Corps was then arriving near headquarters. Hancock was a career soldier, a graduate of West Point's class of 1844 and one of the best general officers to don the Union blue. His skilled leadership and tough battlefield prowess had already earned him the title of "Hancock the Superb." Meade had such faith in Hancock and had so trusted his judgment that at 1:30 p.m. he ordered him to Gettysburg to take command of the forces there, taking the place of Howard. Meade further directed Hancock "to make an examination of the ground…and to report to me, without loss of time, the facilities and advantages or disadvantages of that ground for receiving battle." With these instructions, Hancock turned command of his corps over to General John Gibbon and then set off on the long journey to Gettysburg, riding for several miles along the way in the back of an ambulance in order to study maps of the surrounding area.

Hancock was well on his way to Gettysburg when the battle there resumed, for Rodes, from atop Oak Hill, had reopened the ball.

Rodes's artillery had announced his arrival on Oak Hill. With these guns now firing from their right and with A.P. Hill's cannons continuing to bark to their front, the Union First Corps soldiers now found themselves caught up in a vicious crossfire, the supposed lull in the fighting being anything but quiet for these men forced to endure this iron storm. With their right flank exposed to Carter's sixteen guns, Cutler's men fell back to the shelter of Sheads's Woods, while at the same time, Colonel Roy Stone shifted two of his three regiments to align along the Chambersburg Pike and face north, thus reducing the flanking fire from Carter's cannons. But this shift in position only exposed their left flank to the Confederate cannon fire coming from the west.

Knowing that the Confederate gunners were targeting his regiments' flags, Stone ordered the color guard of the 149th Pennsylvania to take up a position some fifty yards to the left-front of the brigade. The trick worked, and Stone's men, excepting those stalwart few with the flags of the 149th, were relieved from much of the fire. Finally, with Rodes's men arriving on Oak Hill, Doubleday called on Brigadier General John Robinson, whose division had been held in reserve near the Seminary buildings, instructing him to send at least one of his brigades north in order to meet the new threat. Robinson, in turn, gave the nod to Henry Baxter, who quickly led his six regiments northward, behind the crest of Oak Ridge and toward the right of Cutler's men in Sheads's Woods.

On Oak Hill, both Ewell and Rodes watched with growing alarm as Baxter's men began emerging from the woodlot to their left-front. With the Eleventh Corps continuing to deploy on the fields north of town and on their left flank, they believed that the Union forces were gathering for an attack. Better to strike first, they thought, before being struck. By this time, staff officer Brown had returned from his meeting with Lee and repeated Lee's instructions not to bring on a fight. But just like Heth earlier that morning, Ewell believed that a battle was by now unavoidable. As he later reported, "[I]t was too late to avoid an engagement without abandoning the position taken up and I determined to push the attack vigorously."

Rodes hashed out a plan to attack south from Oak Hill with the brigades of Edward O'Neal, Alfred Iverson and Junius Daniel. Doles's Brigade, operating on Rodes's far left, would keep the Eleventh Corps occupied until Early's Division arrived, while Rodes's final brigade, under Stephen Ramseur, would be held in reserve. Rodes's plan was to come crashing down on the right of the First Corps line and drive it from the field. However, poor communication, vague directives, uninspired leadership and an imperfect understanding of the Union positions would all combine to result in a series of disjointed, costly assaults.

Advancing just after 2:00 p.m., O'Neal's Brigade would be the first to come to grief. For various reasons, Rodes had detached two of O'Neal's regiments, while the remaining three moved out to the attack with nothing in the way of direction since O'Neal decided to remain in the rear. The three Alabama regiments swept south across the eastern slopes of Oak Hill, past the McLean farm buildings and directly into a wall of musket fire delivered at close range by Baxter's men lined up to their front. Moving north out of Sheads's Woods, Baxter, just a few minutes earlier, had formed his six regiments in the shape of a backward "L," with the base, two regiments strong, lining up along Oak Ridge and facing west and the long end of the "L," four regiments strong, deploying in a grove of oak trees in a line of battle that ran southeasterly and parallel to the Mummasburg Road, which cut across the ridgeline.

As O'Neal's men approached, they were greeted with a series of volleys that staggered their advance. They were also taking fire on their exposed left by the Eleventh Corps soldiers of the 45th New York, just then advancing as a heavy skirmish force. Canister fire delivered by Captain Hubert Dilger's Eleventh Corps battery also raked O'Neal's lines. The attack foundered after just fifteen minutes, and scores of Alabamians lay dead or wounded. Many more had fallen into Union hands as prisoners of war, gobbled up by the advancing 45th New York. Yet, having driven back O'Neal, Baxter's men would get little in the way of a respite, for just minutes later, Iverson's Brigade of North Carolinians came sweeping southwesterly toward their position on Oak Ridge.

To confront Iverson, Robinson directed Baxter to reform his line along the crest of Oak Ridge and face west. Baxter very quickly effected this change in position, his six regiments now in a line behind a stone wall that stretched south along the eastern crest of Oak Ridge. The blue-coated soldiers lay down behind this stone wall, patiently awaiting the approach of Iverson's four regiments.

Iverson's men stepped off to the attack soon after O'Neal's, with instructions to advance to the right of the Alabamians. Because of the terrain, however, Iverson's men could not see O'Neal's men advancing. In an effort to thus close up on O'Neal's right, they wheeled to the left, angling across a swale of ground that rose gently up to form Oak Ridge. Baxter's men, ensconced behind that stone wall, were entirely out of view from Iverson's serried ranks; the North Carolinians thus advanced in tragic ignorance of the 1,400 Union soldiers directly to their front. A soldier of the 88th Pennsylvania later wrote that Iverson's men "came sweeping on in magnificent order, with perfect alignment, guns at right shoulder and colors to the front—to many a dead march." And indeed it was.

When Iverson's gray line approached to within one hundred yards of their position, Baxter's men rose and delivered a murderous volley that dropped North Carolinians by the hundreds. Those who survived that first devastating blast fell to the ground, doing their best to weather the leaden storm that swirled around their heads. They could not rise, either to advance or retreat. "I believe every man who stood up was either killed or wounded," attested one of Iverson's survivors. They simply hugged the ground while Baxter's men continued to pour in a deadly fire. It was not long before Baxter's men saw handkerchiefs being raised in surrender by the trapped Southerners to their

One man famously wrote that General John Robinson "was the hairiest general…in a much bearded army." On July 1, his two brigades withstood repeated attacks from Rodes's Division on Oak Ridge before ultimately being forced off the field. *Library of Congress.*

front. With bayonets fixed, Baxter's men surged up and over the wall and were very quickly upon the prone North Carolinians, hundreds of whom were now being herded to the rear. The flags of the 20th and 23rd North Carolina were also captured by Baxter's victory-flushed soldiers.

Iverson, like O'Neal, had remained in the rear and now watched in horror as his brigade was nearly annihilated. Within a matter of minutes, he had lost nearly 800 of his 1,300 men. It was an experience the survivors would never forget. Long after the war, in an oft-quoted précis of their attack on Day One at Gettysburg, one of Iverson's men lamented, "[U] unwarned, unled as a brigade, went forward Iverson's deserted band to its doom. Deep and long must the desolate homes and orphaned children of North Carolina rue the rashness of that hour."

Having turned back O'Neal and Iverson and with their ammunition running low, Baxter's men moved into position next to Cutler's men in Sheads's Woods, their place on Oak Ridge having been taken up by Gabriel Paul's fresh 1,500-man brigade, which had been summoned earlier by Robinson.

Though O'Neal and Iverson were repulsed with heavy losses, the fighting only momentarily abated, as more of Rodes's men were being fed into the fight. Junius Daniel's large brigade, 2,100 strong, advanced two hundred yards to the right-rear of Iverson. As his North Carolinians were getting slaughtered, Iverson appealed to Daniel for support. Daniel led his brigade southward, sweeping across the fields to the rear of Iverson's prone men. He was in a tricky spot. He wanted to support Iverson and at the same time deal with the Union soldiers in Sheads's Woods, but his men were also coming under fire from Union troops positioned directly to his front—Roy Stone's Pennsylvanians, along the Chambersburg Pike. He thus decided to divide his brigade, swinging two of his regiments to the left, to deal with the Union troops in the woodlot, while advancing his remaining three regiments to the south toward Stone's Pennsylvanians along the pike.

Watching as Daniel's line drew nearer, Colonel Roy Stone ordered the 149th Pennsylvania forward to the Railroad Cut. There they waited until Daniel's men got to within point-blank range before opening a withering fire. The soldiers of the 143rd Pennsylvania, still along the pike, added their fire to the din, as did a number of First Corps batteries posted along Seminary Ridge. This combined fire sent Daniel's North Carolinians reeling and falling back in confusion. But Daniel would demonstrate a remarkable doggedness that afternoon. He rallied his men for another attack, while Stone ordered the 149th to fall back to the Chambersburg Pike. The panting Pennsylvania soldiers raced back to their original position, to the left of the 143rd. They were joined there by Stone's third regiment, the 150th Pennsylvania, which had swung north from its position in front of the McPherson house. These raw Pennsylvania troops, engaged that afternoon in their first serious combat since being mustered into service the previous summer, pulled back the hammers on their muskets and braced for another attack.

Daniel's three regiments again swept forward and again met a heavy fire. But they pushed on, this time all the way to the now vacant Railroad Cut. However, for many of Daniel's men, the cut was too deep, and just like Davis's men earlier that morning, they found themselves trapped. Stone ordered the

149th to charge toward the cut, where they captured scores of Daniel's North Carolinians. The rest of Daniel's line retreated, his second attack now driven back. The cost of these attacks had been heavy on both sides. Colonel Roy Stone had fallen, shot through the hip, and command of the brigade had passed to Colonel Langhorne Wister, but it was not long before he, too, fell with a grievous wound, shot through the face while shouting out commands. Despite his heavy losses, Junius Daniel again prepared for another strike.

The Union First Corps was putting up a tenacious defense, yielding not a foot of ground and turning back repeated assaults. For the moment, the men were holding their own on the fields west of town, but it would not be long before the tide of battle would reverse its bloody course.

From atop Herr's Ridge, Henry Heth had watched as Rodes's attacks unfolded. He was eager to reenter the fight, especially after noticing First Corps units shifting positions to his front in order to meet Rodes's attacks while his own division stood idly by, spectators to the grand drama unfolding before them. Heth appealed twice to Lee, who had by this time arrived on Herr's Ridge. But Lee, trying to make sense of what was happening, was reluctant to commit any more troops to battle. When Heth first asked if he should advance, Lee answered with an emphatic *no*; he was not yet prepared for battle since Longstreet was not yet up with his First Corps.

At about the same time, the Confederate army commander at long last learned of the whereabouts of Jeb Stuart and his absent brigades of cavalry. One of Stuart's staff officers found Lee and reported that Stuart was all the way up in Carlisle, thirty miles away. Lee immediately sent the officer galloping back to Carlisle with instructions for Stuart to make his way to Gettysburg as soon as possible. Of course, with Stuart that far away and in the absence of any report from him, Lee remained in total ignorance of the size and strength of the Union force to his front. As he had told Richard Anderson earlier that afternoon, it could have been the whole Army of the Potomac or only a part of it—there was simply no way for him to know.

Still, despite his reservations, Lee could sense that events were beginning to spiral beyond his control. Rodes's men were heavily engaged, and Lee knew that Jubal Early's division would soon be arriving, farther to the north, to the left of Rodes. Seizing the moment and attempting to take control of the escalating situation, Lee decided that it was time to press the attack home, and at 2:30 p.m., he sent orders for Heth to advance.

To lead this effort, Heth called on his two brigades that had been kept out of the morning fight, those under John Brockenbrough and Johnston Pettigrew. Forming into lines of battle south of the Chambersburg Pike and less than half a mile west of McPherson's Ridge, Brockenbrough's 800 Virginians held the left of Heth's line, while Pettigrew's all–North Carolina brigade—the largest brigade in Lee's army at 2,500 men strong—formed up to Brockenbrough's right. What remained of Archer's Brigade would advance to the right of Pettigrew in support. Heth's instructions were simple: Brockenbrough and Pettigrew were to push straight ahead, directly toward the Iron Brigade formed up in Herbst's Woods and toward Colonel Chapman Biddle's New York and Pennsylvania soldiers farther back on McPherson's Ridge.

Stepping off in parade-like precision, Heth's men immediately came under artillery fire, but they closed ranks and continued driving forward. In Herbst's Woods, soldiers of the Iron Brigade marveled at the Confederate advance. One member of the 2nd Wisconsin wrote, "Their bearing was magnificent and their alignment seemed to be perfect," while another recorded, "They kept coming steadily on, and in as good a line as ever troops did upon parade, and their muskets a glittering. It was an awe-inspiring sight to observe them." The Iron Brigade, under orders to hold on to the woodlot "at all hazards," waited patiently for the Confederates to get well within range before opening fire.

To the right of the Iron Brigade, Colonel Edmund Dana, commanding Stone's brigade, pivoted his three regiments to meet Brockenbrough's advance, bringing the Virginians' advance to a temporary standstill. To the right of Brockenbrough's stalled line, Pettigrew's men continued to move forward, directly in the face of a destructive fire poured forth from the stalwart Iron Brigade. Casualties were especially high as the North Carolinians negotiated their way across Willoughby Run and began climbing its steep embankments. The struggle within the woodlot was fierce beyond description—soldiers in blue and gray firing at close quarters, in some cases just forty yards apart, and filling the woodlot with a thick, sulfurous smoke.

The losses on both sides were horrific. The 26th North Carolina, advancing in the center of Pettigrew's Brigade, lost 550 of the 800 men it took into the fight, including no fewer than 14 men who carried the regimental flag, as well as its brave twenty-one-year-old commander, Colonel Henry King Burgwyn, the youngest colonel in Lee's army, who fell with a mortal wound. All 91 men of Company F were either killed or wounded. In front of the 26th North Carolina stood the 24th Michigan, the junior regiment of the storied Iron Brigade having joined up with it the previous fall. In Herbst's Woods that afternoon, these Michigan men proved themselves equally as tough and as determined as their fellow black-hatted comrades from Indiana and Wisconsin. In its fight with Pettigrew, the 24th Michigan lost 365 men, including 99 killed in action.

Despite their tough stance, it was not long before the Iron Brigade found itself in a precarious situation. Soldiers of the 11th North Carolina were able to work their way around the exposed left flank of the Iron Brigade, held by the 19th Indiana. Said one Hoosier, "The slaughter in our ranks became frightful beyond description." Under fire from the front and flank, the 19th fell back. Its withdrawal, in turn, exposed the left flank of the 24th Michigan in the woodlot; soon, all the regiments of the Iron Brigade were in retreat, the men falling back stubbornly all the way to Seminary Ridge.

As the 26th and 11th North Carolina pried loose the Iron Brigade from Herbst's Woods, farther south, the soldiers of Pettigrew's other two regiments—the 47th and 52nd North Carolina—slammed head-on with Chapman Biddle's men on McPherson's Ridge. The combat there was equally terrific, the casualties equally appalling. But there, too, the right of the Confederate line extended well beyond Biddle's left. Unable to hold, Biddle's New Yorkers and Pennsylvanians also began falling back.

The First Corps' line on McPherson's Ridge was collapsing. The retreat of both Biddle's brigade and the Iron Brigade left only the Pennsylvanians of Stone's brigade atop the ridgeline, near the McPherson house and barn. Brockenbrough's men had by now renewed their attack, advancing from the west; so, too, had the indefatigable Junius Daniel, whose North Carolinians advanced, for the third time, from the north. Under severe pressure and alone on the ridgeline, Colonel Dana ordered his men to retreat. Brockenbrough's Virginians swept forward to the McPherson buildings. In the barn, they rounded up 350 prisoners, mostly wounded Union soldiers who had sought shelter there, including Colonel Roy Stone. Stone's three Pennsylvania regiments, never before in combat, had proven themselves hearty warriors. They entered the fight with a total of 1,350 men; 850 were now casualties of war, a staggering 65 percent loss.

Stone's survivors fell back to Seminary Ridge, where a new line of defense was being patched together. The battered remnants of the Iron Brigade were there, as were those of Biddle's brigade farther south, while First Corps artillery chief Charles Wainwright lined the ridge with an impressive array of guns. There, they determined to make one more stand, preparing for yet another Confederate advance, which was not long in arriving. This one, though, would be led by the soldiers of Dorsey Pender's fresh division, which had made its way to the front, sweeping past Heth's shattered ranks. In their attack, Brockenbrough and especially Pettigrew

A.C. Redwood illustration depicting Virginians of John Brockenbrough's brigade sweeping past the McPherson barn. *From* Battles and Leaders of the Civil War.

had suffered tremendous loss, and their offensive punch had been spent. Heth himself was among the wounded, having been struck in the head and knocked unconscious while spurring his horse through Herbst's Woods. Pettigrew took Heth's place in divisional command, while the soldiers of his own brigade regrouped from their savage fight and watched as Pender's troops moved forward to the attack.

Farther north, elements of Daniel's Brigade, aided by portions of Iverson's and O'Neal's, kept up a steady pressure on Cutler's and Baxter's men in Sheads's Woods. As the minutes ticked by, the fire from the trees continually dwindled as the Union troops there simply began to run out of bullets. To the right of Cutler's and Baxter's men, on Oak Ridge, General Gabriel Paul's mixed brigade of Pennsylvania, New York, Massachusetts and Maine men also had their hands full as Robert Rodes kept up his relentless attack. Like Baxter earlier, Paul had formed his brigade into the shape of a backward "L," his men lining up either along the crest of the ridgeline or down its eastern slope in order to meet attacks from both the north and west.

No sooner had Paul's men replaced Baxter's in position there than they came under assault, this time from Stephen Ramseur's one-thousand-man brigade, sweeping south from Oak Hill. Of the action there, Captain Abner Small of the 16th Maine later wrote, "I remember the still trees in the heat, and the bullets whistling over us, and the stone wall bristling with muskets, and the line of our men, sweating and grimy, firing and loading and firing again, and here a man suddenly lying still, and there another rising all bloody and cursing and starting for the surgeon."

Gabriel Paul, a Missouri-born career soldier of French ancestry and a West Point graduate, fell from his saddle with a horrific wound, shot through the head by a bullet that entered his right temple and exited through his left eye socket. The wound would, of course, leave him blind, but somehow the tough old soldier would survive. In very quick succession, the next two officers who assumed command of Paul's brigade were also struck down wounded. Paul's men were putting up a stout fight, but the pressure, coming in from two sides, was becoming too great for them to bear.

It was now 3:00 p.m., and like an irresistible tide, Confederate forces were pressing the entirety of the Union lines beyond Gettysburg, for not only were Heth's and Rodes's men then advancing, but farther north, so too was General Jubal Early's division, which at last came sweeping onto the field, descending like an avalanche on the far right of the Union line, manned by the soldiers of Francis Barlow's division of the Eleventh Army Corps.

Oliver Howard had hoped to connect his Eleventh Corps directly to the right of Doubleday's First Corps line, but the timely arrival of Rodes's command on Oak Hill had prevented that. Thus, when the Eleventh Corps arrived on the fields north of town, there developed a quarter-mile gap between the two corps. Howard placed the deployment of the Eleventh Corps in the capable hands of Carl Schurz, then galloped all the way south to Seminary Ridge, where he met Abner Doubleday. Howard told Doubleday that if his men were driven back, they were to retreat through town and rally on Cemetery Hill, where he had already placed Von Steinwehr's division. Howard then made his way back through town to his headquarters on Cemetery Hill, where he sent off messages to both Major General Henry Slocum (whose Twelfth Corps was just five miles at Two Taverns) and Daniel Sickles (whose Third Corps was guarding the army's left flank at Emmitsburg), urging them to bring their commands to Gettysburg.

The position taken up by the Eleventh Corps was a poor one, ill-suited for defense, with nary a ridgeline or a woodlot to better shelter the troops. Schurz's division, under the direct command of Alexander Schimmelfennig, formed on the left of the line, its two brigades—under Colonel George von Amsberg and General Wladimir Krzyzanowski—stretching across the broad,

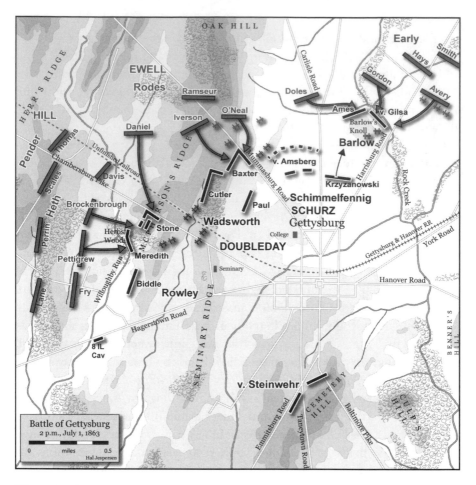

Like an irresistible tide, the soldiers of four Confederate divisions swept forward to the attack on the afternoon of July 1, overwhelming the outnumbered First and Eleventh Corps. *Map by Hal Jespersen.*

open fields between the Mummasburg Road on its left and the Carlisle Pike on its right. Immediately upon taking up this position, the men of these two brigades came under fire from Carter's guns on Oak Hill, as well as from the Georgians of George Doles's brigade, stretched out to their front. Francis Barlow's division formed to the right of Schimmelfennig, stretching from the Carlisle Pike in an easterly fashion, in front of the county almshouse and to the Harrisburg Road.

Francis Barlow was a clean-shaven Harvard graduate and New York City lawyer whose boyish looks made him appear even younger than his twenty-nine years. He had neither formal military training nor any prewar military experience, but he was a fierce fighter who had risen rapidly from captain to colonel to brigadier general. Earlier that spring, he was given divisional command in the Eleventh Corps, an assignment he did not particularly like. Barlow did not think highly of the men under his command, once referring to them as "miserable creatures." But neither did his men care much for Barlow, finding him excessively strict and overbearing.

Not liking the position taken up by his men, Barlow decided to advance his 2,100-man division to the only high ground on this area of the field, a modest rise known as Blocher's Knoll to his front. It seemed a natural thing to do, to take possession of the high ground. But Barlow's decision to advance would soon spell disaster for the Eleventh Corps, for not only did it force Schurz to further extend Schimmelfennig's line in order to maintain contact with Barlow's, but it also placed Barlow's own exposed right flank directly on the Harrisburg Road, making it an all-too-inviting target for Jubal Early's men, who were just then advancing down that very same roadway.

As soon as Rodes's attack had commenced, Ewell had sent an aide galloping off to find Early with instructions to hurry forward and attack.

Blocher's Knoll would forever afterward become known as Barlow's Knoll, named for the boyish-looking Francis Barlow, who had advanced his division to this rise of ground. *Library of Congress*.

Early received these orders when he was within just a few miles of town, and he immediately sprang into action. His artillery raced to the front, taking up positions on some high ground north of Rock Creek, where they began shelling Barlow's lines. Early's infantry also deployed. The soldiers of Brigadier General John Gordon's brigade filed to the right of the Harrisburg Road, while to the left of Gordon went the brigades of Harry Hays and Isaac Avery on Early's far left flank. Early's fourth brigade, under William Smith was held in reserve. Early recognized that his men were heading directly toward the Federal flank and that the Union line was actually angling away from his front, since Barlow's men, for the moment, were focused on George Doles's brigade to their front and left. Sensing a great opportunity, Early gave the order for his men to attack.

Gordon's Brigade led the effort, its 1,200 Georgians sweeping forward and quickly driving back Barlow's skirmishers before encountering Colonel Leopold von Gilsa's small brigade of just 900 men in position in a narrow line of trees that skirted Rock Creek, in front of Blocher's Knoll. Behind

John Gordon had no military education nor any prior military experience before the outbreak of the Civil War. Still, he would become one of Lee's best and hardest-fighting officers, rising in rank from captain to major general by war's end. *Library of Congress*.

Lieutenant Bayard Wilkeson directs the fire of his battery from atop Blocher's Knoll just moments before falling with a mortal wound. *From* Battles and Leaders of the Civil War.

Von Gilsa's thin line, on the knoll, the guns of Battery G, 4th U.S. Artillery, were blazing away in a desperate contest with Early's guns. Among those struck down in this unequal fight was nineteen-year-old Lieutenant Bayard Wilkeson, commanding the outgunned Union battery. A Confederate shell crashed into his right leg and killed his horse. Falling to the ground, Wilkeson very coolly wrapped a handkerchief around his mangled limb as a tourniquet and then took out his penknife and amputated his leg, which had been hanging on by shreds. He was carried back to the almshouse, where, later that night, the brave young officer passed away.

After an obstinate fight, Von Gilsa's outnumbered troops fell back, racing their way up and over the knoll where Barlow's second brigade, under General Adelbert Ames, had taken up position. Ames had roughly 1,200 men in his four regiments, troops from Connecticut and Ohio, who were already hotly engaged with Doles's persistent Georgians. Ames's men were holding their own, but the collapse of Von Gilsa's brigade and the subsequent retreat of Wilkeson's battery, which had limbered up and galloped away at the approach of the Confederate infantry, had now exposed their own right flank to the rushing gray tide. Gordon's men splashed across Rock Creek and swept up the rising ground, forming a connection with the left flank of Doles. Together, the two all-Georgia brigades pushed forward, "yelling like savage Indians in making a savage charge," said one man, and effecting heavy losses on Ames's outnumbered troops. The 25th Ohio, for example, lost no fewer than 160 of its 220 men, while the 17th Connecticut lost nearly 200 of the 385 taken into the fight, including its commanding officer, Lieutenant Colonel Douglas Fowler, who was decapitated by a Confederate artillery shell atop Blocher's Knoll. Ames's men took to their heels, falling back toward the almshouse, where Union officers frantically tried to piece together a new line of defense. Seeing the collapse of his division, Barlow tried desperately to rally his men, but to no avail. He was shot down, seriously wounded, and soon fell into Confederate hands.

Carl Schurz watched as the Eleventh Corps began to unravel. With the retreat of Barlow's division, Schurz, the German-born revolutionary, sent a desperate plea for reinforcements back to Howard on Cemetery Hill and then advanced Wladimir Krzyzanowski's brigade, from Schimmelfennig's division, to help meet the Confederate advance. Krzyzanowski's men poured

Like many others, General Wladimir Krzyzanowski's brigade was torn to pieces on July 1 at Gettysburg. His 119th New York and 26th Wisconsin each lost 100 men. His 82nd lost 142 of the 250 men taken into the fight, while his 75th Pennsylvania lost 111 of its 194 men. *Library of Congress.*

volley after volley into surging lines of Georgians, their bullets, said one Confederate, humming "about our ears like infuriated bees." The gunners of Dilger's and Wheeler's batteries turned the barrels of their cannons to the right, adding their thunder to the din. Krzyzanowski, an émigré from Poland, rode back and forth behind his lines, encouraging his men, before being thrown from the saddle when his horse was struck down. In later describing the action that morning, Krzyzanowski said simply that "[t]his portrait of battle was the portrait of hell."

"The Yankees fought more stubborn than I ever saw them or ever want to see them again," admitted one of Doles's Georgians. Krzyzanowski helped to explain why, saying, "The fate of the nation was at stake. I felt it, the leaders felt it, the army felt it, and we fought like lions." But though fighting like lions, Krzyzanowski's line broke after just twenty minutes of intense combat, his regiments taking fearful losses. In a last-ditch effort to brace Krzyzanowski's rapidly dwindling line, Schimmelfennig threw forward the 157th New York of Von Amsberg's brigade. The New Yorkers swept forward, wheeling to the right, and were initially successful in turning Doles's flank, but it was not long before Doles's men rallied and surrounded the New Yorkers on three sides. The 157th fled, its ranks reduced by 75 percent.

Doles's and Gordon's Georgians swept two Union divisions off the field, inflicting heavy losses while their own casualties were comparatively light. At the same time but to the left of Gordon, Hays's and Avery's Brigades continued their advance along the axis of the Harrisburg Road, quickly overrunning an ad hoc line of troops pieced together by Adelbert Ames near the almshouse before descending on another line of Union infantry on the northern outskirts of town.

In response to Schurz's plea, Howard had sent forward Lewis Heckman's Ohio battery, as well as Colonel Charles Coster's brigade from Von Steinwehr's division, leaving only Orland Smith's brigade behind on Cemetery Hill. Coster led his 1,200 men through town, already thick with retreating Eleventh Corps soldiers. Heckman's pieces dropped trail and swung into position on Carlisle Street, near the college grounds, while the 73rd Pennsylvania halted near the railroad station. Coster's other three regiments, roughly 900 men, continued north along Stratton Street before hastily forming a line of battle near the kilns of John Kuhn's brickyard. Hardly were these three regiments in position before Hays and Avery struck. Outflanked and outgunned, it was not long before Coster's line was smashed. Within twenty minutes, Coster lost 550 of the 900 who lined up in Kuhn's brickyard, a number that included 300 captured. Only 18 of the 270 soldiers in the 154th New York made it safely back to Cemetery Hill. Simultaneously, Heckman's artillerists, after throwing a few rounds of canister in Hays's advancing Louisianans, were also overrun, two of their four guns captured.

The Eleventh Corps was in full retreat, the men racing their way through the streets of town, with Early's victory-flushed men close behind them. At the same time, Union troops were also pouring into town from the west—the First Corps had finally collapsed.

Driven off McPherson's Ridge, the battered First Corps had fallen back to Seminary Ridge, where it formed a last line of defense, stretching nearly half a mile in length from near the Railroad Cut on the right to the Fairfield/Hagerstown Road on its left. South of this roadway, in the trees of Schultz's Woods, went the horsemen of Colonel William Gamble's brigade, placed there by Buford to provide flank support. Forming up in front of the buildings of the Lutheran Seminary, some of these First Corps troops took shelter behind the improvised breastworks constructed earlier that day by Robinson's men. The ridgeline also bristled with artillery; eighteen guns massed on what was a narrow front. The gunners and their infantry support now girded for a renewed Confederate attack.

Heth's men had been entirely used up, their place taken by the soldiers of Pender's Division. The North Carolinians of Alfred Scales's brigade swept past the McPherson buildings and over the prone men of Brockenbrough's Brigade, their left anchored on the Chambersburg Pike. To their right and making their way through Pettigrew's shattered regiments advanced the South Carolinians under Abner Perrin. With a combined force of just under three thousand men, Scales and Perrin now faced a daunting task, having been ordered to advance straight ahead, across the swale of ground between McPherson's and Seminary Ridges and directly toward the First Corps' new line and its massed cannons. Lieutenant Colonel Joseph Brown of the 14th South Carolina spoke for many of Scales's and Perrin's men when he later described the ground to their front as "the fairest field and finest front for destruction on an advancing foe that could well be conceived."

The two brigades stepped forward to the attack, and immediately Perrin encountered trouble, his right flank coming under such a withering fire from Gamble's horsemen in Schultz's Woods that his advance grounded to a halt. Until Perrin could get his men once more in motion, Scales's men were forced to advance alone, with all the Federal muskets and cannon barrels pointed directly at them. Scales's North Carolinians moved forward at a double-quick, down the eastern slope of McPherson's Ridge and directly into a wall of iron and lead. First Corps artillerists packed their cannons with deadly and devastating rounds of canister. "Every discharge," said one of Scales's men, "made sad loss in the line." Scales's attack stalled at the bottom of the swale, one hundred yards from the Union line. They could neither advance nor retreat, and hundreds fell, including Scales, who went down with a savage wound. Such was the destruction of his brigade that the wounded warrior later wrote that "only a squad here and there marked the place where regiments rested." By day's end, Scales lost 900 of the 1,400 he took into the fight. Of the 180 soldiers in the 13th North Carolina, only 30 survived the storm unscathed.

Scales's men valiantly stood their ground while Perrin finally got his line moving forward once again. The South Carolina–born brigade commander angled his two right-most regiments toward Gamble's horsemen while leading his other regiments forward. Perrin, who would lose 600 of his 1,500 in the next twenty minutes, led the way on horseback, instructing his soldiers to charge directly forward and not to stop to fire until ordered to do so. They were greeted with the same destructive fire that had met Scales minutes earlier, a fire Perrin later described as "the most destructive fire of musketry I have ever been exposed to." Still, in the face of this "furious storm," Perrin's men surged forward, bearing down on the Union line on Seminary Ridge.

One of the Union artillerists posted atop the ridgeline would later vividly describe the scene as Scales's and Perrin's men advanced and as Confederate shells, fired from both Herr's Ridge and Oak Hill, tore into the blue ranks: "Up and down the line, men reeling and falling; splinters flying from wheels and axles where bullets hit; in rear, horses tearing and plunging, mad with wounds or terror; drivers yelling, shells bursting, shot shrieking overhead, howling about our ears or throwing up great clouds of dust where they struck; the musketry crashing on three sides of us; bullets hissing, humming and whistling everywhere. Smoke, dust, splinters, blood, wreck and carnage indescribable."

"To stop was destruction. To retreat was disaster. To go forward was 'orders,'" said Lieutenant Colonel Brown as Perrin's South Carolinians continued their advance. Perrin detected a weak point near the left of the Federal line, and through deft maneuvering, he angled his men to exploit it. Coming under fire from front and flank, with ammunition running low, Union officers at last ordered their men to retreat, the pressure simply too strong for the men to bear any longer. Artillerists limbered up their pieces while the infantry fled past. With a cheer, Perrin's men swept over Seminary Ridge, finally driving the First Corps troops into town.

Meanwhile, on Oak Ridge, General John Robinson watched as the Eleventh Corps line to his right crumbled. To his left, the soldiers of Baxter's

Union First Corps troops desperately try to fend off Pender's Division from atop Seminary Ridge. *From* Battles and Leaders of the Civil War.

and Cutler's brigades, entirely out of bullets, withdrew from their positions in Sheads's Woods. With the line of Seminary Ride on the verge of collapse, Doubleday sent orders for Robinson to retreat as well. The question now became how best to extract Paul's brigade, which was still heavily engaged with Rodes's men. Robinson called on Colonel Charles Tilden, commander of the 16th Maine. Robinson ordered Tilden to advance his regiment to the angle of the stone wall that both lined Oak Ridge and ran parallel to the Mummasburg Road, instructing the Maine colonel to "hold out to the last."

Realizing his regiment was to be sacrificed, Tilden faithfully carried out his orders and advanced his 275 men to the designated position, where they immediately opened fire on the waves of Confederates advancing from the west and north. These were Ramseur's men, supported on both sides by various elements of Rodes's other brigades. Captain Abner Small of the 16th Maine remembered that "the attacking line came on, and following behind it was another, and we knew that our little regiment could not withstand the onset." The Maine troops turned to see the other regiments of Paul's brigade retreating, heading toward town. They were now the only Union troops left on the field.

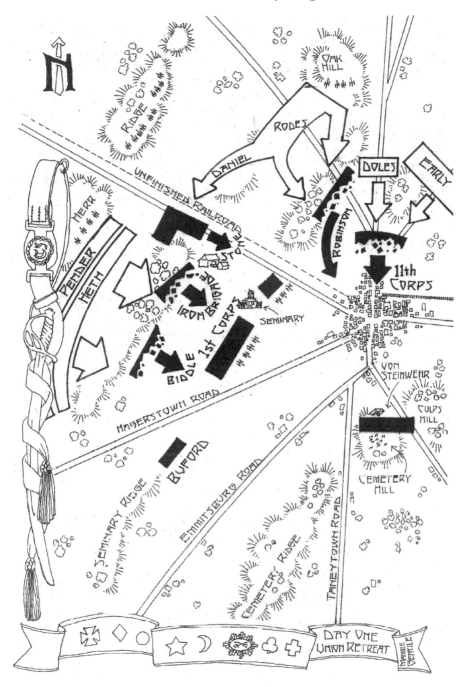

Late in the afternoon, what remained of the First and Eleventh Corps was driven back through the streets of Gettysburg before rallying on Cemetery Hill. *Map by Mannie Gentile.*

With Ramseur's men continuing to advance toward his rapidly dwindling line and believing that his regiment had sacrificed enough, Tilden, after what must have seemed a few long minutes, ordered a retreat. The Maine men fled south, through Sheads's Woods and toward the Railroad Cut, being closely followed by Rodes's men. Then, advancing from the west came elements of Daniel's Brigade. "We were caught between two fires," concluded Small. "It was the end." To prevent their flag from falling into Confederate hands, the Maine troops quickly tore it to shreds before most of them raised their own hands in surrender. The 16th Maine had, indeed, been sacrificed. Of its 275 members, 232 were now dead, wounded or marching to the rear as prisoners of war.

By 4:30 p.m., some nine long hours after Marcellus Jones fired the battle's first shot and after a determined stand north and west of Gettysburg, the Union First and Eleventh Corps had finally collapsed, crumbling under the weight of superior numbers. The streets of town were now thronged with the fleeing men. In a few cases, the retreat took on the appearance of a

Dorsey Pender's men finally pushed the Union First Corps off the fields west of town. A hard fighter, Pender would be struck by shell fragment on July 2 and mortally wounded. *From* Battles and Leaders of the Civil War.

rout, with some men overcome with panic; in other cases, the retreat was more orderly. Despite the best efforts of some officers, regiments quickly lost cohesion, and the mass of Union troops became a jumbled mob in the narrow streets of town. A soldier of Stone's brigade remembered that they retreated "without semblance of military order with every man for himself and the Rebs take the hindmost." With Confederates entering town behind them, the fleeing Union soldiers turned blind corners, hopped over fences and trampled gardens underfoot as they made their way rearward. Hundreds, unable to get away, were rounded up and captured, while in the town square, or diamond, soldiers of the 1st South Carolina of Perrin's Brigade triumphantly raised the Confederate banner up the town's flagpole as valiant General Pender reined up beside them and congratulated them on what he deemed a "glorious day's work."

The people of town, caught up in the whirlwind of the retreat, clustered in their basements, doing their best to ride out the storm. Salome Myers remembered that she "knelt shivering and prayed [while] The noise above our heads, the rattling of muskets, the unearthly cries mingled with the sobbing of children, shook our hearts." Other residents, more curious, watched the wild scenes unfold from upstairs windows, including one woman who later famously wrote that the crowd beneath her window was so thick that she believed she could have walked from one side of her street to the other just by stepping on the heads of the soldiers. The occasional shell crashed into some of the buildings of town, while bullets ricocheted off the bricks or splintered windowsills and doorframes. In some instances, Union troops broke into homes seeking a refuge, only to be rooted out and captured once the Confederates occupied town.

Perhaps the best remembered incident of the retreat, though, has to do with a Union soldier who *was* successfully able to evade capture. While making his way back to Cemetery Hill, Brigadier General Alexander Schimmelfennig found himself cut off in the backyard of Anna Garlach on Baltimore Street. Seeing no escape, the Prussian-born officer hid behind Garlach's small woodshed, where he remained for the next three days, finally emerging, very sore but very much relieved on the morning of July 4 once he was certain that the Confederates had vacated the town.

Chased from town, the retreating Union soldiers at last arrived at their designated rallying point on Cemetery Hill, where for the moment, chaos reigned. Rufus Dawes of the bloodied 6th Wisconsin recalled that as he looked around he saw nothing but a "confused rabble of disorganized regiments of infantry and crippled batteries." The only organized force there was Colonel Orland Smith's brigade of Von Steinwehr's division, which stood poised to resist any immediate Confederate attack. Union officers of all ranks worked feverishly to rally the troops and restore order. Notable among them was Oliver Howard, whose presence and calm demeanor amid all the chaos went far in inspiring the men, one of whom later wrote that there was "[n]o hurry, no confusion in his mind. He knew that if he could get his troops in any kind of order…the country was safe.

Assisting Howard in rallying the troops was Major General Winfield Scott Hancock. Sent by Meade to take charge of the forces at Gettysburg and to report on the nature of the terrain, Hancock arrived on Cemetery Hill sometime around 4:30 p.m., just as the First and Eleventh Corps were "retreating in disorder and confusion from the town," Hancock later related, "closely followed by the enemy." But even with Federal forces in retreat, Hancock, like most of the Union brass before him, liked what he saw of the ground south of Gettysburg and especially on Cemetery Hill, allegedly telling Howard that "this is the strongest position by nature on which to fight a battle that I ever saw."

Although Howard in his calm and collected manner had already rallied many of his men on Cemetery Hill, the soldiers' spirits were especially buoyed when they spotted the gallant Hancock. "They all knew him by fame," explained Carl Schurz, "and his stalwart figure, his proud mien, and his superb soldierly bearing seemed to verify all the things that fame had told about him. His mere presence was a reinforcement, and everybody on the field felt stronger for his being there." Another man wrote that Hancock's "bearing was courageous and hopeful, while his eyes flashed defiance," while another remembered that Hancock was "all excitement—not nervous—looking in a thousand ways every minutes and giving directions…he was saying to this man and that: 'Take your guns in that direction'; 'Collect your men'; 'Prepare for immediate action.'" Under their inspired leadership, Howard and Hancock together fashioned a new line of defense.

Cemetery Hill rose roughly one hundred feet in height. Artillery positioned there could sweep the open fields surrounding it to the east and west, and any attack up its northern slopes would have to be launched through narrow streets of town, a most difficult challenge. Because of its inherent military value, it is little wonder why so many Union officers recognized Cemetery Hill as the key ground near Gettysburg. However, in order to hold Cemetery Hill, Union forces would also have to secure Culp's Hill, a higher eminence that towered almost one hundred feet above Cemetery Hill to the southeast. Hancock dispatched

Major General Winfield
Scott Hancock. *Library
of Congress.*

Captain Greenleaf Stevens's 5th Maine battery to occupy a rise of ground
known as McKnight's Knoll, which rose up between the two hilltops, while at
the same time directed Doubleday to send the battered remnants of the Iron
Brigade to occupy Culp's Hill. These men, later joined by various other units
of the First Corps, immediately began constructing earthworks on Culp's Hill
before darkness brought an end to their labors.

On Cemetery Hill any panic that might have taken hold of some of the
men subsided as order was finally, gradually, restored. Charles Wainwright
and Major Thomas Osborn, commanding the artillery of the First and
Eleventh Corps, respectively, established a formidable line of guns on the
hilltop, wheeling no fewer than forty-three cannons into position, ready to
punish any Confederate force that might make an effort to storm the hill.
The infantry settled into position as well, behind the stone walls that lined
the hilltop and among the tombstones of the Evergreen Cemetery, which
crowned its summit. The heavy losses sustained that day by the First and
Eleventh Corps had now become all too readily apparent. Of the 8,200 First

Corps troops who marched into battle that day, fewer than 2,500 remained. Eleventh Corps casualties neared 3,200, more than 40 percent of the 7,600 men it took into the fight. Included among these stunning losses were more than 3,000 men who had fallen into Confederate hands as prisoners of war.

With the sun fast setting over the crimson-colored fields west of Gettysburg, roughly seven thousand Union soldiers, backed up by forty-three guns, held on to Cemetery and Culp's Hills. It was a small, battered force to be sure, but the men, though exhausted from their exertions of the day, did hold commanding positions, and additional Union forces were not long in arriving.

First to arrive were the soldiers of Major General Henry Slocum's Twelfth Corps, its two divisions going into position that evening on either end of embryonic Union line. At eleven o'clock that morning, the Twelfth Corps had arrived at Two Taverns, a small hamlet just five miles southeast of Gettysburg. From there, Slocum could plainly hear the distant sounds of battle, but despite several pleas sent by Howard for the Twelfth Corps to hurry on to Gettysburg, Slocum opted to remain at Two Taverns, his men whiling away the afternoon while the First and Twelfth Corps got shot to pieces.

Finally, at 3:00 p.m., Slocum at last decided to set his men in motion. Unlike Reynolds and Howard, Slocum had, earlier that morning, received the Pipe Creek Circular, and he was understandably reluctant to advance on to Gettysburg without orders from Meade to do so. Not so with Daniel Sickles, commanding the Third Corps. Sickles had marched his men to Emmitsburg that morning, guarding the army's left. He, too, had received the Pipe Creek Circular, as well as another order from Meade to maintain his position. But in Sickles's mind, Howard's reports of the fighting at Gettysburg and his calls for help trumped Meade's instructions. He kept only a small portion of his corps—two brigades—behind at Emmitsburg while vigilantly marching the rest to Howard's support, arriving near Gettysburg later that evening.

With daylight fast fading and with additional troops not long in arriving, fears of a Confederate attack on Cemetery Hill began to give way. As things settled down, Hancock sent off a note to army commander Meade, informing him that the fighting had ended and predicting that the troops would be able to hold on until night. "I think we can retire," reported Hancock. "[I]f not, we can fight here, as the ground appears not unfavorable with good troops." When Slocum arrived on the scene sometime around 7:00 p.m., Hancock turned over command to him and then made his way back to army headquarters at Taneytown, where he reported directly to Meade. Well before Hancock would arrive, however, Meade had already scrapped any idea he might have still had of fighting at Pipe Creek and decided to concentrate his forces at Gettysburg, the orders going out at 7:00 p.m. for all his corps commanders to make their way toward the crossroads town.

Meade's opponent, General Robert E. Lee, had neither expected nor wanted a battle that day and only reluctantly committed his forces in an attempt to exert control over the escalating engagement. Still, four of his divisions had crippled two Union corps, chasing them off the fields north and west of Gettysburg. After Pender's men swept the First Corps off Seminary Ridge, Lee rode toward town, passing by the blood-soaked fields and establishing headquarters near a small grove of trees along the Chambersburg Pike, across from a small stone house belonging to the widow Mary Thompson. From there, Lee could see Union forces rallying on Cemetery Hill south of town. Hoping to drive the Federals off the hilltop and gain this high ground, Lee sent his chief of staff, Major Walter Taylor, galloping off with a message to Ewell, telling his Second Corps commander that it was "only necessary to press those people in order to secure possession of heights" and instructing him to seize Cemetery Hill, but only if it was "practicable."

Taylor found Ewell in town and discovered that he had already been contemplating an attack on Cemetery Hill. Ewell told Taylor that his men would attack, but only *if* they were supported on their right. Taylor immediately reported this back to Lee. Lee did have some fresh troops available in the form of Richard Anderson's division of Hill's Corps, which at some seven thousand men strong was by itself equal to the Union force just then on Cemetery Hill, but Lee, of course, had no way of knowing this, and with the head of Longstreet's corps still six miles away, he decided to hold Anderson's men back as a general reserve. Of Hill's other troops, Heth's Division and two of Pender's brigades had been badly mauled and were in no condition to continue the attack. Lee sent word of this back to Ewell, telling him that if Cemetery Hill was to be carried, it would be entirely up to him and his men.

The willingness Ewell had initially professed in attacking Cemetery Hill dissipated once he rode south along Baltimore Street and got a better look at the Union defenses on the hilltop. It was too heavily defended, decided Ewell, and besides, if he was to launch an attack, it would have to be made through town with little, if any, artillery support since there were no good positions to place his cannons. Ewell knew that Rodes's Division had sustained heavy losses in its attacks against Oak Ridge that afternoon, and like much of Hill's men, they were not in any kind of condition to attack. Early's Division had suffered far fewer losses in its attack against the Eleventh Corps, but its brigades were widely scattered in the streets of town.

What was more, soon after Early rode into Gettysburg, he received an alarming report from Billy Smith, whose brigade advanced east of town on the far left of the Confederate line. Smith reported what seemed to be a large Union force advancing from the east, along the York Pike, and although this report would later prove unfounded, in the absence of any cavalry to determine is veracity, it caused Early, with Ewell's approval, to send John Gordon's brigade to Smith's assistance. With two of his brigades thus sent east to guard the York Pike against this phantom menace, Early was left with only his two remaining brigades, under Hays and Avery, who formed up east of town, along Winebrenner's Run and near the Henry Culp farmstead, where they came under fire from Stevens's guns on McKnight's Knoll and from other Union batteries on Cemetery Hill.

For all of these reasons, Ewell prudently decided against an attack on Cemetery Hill; it was simply not "practicable," he thought. Nevertheless, this decision brought about yet another of those long-standing Gettysburg controversies. Ewell would later suffer much from the criticisms of those who sought to hold Lee blameless for the defeat at Gettysburg and instead place the burden for the loss squarely on the shoulders of his subordinates. Many would later lament the absence of Stonewall Jackson at this critical moment, their argument being that if Jackson had been there, Cemetery Hill would have been taken and the Confederates would have prevailed. There is, of course, no way of knowing what Jackson might have done and whether any Confederate attack on Cemetery Hill that evening would have met with success or been turned back with great slaughter. In the end, the matter was left to Ewell, and he made the right decision.

But Ewell had not entirely given up. Having decided against attacking Cemetery Hill, his focus turned to Culp's Hill, believing that if his men could secure this high ground, they would be in a position to threaten both the Union right flank and rear and thus prompt the men there to abandon Cemetery Hill. His subordinates agreed, with Early allegedly warning his one-legged corps commander that if he did not seize Culp's Hill that night, "it would cost you ten thousand men to get up there tomorrow." To seize Culp's Hill, Ewell called on his final division, under Edward Johnson, which was just then approaching Gettysburg from the west, having begun the day on the other side of South Mountain and having already marched twenty-five miles along the Chambersburg Pike in what was a vast procession of Confederate infantry and wagons. Johnson had ridden into Gettysburg in advance of his men and reported to Ewell. After a brief meeting, Ewell sent Johnson back with orders to bring up his division, march it around to the east side of town and then seize Culp's Hill if he found it to be unoccupied.

By this time, Robert E. Lee, like Meade, had already decided that he would commit to battle at Gettysburg, no matter whether Ewell was successful that night in securing the high ground south of town. Lee's decision to fight at Gettysburg drew an immediate objection from his longest-serving and most trusted subordinate, General James Longstreet. Shortly after 5:00 p.m., Lee's "Old War Horse" arrived at army headquarters, having galloped well ahead of his First Corps as it continued to snake its way over South Mountain. The two generals rode south along Seminary Ridge, their eyes gazing eastward toward the Union positions on the high ground on the other side of town. Longstreet did not like what he saw. Throughout the campaign, Longstreet was under the impression that Lee had undertaken the drive north with the intention of luring the Army of the Potomac after them and then taking up a favorable defensive position, thus forcing the Union army to attack and not the other way around—to conduct, in short, an offensive campaign while seeking a defensive battle. Longstreet even later alleged that Lee had promised him as much, a claim Lee would adamantly deny, and that evening on Seminary Ridge, Lee would very quickly disabuse Longstreet of any such notion.

Seeing Union troops in position on Cemetery Hill, Longstreet suggested that the army disengage and swing around the Federal left, moving south in order to get between Meade's forces and Washington, but Lee would not hear of this. Pointing toward Cemetery Hill, the army commander emphatically stated that "[i]f the enemy is there tomorrow, we must attack him." Longstreet protested, telling Lee, "If the enemy is there, it is because he is anxious that we should attack him—a good reason, in my judgment for not doing so." But Lee would not be dissuaded. As Longstreet later wrote, the army commander "got a taste of victory" on July 1, and his appetite was not yet sated.

Some students of the battle—again engaging in speculative, counterfactual history—would take up the cry that "if Lee had only listened to Longstreet" and adopted this proposed flanking maneuver, things would have turned out much differently for the Confederates. But following such a course of action would have been incredibly tricky and not entirely feasible. Lee still had no idea as to the whereabouts of all the Union corps, and Stuart had yet to arrive to properly screen such a movement south. Longstreet's plan was also predicated on the assumption that Meade would simply remain in place while the Army of Northern Virginia maneuvered around him, a very unlikely scenario.

Like Richard Ewell, Lieutenant General James Longstreet would suffer much from those seeking to exonerate Lee from any blame for the defeat at Gettysburg. Longstreet did not like the prospects of fighting at Gettysburg and made his objections known several times. *From* Miller's Photographic History of the Civil War.

In his official report on the campaign, Lee would later explain his reasons for giving battle at Gettysburg. "It had not been intended to deliver a general battle so far from our base unless attacked," admitted the army commander, "but coming unexpectedly upon the whole Federal army, to withdraw through the mountains with our extensive trains would have been difficult and dangerous. At the same time we were unable to await an attack, as the country was unfavorable for collecting supplies in the presence of the enemy...A battle, had, therefore," concluded Lee, "become in a measure unavoidable, and the success gained [on July 1] gave the hope of a favorable issue."

Having thus resolved to fight at Gettysburg, Lee began weighing his options on how to best go about positioning his forces to strike at Meade. After Longstreet departed to return to his command, Lee saddled up and rode into town, where he met with Ewell, Early and Rodes, each of whom reported that although their men were still full of fight, the enemy lines to their front were formidable and their own position was not at all conducive to offensive action. Hearing this, Lee asked if it would not make sense, then, for Ewell to pull his troops out of town, march them behind Seminary Ridge and take up position on the army's right flank, thus threatening Meade's more exposed left. Ewell and his two subordinates balked at this idea, arguing that such a move would demoralize the men who had fought so hard to gain possession of the town.

Lee let it go at that, but once he returned to headquarters, he thought better of it and sent instructions back to Ewell: if he felt he could not successfully carry Cemetery Hill that night, he was to abandon the town and take up a position on the army's right. This prompted Ewell to ride to army headquarters and again voice his objections, this time informing Lee of his new plan to occupy Culp's Hill with Johnson's Division. Lee again relented, and Ewell returned to his headquarters, again issuing orders for Johnson to occupy Culp's Hill if he had not already done so. The response he got was not at all what Ewell had wanted or had hoped to hear: Culp's Hill, said Johnson, was already occupied by Federal troops.

It was well after nightfall when Johnson deployed his division east of town and prepared for what promised to be a treacherous advance in the darkness, up the steep, boulder-strewn slopes of Culp's Hill. Before moving forward, however, Johnson naturally wanted to determine whether the hilltop was occupied or if it would be his for the taking. He sent forward a scouting party, some twenty-five men who crept forward cautiously and quietly. The men climbed their way up the slopes of Culp's Hill and directly into a Federal picket line. A short time earlier, Colonel Ira Grover's 7th Indiana had taken up a position to the right of the Iron Brigade, near the summit of Culp's Hill. Grover sent forward pickets in all directions down the slopes, and it was these men Johnson's scouting party had met. A few scattered shots rang out, and two of the Confederates were captured. The rest fled.

On their way back to Johnson, the survivors of this harrowing scouting expedition themselves happened upon and captured a Union courier who was bearing a dispatch addressed to Henry Slocum and signed by order of the Union Fifth Corps commander George Sykes. Sykes was attempting to notify Slocum that his Fifth Corps had arrived in a position just four miles east of Gettysburg and that he would be resuming his march at 4:00 a.m. on the morning of July 2. Thus, not only did Johnson discover that Culp's Hill was occupied, but he also learned that an entire Union corps was just a few miles away on his left flank. He wisely decided to hold his position and so ended any chance Confederate forces might have had of gaining the high ground south of Gettysburg that Wednesday night.

In the end, Lee's men had crushed two Federal corps, but the victory that day was an incomplete one since the Army of the Potomac was able to hold on to the dominating defensive positions south of town. Committed to the offensive and determined to renew his attacks the following day, the question now on Lee's mind was where best to strike. And While Lee considered his options, General George Meade, at the end of just his fourth day as commander of the Army of the Potomac, arrived on Cemetery Hill, having set out from Taneytown at 10:00 p.m., riding north in the moonlight. Meade had already conversed with Hancock about the ground south of Gettysburg, and he now asked his other generals their thoughts. "Is this the place to fight the battle?" he inquired of Oliver Howard. "I am confident we can hold this position," replied the Eleventh Corps commander. Others agreed, including Slocum, who mentioned simply that the ground was "good for defense," and Sickles, who told Meade that it was "a good place to fight from." "Well, I am glad to hear you say so, gentlemen," was Meade's famous reply, "for it is too late to leave it."

CHAPTER NOTES

Each of the three days of battle has been subjected to many great and detailed studies, and any study of the first day's Battle at Gettysburg must begin with Harry Pfanz's *Gettysburg: The First Day* (2001). Pfanz's masterful and insightful studies have defined modern understanding and interpretation of the battle and have shaped the narrative of this present work. For a more in-depth examination of the first day's battle, see *Gettysburg: July 1* (1996) by David G. Martin. Other studies of the battle of July 1 include Warren Hassler's *Crisis at the Crossroads* (1970) and Richard Shue's *Morning at Willoughby Run* (1998). See also Grimsley and Simpson (pages 9–57); Coddington, chapters 11–12 (pages 260–322); Sears, chapters 7–9 (pages 154–245); Trudeau, chapter 12 (pages 152–276); and Woodworth, chapters 4–5 (pages 47–103). For the actions of particular units during the first day's battle, see *Stone's Brigade and the Fight for McPherson's Ridge* by James Dougherty; *Those Damned Black Hats!: The Iron Brigade in the Gettysburg Campaign* by Lance Herdegen; and *Covered with Glory: The 26th North Carolina Infantry at the Battle of Gettysburg* by Rod Gragg. For a series of excellent, insightful essays on various aspects of leadership on the First Day at Gettysburg, see *The First Day at Gettysburg: Essays on Confederate and Union Leadership*, edited by Gary Gallagher (1992).

Chapter 3

"A Scene Very Much Like Hell Itself"

The Second Day, July 2, 1863

DAY TWO OVERVIEW

The second day's battle at Gettysburg remains a day mired in controversy and shrouded in legend. It witnessed some of the most intense combat of the entire war and also exacted the heaviest of all the three days' tolls, with more than eighteen thousand casualties, all sustained, incredibly enough, during just six and a half hours of hellish combat. These casualties made July 2, 1863, by itself, one of the worst single-day actions of the entire war.

Late on July 1, and after having been assured of the defensive value of the ground there, George Meade ordered his army to gather at Gettysburg. Most of it would arrive by midmorning on July 2, taking up a strong defensive position that stretched from Culp's Hill on the right and then curved around Cemetery Hill before running south along Cemetery Ridge toward Little Round Top on the army's left. As the Union army settled into this famed "fishhook" line, Robert E. Lee—seeking to maintain his army's hard-won initiative and hoping for results more decisive than what had been gained the previous day—considered the best way of driving them out of it. The plan he ultimately settled on called for the main assault to be launched against the Federal left using two of Longstreet's First Corps divisions and another from A.P. Hill's Third Corps, which had been kept out of the fight on July 1. And while Longstreet attacked the Federal left, Ewell was ordered to demonstrate against the Federal right and to convert this demonstration into a general assault should the opportunity present itself.

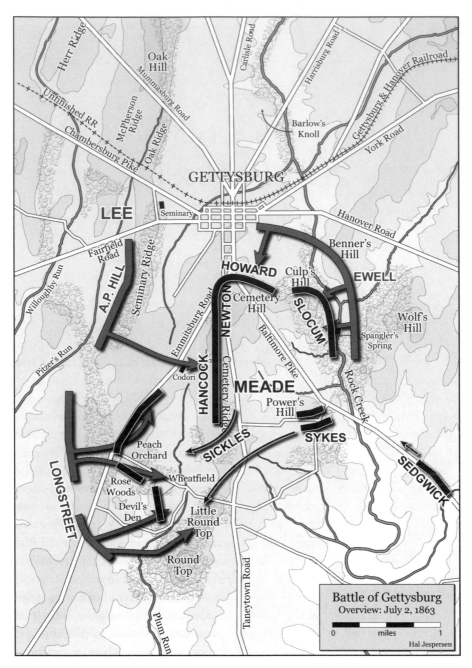

Overview of the Second Day's Battle at Gettysburg. *Map by Hal Jespersen.*

"A Scene Very Much Like Hell Itself"

Sound in theory, Lee's plan was nevertheless based on a faulty understanding of the Federal position, and the attacks that day were not carried out the way Lee had hoped. Most of the day would pass before Longstreet's men were even in position to launch the assault, and once they finally did arrive at the designated jumping-off point, they found the Union army occupying a much different position than had been anticipated. In what continues to rank as one of Gettysburg's most enduring controversies, Union general Daniel Sickles, early that afternoon and without authorization from Meade, advanced his Third Corps some three-quarters of a mile from the position he had been assigned to what he believed was better ground along the Emmitsburg Road and around farmer Joseph Sherfy's Peach Orchard. By doing so, Sickles both disrupted Lee's plan of attack and placed the entire Union army in jeopardy. By the time Meade discovered Sickles's transgression, it was too late to correct it, for Longstreet's assault was just then kicking off.

Once the attack finally commenced—sometime after 4:00 p.m., a full twelve hours after daybreak—it ushered in some of the most intense and horrific combat of the Civil War. Over the next three and a half hours, the soldiers of eleven Confederate brigades—a total of twenty-one thousand hard-fighting men from the divisions of Hood, McLaws and Richard Anderson—pitched into the Union left and center like so many successive waves of an angry sea crashing on the shore. The battle spread like wildfire from Devil's Den and up the rocky slopes of Little Round Top, through John Rose's Wheatfield and Joseph Sherfy's Peach Orchard and all the way north toward a small clump (or copse) of trees near the center of the Union position on Cemetery Ridge. James Longstreet later deemed his soldiers' efforts "the best three-hours' fighting done by any troops on any troops on any battlefield of the war," but the same could have been said of *all* those engaged that bloody Thursday, whether in blue or gray. Launching their own attack a few hours after Longstreet's, portions of Ewell's corps would also fight valiantly, sweeping up Culp's and Cemetery Hills in a series of dramatic nighttime assaults against the Union right.

Several times that day, the Union army seemed to teeter on the brink of destruction, its fate hanging in the proverbial balance. Sickles's Third Corps was mauled, as were portions of the Fifth and Second Corps sent in to restore the Union left. Confederate forces would momentarily pierce the Union center along Cemetery Ridge, achieve a foothold on Culp's Hill and briefly crest east Cemetery Hill. But their gains would prove fleeting, each of their attacks either thwarted by timely arriving Union reinforcements or hindered by a lack of support. Casualties on both sides were heavy, but the day would end with the Union army still holding much the same ground it had occupied that morning, the boys in blue having weathered the storm and deflected each of the successive hammer blows launched by the Army of Northern Virginia.

Despite this and the myriad problems he experienced in the execution of his plans, Lee nevertheless believed that his men had come within a hair's breadth of inflicting a fatal blow to the Army of the Potomac that day. Thus, late that night, even as the sounds of battle gave way to the cries of the wounded and dying, the determined Confederate army commander resolved to renew the fight the next day, on Friday, July 3. At the same time, at a famed council of war held that night at army headquarters, Meade and his generals unanimously agreed that the Union army would hold its position and, in the words of General Henry Slocum, "stay and fight it out" the following day.

* * *

Thursday, July 2, dawned quiet, peaceful even. The skies around Gettysburg began to lighten around 4:15 a.m., and by 7:00 a.m., the temperature was at a pleasant seventy-four degrees. Jacob Smith of the 107th Ohio, who awoke that morning on Cemetery Hill, remembered that daybreak on July 2 was "fresh, balmy and pleasant. The sun shone mildly through an atmosphere still smoky from yesterday's conflict giving it the appearance of a huge fire ball. All the world was quiet and at rest." Continued Smith, "There was nothing outside our immediate surroundings that would indicate…the dreadful struggle that was before us."

On the hilltop behind Smith and the men of the 107th Ohio was the ordinarily serene Evergreen Cemetery, where generations of Gettysburg residents had been laid to rest in the hopes of eternal peace. But that cemetery was now "trodden under, laid a waste, desecrated," wrote one Union artillery officer. "The fences are all down, the many graves have been run over, beautiful lots with iron fences and splendid monuments have been destroyed or soiled, and our infantry and artillery occupy those sacred grounds where the dead are sleeping. It is enough to make one mourn."

Late the night before, a disheveled George Meade, worn out from his moonlight ride from Taneytown, arrived at the distinctive arched gatehouse

Post-battle photograph of the Evergreen Cemetery Gatehouse. *Library of Congress*.

of the Evergreen Cemetery, where he met with Generals Howard, Slocum and Sickles, each of whom echoed the others in their thoughts about the defensive value of the ground there, on the hilltop and on the heights and ridgelines south of town. Having already heard much the same from the trusted Hancock, Meade had hours earlier already issued orders for the rest of his army to gather there.

Meade got no rest that night. After a quick survey of the position on Cemetery Hill, the army commander set out with his staff and several of his generals on an examination of the ground south of Gettysburg. As the cavalcade of officers rode south along what would later be dubbed Cemetery Ridge and toward two eminences later to become known as Big and Little Round Top, one of Meade's engineers did his best to sketch a map of the terrain while Meade designated the locations where he wanted each of his various corps to position themselves upon their arrival. At about 4:00 a.m., with the survey complete and dawn now breaking, Meade and his staff dismounted at the small, modest home of the widow Lydia Leister that sat alongside the Taneytown Road just south of Cemetery Hill and on the eastern slope of Cemetery Ridge. For the duration of the battle, Leister's home would serve as Union army headquarters.

Meade was understandably nervous as the skies continued to lighten. Only a portion of his army had arrived and had taken up positions by then, and Meade simply could not know whether his ever-aggressive counterpart Lee was planning for an early morning assault. Yet with each passing hour—as more and more of his commands came trampling in and as the Confederate army remained quiet—Meade's anxiety lessened.

By midmorning, most of his army was on the field. The Twelfth Corps and portions of the First took up positions on Culp's Hill, on the right of the Union line, while the Eleventh Corps maintained its position on Cemetery Hill, the keystone of the entire Union line. Hancock's Second Corps formed to the left of the Eleventh Corps, taking up a line of defense that ran southward along Cemetery Ridge. To the left of Hancock went the soldiers of the Third Corps, commanded by Daniel Sickles, who had been instructed to extend his line south toward Little Round Top, a rocky eminence that rose 150 feet above the surrounding valley floor. General John Buford's cavalrymen patrolled the area around Sherfy's Peach Orchard, some three-quarters of a mile in front of Sickles's position, where they also provided flank support. George Sykes's Fifth Corps, reaching the field at about 10:00 a.m., took up position behind the lines, where it was held in reserve.

The only force not yet on the field that morning was the Sixth Corps, commanded by John Sedgwick. Having received orders late on July 1 to make their way without delay to Gettysburg, Sedgwick's men set out from Manchester, Maryland, on what would be a marathon march, covering more than thirty miles during nineteen hours of almost continuous marching and finally arriving at Gettysburg late on the afternoon of July 2.

From flank to flank, the Army of the Potomac stretched some three miles in length and, from above, would have resembled a large fishhook. Culp's Hill on the army's right was the barb of the hook. From there, the bend of the hook curved around Cemetery Hill, while the long shank of the hook—held by the Second and Third Corps—ran south along Cemetery Ridge. The eye of the hook was Little Round Top, on the army's far left. Both flanks were anchored on high ground, and the compact nature of his Union position provided Meade the benefit of strong interior lines, which would enable him to shift and shuffle troops to threatened parts of his position if need be. Although Meade briefly flirted with the idea of launching an attack of his own that morning, he ultimately decided to dig in his heels and await Lee's next move.

"A Scene Very Much Like Hell Itself"

The Confederate army commander had awoken shortly before dawn that Thursday morning, determined to attack—and the sooner the better, he thought, before the Union army had time to fully concentrate. But before he could pitch in—indeed, before he could even develop a plan of attack for the day ahead—Lee had to first get a better idea of the ground south of Gettysburg, and more importantly, he had to find out exactly what kind of position his opponent had taken up. Here again the absence of Stuart, his most trusted and reliable intelligence-gatherer, would be felt. Since Stuart would not arrive until noon that day, Lee was forced to rely on a number of his staff and other officers to perform reconnaissance duty. Several of them set out that morning following Lee's instructions to both survey the ground and fix the locations of the Union army. Lee knew that the Union right was well positioned on the high ground southeast of town—on Culp's and Cemetery Hills—so his strongest focus was on the Union left. To find out exactly where that was, Lee sent out one of his engineers, Captain Samuel Johnston, who, along with Major James Clarke of Longstreet's staff, set out just after 4:00 a.m., riding south in an effort to locate the Union left.

As Johnston and Clarke galloped away, Lee made his way to a point near the Lutheran Seminary building where he could get a better view of the Union positions on the other side of town. There he met up with Longstreet. Just as he had the previous afternoon, Longstreet greeted Lee that morning by advising against an attack and again expressing his opinion that the army should side-step to the right, work its way south around Meade's army and take up a defensive position somewhere between it and Washington, where it could settle in and await Meade's attack. But just as *he* had done the day before, Lee dismissed this idea and instead continued to think about the best way of attacking Meade there at Gettysburg. A number of other Confederate officers soon arrived, including John Bell Hood, a hard-fighting Kentuckian who commanded one of Longstreet's divisions. To Hood, Lee appeared anxious that morning as he paced back and forth, stopping every now and then to gaze through his binoculars. Lee "seemed full of hope," said Hood, "yet at times, buried in deep thought."

Sometime around 7:00 a.m., Johnston and Clarke returned from their expedition. Lee invited the engineer to step forward and then listened carefully as Johnston reported what he and Clarke had discovered about the Union left. On a map, Johnston traced the route they had just taken. They had set out, said Johnston, by riding south to the right, or west, of Seminary Ridge until arriving at the Millerstown/Wheatfield Road. From there, they turned left, crested the ridge and rode south a few hundred more yards before cutting eastward across the Emmitsburg Road, south of Sherfy's Peach Orchard, and continuing all the way up to the very summit of Little Round Top, which Johnston reported was entirely unoccupied.

Almost unbelieving, Lee pointed to this rocky eminence on the map and asked, "Did you get *there?*" Johnston assured Lee that they had. Even more incredibly, excepting a small cavalry patrol that they had narrowly avoided on the return trip, Johnston reported that they had neither come across nor detected any Union troops along the way or in the vicinity of the Little Round Top, meaning that Meade's flank did not extend that far south. Without Stuart, Lee had no choice but to trust in Johnston's findings, which seemed to confirm what he had already suspected about the Union left: it was exposed, or "in the air," and perfectly ripe for a crushing flank attack.

Visions of Chancellorsville flooded Lee's mind. There, two months earlier, Stonewall Jackson had executed a wide flanking maneuver, marching his men to a position opposite the exposed Union flank before crashing down on it like an avalanche. The same thing, he thought, could happen here. Jackson was gone, of course—already seven weeks in the grave—but Lee still had Longstreet. Most of Longstreet's corps had arrived by this time, including all of McLaws's Division and most of Hood's. Of Hood's four brigades, only Evander Law's had yet to arrive. Law's Alabamians awoke at 3:00 a.m. in New Guilford and soon set off on what would prove to be an exhausting twenty-four-mile march to Gettysburg, arriving there just before noon. Longstreet's final division—some 5,500 Virginians under George Pickett—were even farther away, guarding army trains near Chambersburg, and would not arrive in time to participate in any action that day.

Longstreet did not like the prospects of going into battle without Pickett; it was like going into battle, he famously told Hood, "with one boot off." But Lee would not wait for Pickett to arrive. Instead, he would direct Longstreet to move south with Hood and McLaws—some 14,500 men in all—and circle around the presumably exposed left flank of the Union army. From there, they were to turn left and come crashing down on the Union line, rolling it up as they advanced in a northerly fashion. Adding weight to the assault would be the 7,000 soldiers of Richard Anderson's Third Corps division. Anderson, whose five brigades had been kept out of the action on July 1, was instructed to position his men along Seminary Ridge, wait for McLaws and Hood to attack and then advance straight ahead toward the Emmitsburg Road and toward the center of the Union line on Cemetery Ridge beyond, delivering the proverbial left jab after Longstreet's men delivered the punishing right hook.

This plan may have been sound in theory, but as it turned out, it was one based almost entirely on faulty intelligence and a false perception of the Union line. One of the enduring mysteries of the Battle of Gettysburg is that early morning reconnaissance expedition undertaken by Johnston and Clarke. Johnston reported to Lee that not only had he and Clarke made it all the way to the summit of Little Round Top but also that they had detected no Federal troops in its vicinity, lending further credence to the army commander's thoughts about the Union left being exposed. But early that morning, the areas where Johnston claimed he traveled were, in fact, swarming with Union troops. Buford's cavalrymen patrolled the area around the Peach Orchard and southward along the Emmitsburg Road, while two Union brigades, left behind by Sickles at Emmitsburg the previous day, were that morning marching north along the same roadway. Additionally, General John Geary's Twelfth Corps division was bivouacked early that morning on the northern slopes of Little Round Top, and when Geary's men departed to take up positions on Culp's Hill, their place was soon taken up by Sickles's Third Corps. Surely, if Johnston had made it to Little Round Top, he would have at least detected some of these men. Exactly *where* Johnston and Clarke actually got to that morning remains unknown, but most historians believe that it was not Little Round Top. Nevertheless, Johnston believed that they had, and it was on his report that Lee had based his plan of attack.

With his division slated to lead the attack, General Lafayette McLaws listened carefully as Lee explained exactly what he wanted him to do. On the map, Lee used his finger to trace a line that ran perpendicular to the Emmitsburg Road south of the Peach Orchard, telling the heavily bearded Divisional commander that he wanted him to place his division across the roadway and "to get there if possible without being seen by the enemy." Hood's Division, moving out behind McLaws, would then form up to his left. Just then, General Longstreet chimed in on the conversation. Perhaps he did not care about the prospects of such an attack, or perhaps he did not appreciate Lee giving instructions directly to one of his own division commanders, but whatever the case, Longstreet traced a line on the map at right angles to the one traced out by Lee and one *parallel* to the Emmitsburg Road, telling McLaws that this is how he should place his division. "No, General," snapped Lee, "I wish it placed just the opposite." Already at this early hour, nerves were fraying and patience was wearing thin. To McLaws, Longstreet "appeared as if he was irritated and annoyed, but the cause I did not ask."

Of course, Longstreet's role in the day ahead was only one part of the equation. The question of what to do with Ewell still remained. With his

Major General Lafayette McLaws, slated to lead the Confederate attack on July 2, would find himself frequently exasperated that day. *From* Miller's Photographic History of the Civil War.

meeting with McLaws and Longstreet adjourned, Lee next rode into town, where he met up with his Second Corps commander. As he had done the evening before, Lee again broached the idea of shifting Ewell's men south, to take up positions along Seminary Ridge in order to add a greater punch to the attack against the Union left and center, but again Ewell objected and again Lee relented. But with one-third of the army, Ewell simply could not remain idle. Lee therefore instructed him to await the sounds of Longstreet's attack and then to launch a demonstration against Culp's and Cemetery Hills, to create a diversion that, at the very least, would prevent Meade from stripping troops from his right to reinforce his left. But if Ewell sensed an opportunity to turn this demonstration into a general assault, then he was to do so. With that, Lee made his way back to Seminary Ridge.

In their efforts at absolving Lee of any blame for the defeat at Gettysburg and placing it instead on the shoulders of Longstreet, many of Lee's defenders would afterward claim that Lee was angry when, upon his return, he discovered that Longstreet had yet to begin his march, but it does not seem likely that Lee would have given Longstreet orders to do so before he first met with Ewell to discuss the role of his Second Corps in the fight ahead. Longstreet claimed that he did not get the orders to begin his flanking march until *after* Lee returned, which makes sense considering that Lee was still thinking about shifting the Second Corps to the south and especially considering that Lee may not have wanted to issue orders until after being assured that Ewell's own left flank was secure.

Further, since Longstreet's men would be taking up a position to the right of Anderson's Division, Anderson had to necessarily get his five brigades into position first, something that would not be completed until shortly after noon. And although Lee may have been a bit irritated when he discovered that Hood and McLaws had been inactive during his meeting with Ewell—as some of his supporters later alleged—when he finally did give Longstreet orders to begin his march, sometime around 11:00 a.m., he just as soon relented to Longstreet's urging that he await the arrival of Law's Brigade before doing so. If Lee was upset with Longstreet for allegedly remaining idle, the question, then, is why he would have agreed to delay even further to wait for Law. Regardless, it would take another forty-five minutes before Law's exhausted men finally did arrive, and it was already fast approaching noon when Longstreet got his men moving south.

Lee's plan, which had taken much of the morning to fully develop, was at last set in motion, but things would very quickly begin to unravel for the Confederate army commander. Just as it was with Jackson at Chancellorsville, surprise was to be a critical element in Longstreet's flank attack that afternoon, and he and his generals were cautioned to take up positions opposite the Union left without being seen. But soon after setting out, McLaws encountered a "high, bare place," where the ground rose considerably. Had his column continued up and over this rise of ground, it would have been spotted by the observant Union signalmen in position atop Little Round Top. An aggravated McLaws—who was, said one man, "saying things I would not like my grandson...to repeat"—ordered a halt while he sought another route south.

It was not long before Longstreet arrived on the scene, wanting to know why his men had halted. McLaws led the corps commander to that "high, bare place" to see for himself. "Why, this won't do," said Longstreet. "Is there no way to avoid it?" McLaws said that he had found an alternate route but that taking it would require a good degree of backtracking. If that was the case, asked Longstreet, why not just have everyone about-face, or simply turn around and have Hood's men, stacked up in columns behind McLaws's, lead the way? McLaws demurred, claiming that Lee had specifically wanted his division to lead the attack. Longstreet yielded to McLaws's views, and there then began a great untangling of the stacked gray columns as McLaws's and then Hood's men retraced their steps almost all the way back to their starting point on Herr's Ridge before taking another route south.

Of course, all of this took time, and it would not be until 3:30 p.m. before the head of McLaws's Division at last neared its jumping-off point. Three and a half hours had passed since they first set off on a march that should have taken about half that time. As his men turned left and now marched east, up the wooded western slopes of Seminary Ridge, McLaws was greeted once again by Longstreet. "How are you going in?" asked the corps commander. "That will be determined when I can see what is in my front," was McLaws's curt reply. "There is nothing to your front," countered Longstreet, "you will be entirely on the flank of the enemy." At most, said Longstreet, there would be just one regiment and perhaps a battery to his front. "Then I will continue my march in columns of companies," answered McLaws, "and after arriving on the flank as far as is necessary will face to the left and march on the enemy." "That suits me," replied Longstreet before galloping away to confer with Hood, and with that, McLaws rode forward to catch up with the head of his division near the crest of the ridge. When he arrived there, a thoroughly exasperated McLaws discovered that his problems were only then just beginning.

"The view...astonished me," McLaws later wrote, "as the enemy was massed in my front, and extended to my right and left as far as I could see." McLaws was at a loss; he was *not* on the Union left, as he had been told and as he had expected. He was, instead, directly opposite a line of Union troops positioned "in greater force than was supposed" just six hundred yards to his front, in and around the Peach Orchard, with their lines running both north along the Emmitsburg Road and southeasterly, it appeared, all the way toward Little Round Top. The enemy was not holding the positions Lee had envisioned, and it was by now readily apparent that his plan of attack was based entirely on a false understanding of the Union line. Worse, as soon as they came within view, McLaws's men drew fire from the Union guns posted to their front. Thus, despite McLaws's and Longstreet's best efforts to avoid detection—despite that lengthy march and countermarch to get into position—there would be no surprise attack that day.

The artillery fire forced McLaws to deploy his brigades into lines of battle on Seminary Ridge, in much the same position Longstreet had earlier traced on the map before being countermanded by Lee. Joseph Kershaw's brigade filed to the right, taking cover behind a low stone wall that ran along the crest of the ridgeline. About 150 yards behind Kershaw's South Carolinians went the Georgians under Paul Semmes. William Barksdale's Mississippians formed to the left of Kershaw, their line extending northward toward the right flank of Anderson's Division. McLaws's final brigade, another all-Georgia outfit commanded by William T. Wofford, took up positions to the rear of Barksdale. At the same time, E.P. Alexander's artillery battalion unlimbered to the front of McLaws's men, its cannons soon trading shots with the Union guns posted in and around the Peach Orchard.

As his brigades settled into position, McLaws was greeted by Major Osmun Latrobe of Longstreet's staff, who had been sent forward to find out why McLaws was not advancing. McLaws responded by saying he would advance as soon as his division was fully deployed. However, he wanted Longstreet to know that the enemy force to his front was much greater than had been anticipated—much greater than just one sole regiment backed up by a single battery.

Latrobe took this information back to Longstreet, but it was not long before he again came galloping back with orders to attack. McLaws said that he would attack but was hoping to delay his advance until the Confederate artillery could further soften up the Union lines. He also told Latrobe that he wished Longstreet would ride ahead and see the situation for himself. Latrobe rode back to the corps commander but soon returned a third time, making it clear that Longstreet's orders to attack were peremptory. Resigned, McLaws promised that he would move forward in five minutes, but even before those five minutes passed, a new order had arrived from Longstreet: McLaws was to now hold off and wait for Hood's men to settle into position—not on his left, as was originally envisioned, but on his right instead. Once in this position, it would be Hood who would now launch the assault, with McLaws to follow. For the Confederates, this was very literally a last-minute change in plans, worked out by Lee and Longstreet, but the situation they encountered once arriving opposite the Peach Orchard required that changes be made.

The Union troops McLaws discovered drawn up to his front in that Peach Orchard belonged to Major General Daniel Sickles's Third Corps, Army of the Potomac. Early that morning, George Meade had assigned these men to a position some three-quarters of a mile *east* of the Peach Orchard, along the southern reaches of Cemetery Ridge, with their right flank connecting to the left of Hancock's Second Corps and their left flank extending south toward Little Round Top. And all throughout the day, Meade had assumed that the Third Corps was holding this designated spot, but Sickles, as will be seen, had other ideas.

Daniel Edgar Sickles remains one of the most colorful and controversial figures of the American Civil War. In an army dominated by West Point–educated, professional officers, Sickles was not a trained soldier. He was, instead, a lawyer and an ambitious politician who never shied away from the spotlight and from scandal. He was notorious for the 1859 murder of Philip Barton Key—son of Francis Scott Key, author of "The Star-Spangled Banner"—who had been carrying on an affair with Sickles's much younger wife; Sickles shot him down in broad daylight in Lafayette Square, just behind the White House. In one of those so-called trials of the century, Sickles was fully acquitted of the charges, his lawyers successfully arguing that he was not guilty by reason of temporary insanity.

A staunch Democrat, Sickles, at the outset of war, proved himself an ardent Unionist and a strong supporter of the Republican Abraham Lincoln. He helped to raise thousands of volunteers, which, combined with the fact that

The colorful, confident and extremely controversial Daniel Sickles. *Library of Congress.*

"A Scene Very Much Like Hell Itself"

Lincoln needed all the support he could get from the other side of the aisle, earned him a general's commission. Sickles had attached himself firmly to Joseph Hooker, and when Hooker assumed army command in early 1863, he appointed Sickles commander of the Third Corps, his lack of military training or experience notwithstanding. Of course, Sickles's champion Hooker was now gone, replaced by the no-nonsense Meade, and thus it was that at Gettysburg, Sickles found himself serving under a commander he did not particularly care for and assigned to a position he did not at all like.

The position assigned to the Third Corps was the poorest of any held by the Army of the Potomac, with much of it along low ground. What most troubled Sickles was his belief that the higher ground that ran almost parallel to his line some three-quarters of a mile to the west, directly to his front, would dominate his assigned position. The Emmitsburg Road ran along the crest of this high ground, which was also crowned by farmer Sherfy's Peach Orchard, where, for the moment at least, Buford's cavalrymen were posted, keeping a careful eye to the west and south and providing flank support. But though it did have its weaknesses, the ground assigned to Sickles simply had to be held in order for the Union army to maintain its compact line of battle. Yet Sickles's attention remained fixed on that higher ground to his front, and as the hours ticked by that morning, the prescient Third Corps commander increasingly became convinced that Lee was preparing for a crushing assault against his position on the left of the Union line. Sometime after 9:00 a.m., Sickles sent his senior staff officer, Major Henry Tremain, to Meade's headquarters to express his concerns. But Meade, at least according to Tremain, seemed indifferent to Sickles's plight.

Sickles's anxieties only continued to mount, especially after he noticed Buford's men galloping away from the Peach Orchard. Earlier that morning, Buford had asked cavalry commander Pleasonton that his men be withdrawn; they were weary and worn out from their fight of the previous day, the grizzled horseman argued, and his horses were tired. Pleasonton ran Buford's request past Meade, who approved, assuming as a matter of course that Pleasonton would replace Buford's men there with another, fresher cavalry force. But Pleasonton unaccountably failed to do this, and thus, when Buford's men trotted away from the Peach Orchard, no one arrived to take their place.

At about 10:00 a.m., Sickles—believing that Meade was not paying enough attention to the army's left and convinced further about the unsatisfactory nature of his position—paid a visit to the army commander at the Leister house. He told Meade of the higher ground to his front, which, he said, would serve as an excellent artillery platform, and expressed his opinion that Lee was gearing up for an attack against his position. He wanted Meade to come see for himself. Meade declined but promised Sickles that he would send Henry Hunt, the army's chief artillerist, south to have a look. Satisfied, Sickles mounted to return to his Third Corps, but before he galloped away, he asked Meade if he could position his men in a way he "should deem most suitable." "Certainly, within the limits of the general instructions I have given you," replied the army commander, "any ground within those limits you choose to occupy, I leave to you."

It was not long before Hunt met up with Sickles. Sickles led the West Point–educated, professional artillerist all the way out to the Peach Orchard, where, Sickles explained, he would much rather prefer to position his men. One of his divisions, proposed Sickles, would extend north along the Emmitsburg Road, while the other would stretch in a southeasterly direction from the orchard, across a rocky, tree-covered hillock, known simply enough as Stony Hill, then through farmer John Rose's ripe field of wheat and finally along a largely forested rise of ground known as Houck's Ridge. His far left would be anchored on Devil's Den, a bizarre collection of massive boulders strewn haphazardly about on the southern end of the ridgeline, about five hundred yards west and *in front of* Little Round Top.

Hunt listened carefully as Sickles made his case. He could clearly see merit in some of the points raised by the uneasy Third Corps commander. The ground there *was* higher than where Sickles had been assigned on lower Cemetery Ridge, and the Peach Orchard would, indeed, serve as a fine position for artillery. But, as Hunt explained to Sickles, advancing that far out would dangerously extend the Union battle line and break Sickles's connection to Hancock's left. Sickles's proposed position would also mean that there would be a perilous salient formed at the Peach Orchard, which could be struck simultaneously from two sides. Most importantly, though, Sickles simply did not have enough troops to defend so lengthy a position, as it would be nearly double the length of the line Meade had assigned him. Sickles remained unconvinced by the artillerist's arguments, and before Hunt departed to attend to affairs on the opposite end of the line, Sickles asked whether he *should* advance his men and take up the line he had proposed. "Not on my authority," was Hunt's gruff reply.

Soon after Hunt galloped away, Sickles ordered Colonel Hiram Berdan of Sharpshooters' fame to lead a reconnaissance expedition into the trees that lined Seminary Ridge just six hundred or so yards to the west in an effort to better discern Lee's intentions. Berdan selected four companies of his 1st

"A Scene Very Much Like Hell Itself"

United States Sharpshooters, a total of 100 men, for the task. Distinctive in their dark-green uniforms, their kepis topped by a black ostrich plume and carrying Sharps breech-loading carbines, Berdan's expert marksmen advanced stealthily across the fields, their force augmented by the 210 soldiers of the 3rd Maine Infantry. Advancing into the woods around noon, they soon made contact with General Cadmus Wilcox's brigade of Richard Anderson's division, just then settling into position in preparation for the Confederate assault. A sharp firefight ensued, the two sides battling it out for more than half an hour before Berdan, facing far superior numbers and having already lost 70 of his men killed or wounded, ordered a retreat. While his men made their way back to Union lines, Berdan reported to Sickles that the woods to his front were swarming with Confederates.

It was this report that finally clinched it for Sickles, now fully convinced—and rightfully so—that Lee was preparing for an attack against his position. All morning, he had tried to alert Meade to this, but the army commander had paid him little heed and had been entirely negligent in minding his left, or at least so thought Sickles. Believing that he had no other choice but to now take matters into his own hands, Sickles, at 2:00 p.m., without orders and without even notifying the army commander, abandoned his designated line and advanced his men forward to what he thought was a much better position, hoping to secure the high ground to his front before Lee had a chance to do so. Sickles justified his decision—and would do so until his dying day—by explaining, "I took up that line because it enabled me to hold commanding ground, which, if the enemy had been allowed to take—as they would have taken it if I had not occupied it in force—would have rendered our position on the left untenable; and, in my judgment, would have turned the fortunes of the day hopelessly against us." There was nothing sinister or villainous in Sickles's movement, he simply did what he thought was best. However, despite his best intentions, by advancing his men Sickles imperiled the rest of the Union line, placing his own corps and the rest of the Army of the Potomac in serious jeopardy.

David Bell Birney positioned the men of his division first, with General J.H. Hobart Ward's mixed brigade of New York, Pennsylvania, Indiana and Maine men forming the left of his line and with Ward's own left resting on the massive boulders of Devil's Den. In describing this geological anomaly, one Union soldier wrote that it was as though "nature in some wild freak had forgotten herself and piled great rocks in mad confusion together." Four guns of Captain James Smith's 4th New York Battery also took up positions atop Devil's Den. Ward's line extended northwesterly from Devil's Den, across the tree-covered Houck's Ridge and toward Rose's twenty-acre field of wheat, where Colonel Phillipe Regis de Kerenden de Trobriand's brigade next took up position. De Trobriand's regiments were stretched paper-thin in the wheat field, over and atop Stony Hill and on toward the Peach Orchard, where the soldiers of Birney's final brigade, under General Charles Graham, took up positions. Facing both to the south and west, Graham's Pennsylvanians formed the salient in Sickles's advanced line. Birney's division was spread dangerously thin, and there developed a number of yawning gaps in the line, gaps that would soon be plugged by artillery from both the Third Corps and from the army's Artillery Reserve.

After Birney's men settled into positions, Sickles next ordered Andrew Humphreys's men forward to the Emmitsburg Road. Humphreys aligned two of his brigades in a line that extended north along the roadway. On his left and connecting to the right of Graham's line north of the Peach Orchard and near the Trostle farm lane were the soldiers of Colonel William Brewster's Excelsior Brigade. Joseph Carr positioned his men to the right of Brewster, his line extending to a point a few hundred yards south of the Nicholas Codori house and barn. The regiments of Humphreys's third brigade under Colonel George Burling, designated as the corps reserve, had already been parceled out to fill gaps in the Third Corps line, with most of them sent over to Birney.

Watching as the Third Corps advanced, a bewildered Winfield Scott Hancock wondered, "What in hell can that man Sickles be doing?" Some of Hancock's men could not help but be caught up in the martial pageantry of it all. One Third Corps soldier, writing well after the war, did his best to capture the moment: "The sun shone brightly on their waving colors, and flashed in scintillating rays from their burnished arms, as with well-aligned ranks and even steps they moved proudly across the field. Away to the right, along Cemetery Ridge, the soldiers of the Second Corps, leaving their coffee and their cards, crowded to their front, where they gazed with soldierly pride and quickened pulse on the stirring scene." But no matter how stirring the scene, Hancock was none too impressed, grimly predicting that it would not be long before Sickles's men would come tumbling back.

Sickles did not bother to notify Meade of his advance, nor did anyone else report it to the army commander who, for the moment, remained in total ignorance of the unfolding situation. From his headquarters, Meade had just finished wiring off a status report to Halleck, reporting that he had been in position all day, awaiting Lee's next move and awaiting the arrival of Sedgwick's Sixth Corps. Around 3:00 p.m., Meade sent off couriers to all his corps commanders, directing them to report to the Leister house for a meeting. Most of the top Union brass soon arrived, but Sickles was noticeably absent. Twice he had turned down Meade's summons, for he was just then too busy repositioning his corps and preparing for an attack. But the third time Meade sent for him, the orders were peremptory. Sickles thus made his way to the Leister house. When he arrived, he found the army commander seething.

When army engineer Gouverneur Warren reined up at headquarters sometime shortly before Sickles's arrival, he reported the rather disquieting news that the Third Corps was *not* in its assigned position; it was, instead, advanced well to the front. This was the first time Meade had learned of Sickles's advance, and when he soon spotted Sickles galloping up, a livid George Meade told him "in a few sharp words" to not even dismount but to instead turn right back around and return to his position; he would soon

ride out and meet him there. "I never saw Meade so angry," said staff officer William Paine. The sound of artillery fire was now distinctly heard off to the south. Confronted now by what was an unfolding crisis, Meade turned to General George Sykes, whose Fifth Corps had been held in reserve, directing him to march his three divisions quickly to the south and to hold the ground originally assigned to Sickles "at all hazards." The army commander, with Warren in tow, then galloped south. On the way, Meade pointed to Little Round Top and directed his chief engineer to continue on that hilltop to attend to matters there, while he would continue to ride out to confer with Sickles.

The artillery fire between the Union guns at the Peach

In his first battle as corps commander, Major General George Sykes was directed to hold the army's left flank at all hazards. *Library of Congress.*

Orchard and the Confederate batteries drawn up to the west and southwest had grown quite lively by the time Meade arrived. The army commander angrily demanded to know what the devil Sickles had done. Sickles did his best to explain himself, telling Meade that he thought he had acted within the scope of the instructions he had given him earlier that morning and that he merely sought to take possession of this higher-ground position before Lee had a chance to do so. Cutting him off and above the roar of the cannons, Meade explained to Sickles that "this is neutral ground, our guns command it, as well as the enemy's. The very reason you cannot hold it applies to them." He further told Sickles that his men were too far extended, that they had advanced well beyond any immediate support and that both of his flanks were now exposed. "You cannot hold this position," barked Meade, "but the enemy will not let you get away without a fight, and it may as well begin now as at any time."

Sickles rather sheepishly asked whether he should pull his men back to their original position. "I wish to God you could," said Meade famously, "but the enemy won't let you." It was much too late. With the artillery now at a fever pitch, Meade told Sickles to hold on as best he could. Sykes's Fifth Corps was on its way, and Hancock would be called on to send support to the right of Sickles's exposed line. For George Meade, much of the day had passed quietly, but now, having discovered Sickles's transgression and with the Confederates poised to launch their attack, he was forced to make the best out of what was truly a bad situation. As he galloped away to hurry along support, Sickles and his men braced for the Confederate tide, just then sweeping forward from Seminary Ridge.

The revised Confederate attack plan called for John Bell Hood's division to now kick off the assault. Forming his division to the right of McLaws, Hood, like McLaws, had stacked up his division with two brigades in front and two in support. Evander Law's exhausted and thoroughly parched Alabamians formed the right of his front line, while General Jerome Robertson's Texas and Arkansas troops formed to the left of Law, their line stretching northerly toward McLaws's right flank. Henry Benning lined up his brigade roughly two hundred yards behind Law, while George T. Anderson's Brigade went into position to the left of Benning, behind Robertson.

Before his men stepped out to the attack, Hood had urged Longstreet several times to allow him to swing his division farther south, around Big Round Top, which his scouts discovered to be unoccupied, and take up positions behind the Union lines. But Longstreet would not—could not—be swayed. The prospects of such a move may have been appealing,

Right: Hard-fighting John Bell Hood had, said one observer, "the face of an old Crusader, who believed in his cause, his cross, and his crown." His left arm was shattered at Gettysburg, and he lost his right leg two months later at Chickamauga. *Library of Congress*.

Below: Confederate artillery keeping up a hot fire against Little Round Top on the Union left. Sketch by Alfred Waud. *Library of Congress*.

but adopting it would require yet another change in plans and would consume even more time, and it was already far too late in the day. Hood later claimed that he appealed three times to Longstreet, but each time he was turned down; the final time, Longstreet made it clear that "[i] t is General Lee's order, the time is up—attack at once!" With that, a resigned John Hood prepared his division for the attack. Galloping to the front of his lines, Hood reined up in front of his old Texas brigade, pointed toward Little Round Top and yelled out, "Forward, my brave Texans! Forward and take those heights!"

It was already well after 4:00 p.m. when the attack finally got underway. Law's and Robertson's men moved out first, while behind them advanced the soldiers of Hood's rear brigades under Benning and Tige Anderson. Confederate artillerists held their fire as the infantry passed through their line of cannons, but by no means did the Union artillery fire abate; indeed, it only seemed to increase in its ferocity. One of Benning's men later wrote, "As soon as we came in sight, a furious blast of cannon broke from the tops of the hills and mountains around and the terrific cry and screams of shells began." But the men moved forward, "undismayed by the terrors that seemed to awake from the infernal regions." Shells crashed among the gray ranks, and Hood's men dropped by the score. Among the first to be struck down was Hood himself. Hood had made it only a short distance forward before a shell fragment tore into his left arm, rendering it useless for the rest of his life. Helped from the saddle, he was then carried to the rear for treatment.

The uneven terrain, broken further by numerous stone fences and the marshy bottomlands of Plum Run, all served to disrupt Hood's formations, as did the steady fire poured into the ranks by Union skirmishers strung out across their front and from James Smith's New York artillerists positioned atop Devil's Den. Yet in the face of this persistent fire, Law's and Robertson's men continued to push forward, steadily driving the Union skirmishers back to their main line. Then, a steady volley erupted from atop Houck's Ridge; the two sides had collided.

The soldiers of the 3rd Arkansas and 1st Texas on the left of Robertson's Brigade were the first struck. Advancing into Rose's Woods, the Arkansas men came under so withering a fire from Hobart Ward's Third Corps soldiers positioned atop the ridge that their advance ground to an abrupt halt. The Arkansans also came under a flanking fire from the soldiers of the 17th Maine of De Trobriand's brigade, lined up along a stone wall that separated the woodlot from the Wheatfield. At the same time but to the right of the 3rd, the 1st Texas also came under a heavy fire as it advanced both

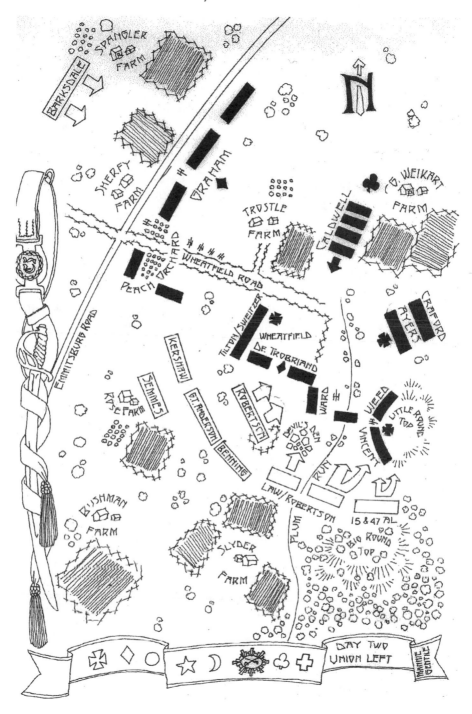

Overview of Hood's and McLaws's attacks against the Union left. *Map by Mannie Gentile.*

through the trees and to the base of an open, irregularly shaped triangular field that led up to the crest of Devil's Den. The Texans advanced with a "fierce, charging yell," but their attack was stymied by a destructive fire poured forth by the 124th New York, holding firmly atop Devil's Den.

Smith's four guns, to the left of the 124th, continued to bang away, their ammunition rapidly dwindling. When he learned that his gunners had expended all their case shot, the gruff Captain Smith hollered, "Give them shell! Give them solid shot! Damn them, give them anything!" Several times the Confederates regrouped and tried to push forward, but each time their advances stalled out. The two sides settled in for a savage firefight that took a heavy toll on both sides. The 20th Indiana, for example, lost 156 of its 268 men, while the 3rd Arkansas regiment lost a staggering 182 men killed or wounded. For the moment, Ward's men were holding their own, but for the Confederate soldiers stalled out in the trees and along the base of Devil's Den, help would not be long in arriving.

Approaching Devil's Den from the south came the 44th and 48th Alabama Regiments from Law's Brigade. When the attack first commenced, these two regiments were on the far *right* of Law's line, but as his brigade drew nearer to the western slopes of Big Round Top, Law halted them and then turned them to the left in order to deal with Smith's gunners on Devil's Den. The two regiments changed direction, marching in a northerly fashion behind the other three regiments of Law's Brigade and now approached Devil's Den from the south. It was a tough go for these Alabama men—the huge boulders in the Plum Run gorge, which separated Devil's Den from Big Round Top, slowed and disrupted their advance, as did the soldiers of the 4th Maine, well positioned among the large granite slabs on the far left of Ward's line, who greeted Law's approaching Alabamians with a shower of bullets. Slowed in their approach, the 44th and 48th were nevertheless determined, and they were able to eventually work their way around the left flank of the 4th Maine, forcing the Maine men to fall back, grudgingly.

As the 44th and 48th Alabama crept up and over the rocks and attacked Devil's Den from the south, the men of the 1st Texas continued their efforts up the western slopes, pushing up that open, triangular field, all the while blazing away at the 124th New York holding on to the crest. Colonel Van Horne Ellis of the 124th watched coolly as his men slugged it out with the determined Texans. With the Texans showing no signs of giving up the fight, Ellis ordered a bayonet charge. At his command, the New Yorkers rushed down the hillside and very quickly drove the Texans back, all the way to the western base of Houck's Ridge. But though the Texans may have been

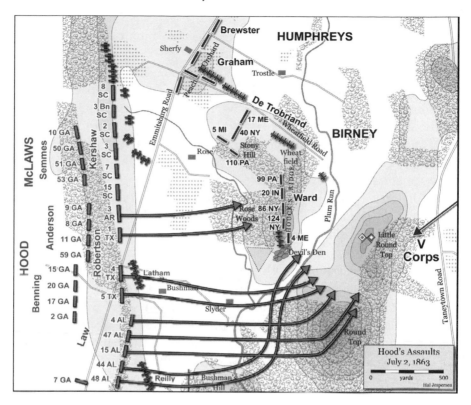

Hood's opening attack on the Union left. *Map by Hal Jespersen.*

driven back, behind them there emerged a solid gray line: Henry Benning's brigade had arrived.

Advancing on the right of Hood's second line, Benning was supposed to follow directly behind Law, but Law's Alabamians had veered too far to the right, and Benning lost sight of them. His advance thus brought his Georgians behind Robertson's fragmented line as they attacked Ward's men on Devil's Den. Approaching Devil's Den just as the 124th charged down the hillside to their front, Benning's men leveled their muskets and delivered a terrific fire into the New Yorkers. One New York officer recalled that the first volley brought down a full quarter of the men. Included among the killed was Colonel Ellis, who fell dead from the saddle when a bullet pierced his brain. What was left of the 124th scrambled back up the slopes, resuming their place on the crest while Benning's men surged forward, joined in their advance by the 1st Texas on their left and the 44th and 48th Alabama on their right. Together, these men advanced up the slopes through the rocks and toward the crest of Devil's Den, bearing down on Smith's now very much exposed and vulnerable battery.

One of Smith's guns, disabled by a Confederate shell, had already been taken out of the fight. With Confederate infantry now approaching from his front and left and not wishing to lose his three remaining pieces, Smith raced over to the shaken remnants of the 124th, imploring them, "For God's sake, men, don't let them take my guns away from me!" But there was little the infantry could do, and there would be no time for Smith to call for his battery's horses. Despairing of any help, Smith realized that his cannons would have to be abandoned. He ordered his men to make their way to safety and to take all of their firing implements with them—their sponge rammers, friction primers and such. Left behind, Smith's guns soon fell into Confederate hands.

Ward's line was crumbling. On his left, Colonel Elijah Walker of the 4th Maine, his men still under a heavy fire, attempted to regain the ground lost on Devil's Den. He led his men up and around the massive boulders, where they were greeted with a few well-directed volleys. The 99th Pennsylvania soon came racing to their support, and together these two regiments held out for a few violent minutes. But theirs was a forlorn effort; there were simply too many Confederates closing in on them and from nearly three sides. By

Confederate forces seize Devil's Den. *From* Battles and Leaders of the Civil War.

this time, Tige Anderson's Confederate brigade had arrived in Rose's Woods to the left of Benning and the men of the 1st Texas, adding weight to the attacks against Ward's men on Houck's Ridge while Law's Alabamians and Benning's Georgians closed in on Ward's men from their front and flank. Having suffered heavily and feeling that he was about to get overwhelmed, Ward ordered his men to fall back. The veteran army officer and grizzled warrior lost fully one-third of his men, and after what one Texan described as "one of the wildest, fiercest struggles of the war," the Confederates gained Devil's Den. But even as the combat was ending there, it continued to rage with great intensity farther east, up the rocky, tree-covered slopes of Little Round Top.

When he first learned of Sickles's advance, George Meade immediately responded by ordering George Sykes to move his Fifth Corps south and by sending his chief engineer, Gouverneur Warren, to Little Round Top, telling him that if "anything serious is going on" he was to "attend to it." A West Point graduate, Warren was thirty-three years old and was recently married, having exchanged vows just two weeks earlier. Forgoing a honeymoon, Warren returned to the army as it made its way north in pursuit of Lee. On July 1, he had assisted Howard and Hancock in establishing a defensive line on Cemetery Hill, but it would be on the afternoon of July 2 that would witness his shining moment; his actions that Thursday earned him the title of "savior" of Little Round Top.

A vast and dramatic panorama spread out before Warren when he reached the hilltop's rocky summit. Longstreet's attack had yet to commence, but Warren watched as the artillery of both sides thundered away. Below him and some five hundred yards to his left-front, Warren could see Ward's men and Smith's gunners on Devil's Den, while to his far right-front, much farther distant, he could see the apex of Sickles's salient in the Peach Orchard, an area that was also alive with artillery fire. Of greatest concern to the apprehensive Warren was the Confederate infantry stacked up deep in the far distant trees along Seminary Ridge. Union signalmen had alerted Warren to the presence of these men, and it only took a moment for him to realize that the Confederates' right flank extended well beyond Sickles's left. Most disconcerting was the fact that, aside from the handful of flag-waving signal corpsmen, Little Round Top—which Warren deemed "the key to the whole position"—was entirely unoccupied. If the Confederates gained possession of this hilltop, Warren believed that it would spell doom for the entire army, making their line along Cemetery Ridge untenable. To Warren, it was readily apparent that Little Round Top needed to be secured and soon.

General Gouverneur Warren atop Little Round Top. His actions on July 2 earned him the title of "savior" of Little Round Top. *Library of Congress.*

Warren immediately sent calls out to both Meade and Sickles for help. One of his staff officers, Lieutenant Ranald Mackenzie, reined up at Third Corps headquarters near the Trostle house seeking men for the vacant hilltop. But Sickles had no troops to spare; his line was thin enough, and Longstreet's infantry was just then moving forward. Sickles told Mackenzie that the Fifth Corps was on its way and that he should seek out Sykes for help. Mackenzie soon located Sykes, who in turn directed him to call on sixty-one-year-old James Barnes, whose division marched at the head of the Fifth Corps.

Barnes would later claim that he responded to Warren's call for help by ordering his lead brigade, under Colonel Strong Vincent, to Little Round Top. A much more widely accepted version of the event has Vincent himself taking the responsibility of leading his men there. Noticing a Fifth Corps staff officer gallop by, Vincent allegedly called out, "What are your orders?" The staffer told him that he was sent to find General Barnes—did Vincent know where he was? Not answering, Vincent again inquired as to the man's orders. "General Sykes told me to direct General Barnes to send one of his brigades to occupy that hill yonder," he said, pointing to Little Round Top. "I will take the responsibility of taking my brigade there," Vincent retorted, and with that, his four regiments set off for Little Round Top. But no matter how it happened, whether it was by Barnes's direction or by Vincent's initiative, some 1,300 men from Maine, Pennsylvania, New York and Michigan were soon making their way up the hillside. And they would arrive none too soon, for just minutes after they took up positions across the southern face of the hilltop, Confederate soldiers emerged from the trees below.

These Confederates were the soldiers of the 4th Alabama of Law's Brigade and the 4th and 5th Texas of Robertson's. In an attempt to maintain alignment with Law's left, the 4th and 5th Texas had become separated from the rest of their brigade, and as the 3rd Arkansas and 1st Texas struck Ward's line along Houck's Ridge, they continued moving eastward, with the 4th Alabama on their right. All three of these regiments then angled left, sweeping across the tree-covered northwestern shoulder of Big Round Top, while at the same time, the remaining two regiments of Law's Brigade— the 15th and 47th Alabama, both under the command of Colonel William Oates—became even further separated, moving up the steep slopes of Big Round Top all the way to its summit.

It is impossible to imagine just how thoroughly exhausted Law's Alabama men were that hot Thursday afternoon. They had already put in nearly *thirty* miles that day and had not a drop of water. Reaching the crest of Big Round Top, the men of the 15th and 47th Alabama were particularly winded. The climb was by no means an easy one, and the Alabamians were under a constant fire from skirmishers of the 2nd U.S. Sharpshooters. The men were "catching to the rocks and bushes and crawling over the boulders in the face of the fire of the enemy, who kept retreating, taking shelter and firing down on us from the rocks and crags which covered the side of the mountain thicker than gravestones in a city cemetery," said Colonel Oates, who added that upon reaching the top, "some of my men fainted from heat, exhaustion, and thirst."

Oates halted his men on the summit, hoping to give them time to catch their breath. But the halt proved all too short. One of Law's staff officers soon arrived with orders for Oates to once again get moving. He was to sweep down the northern slope of Big Round Top and join the 4th Alabama and 4th and 5th Texas in their attacks up Little Round Top. Soon, Oates's tired Alabamians were once again in motion, making their way down the hillside and toward the saddle of land that separated Big and Little Round Top. As Oates's 15th and 47th Alabama neared that saddle, they could hear the sounds of battle raging to their left-front.

After chasing back the blue-coated skirmishers sent forward from Vincent's brigade and after traversing difficult ground covered by rocks that varied, said one man, "from the size of a washpot to that of a wagon bed," the men of the 4th Alabama and 4th and 5th Texas emerged from the trees on the northern slopes of Big Round Top and immediately came under fire from Vincent's men positioned above. "In an instant a sheet of smoke and flames burst from our whole line," said one man of the 83rd Pennsylvania, "which made the enemy reel and stagger, and fall back in confusion." The Confederates did their best to hold out, taking up spots behind the massive granite boulders and returning fire. As Texan Van Giles later wrote, "Every tree, rock and stump that gave us protection from the rain of Minie balls that were poured down upon us from the crest above, was soon appropriated." But Vincent's fusillades proved too heavy, and the Confederate troops fell back. Reforming for another attempt, they lurched forward a second time, and for a second time, they were driven back.

Colonel Strong Vincent may not have had any formal military training or prewar experience, but he was a good soldier and a gifted officer, well-respected by those who served under him. In answer to Warren's call, Vincent quickly led his four regiments up and across the eastern side of Little Round

Colonel Strong Vincent was a twenty-six-year-old Harvard graduate studying the practice of law in his native Erie, Pennsylvania, upon the outbreak of war. *From* Miller's Photographic History of the Civil War.

Top, positioning them mere minutes before coming under attack. Vincent placed Colonel Joshua Chamberlain's 20th Maine regiment on the left of his line—an important post, to be sure, since these 386 men from Maine now constituted the extreme left flank of the entire army. Setting the 20th into place, Vincent told Chamberlain that he was to hold his position "at all costs." To the right of the 20th went the 83rd Pennsylvania, followed by the 44th New York and finally the 16th Michigan, on the far right of Vincent's line. It was a good position, especially for the men of the 44th New York and 16th Michigan, since the ground to their immediate front was particularly steep and dotted with boulders. But until additional troops could arrive, the right flank of the 16th was exposed and vulnerable to attack from the west.

The first two attacks up Little Round Top struck the center and right of Vincent's line, and both times the Confederates were repulsed. But more Confederate troops soon arrived in the form of the 15th and 47th Alabama, led by Colonel Oates. Oates's instructions were to locate "the left of the Union line, to turn it and do all the damage I could." It was not long before he and his men found it. As the weary soldiers of these two Alabama regiments approached the saddle to the right of the 4th Alabama, they were greeted "by the most destructive fire" Oates had even seen; he would also later remember how his line "wavered like a man trying to walk against a strong wind." Much of the fire that welcomed Oates's Alabamians to the brawl came from the left of the 83rd Pennsylvania and from Colonel Chamberlain's 20th Maine on Vincent's left. Private Elisha Coan of the 20th remembered that the line "burst into flames, and the crash of musketry became constant." Recovering from the initial blast, Oates's men soon returned fire, and the fighting now became general along the length of Vincent's line.

As Vincent's men were slugging it out with the Texans and Alabamians on the southern side of Little Round Top, the gunners of Lieutenant Charles Hazlett's Battery D, 5th United States Artillery, were just then laboring up the opposite side of the hilltop, straining to get their pieces to the summit. It was an exceptionally tough task, too much for the horses alone to handle. The artillerists therefore had to help shoulder the burden, pushing and pulling the cannons up the hill, over the rocks and between the trees to the summit. Gouverneur Warren believed that Hazlett's guns would be of little use. There was so little room to deploy the guns, Warren explained, and besides, their barrels could not be depressed enough to fire at Confederate infantry attacking up the hillside. "Never mind that," replied the battery commander, "the sound of my guns will be encouraging to our troops and disheartening to the others, and my battery's of no use if this hill is lost." Convinced by the

Edwin Forbes's depiction of Hazlett's battery, thundering away from atop Little Round Top. *Library of Congress.*

artillerist's argument, Warren helped position Hazlett's six cannons, which soon began throwing shot and shell at the Confederate infantry swarming up and over Devil's Den and into the Plum Run Valley below.

With Hazlett's guns going into position, Warren, bleeding from a neck wound, raced down the hillside, seeking more men to secure Little Round Top. Near the base of the hill, he happened upon the 140th New York, led by Colonel Patrick O'Rorke. The 140th belonged to Stephen Weed's brigade of Romeyn Ayres's Fifth Corps division, and O'Rorke had halted it while Weed rode ahead for orders. That is when Warren galloped up. "Paddy, give me a regiment," Warren exclaimed. O'Rorke explained that he was waiting for Weed to return with his orders. "Never mind that," said the frantic Warren, "bring your regiment up here and I will take the responsibility." Warren's voice made it clear that there was no time to lose, and thus at the engineer's urgings, O'Rorke led the 140th up Little Round Top, arriving on the summit just in time to help throw back yet another Confederate assault and to stabilize Vincent's wavering line.

The 4th and 5th Texas and 4th Alabama would not be denied. Twice they had gone forward, and twice they had been repulsed, but they were now forming up to try it a third time. By this time, Devil's Den had been secured. Ward's men had been driven back, as had the 40th New York and 6th New Jersey, two regiments that had been sent to Ward's assistance from De Trobriand's and Burling's brigades, respectively. With Oates's men heavily engaged on their right and with the soldiers of the 48th Alabama and other regiments advancing into Plum Run Valley to the left, the 4th and 5th Texas crept steadily once more out of the trees, their piercing yells heard above the roar of battle. Again they ran into a sheet of flame, but joined by some of the 48th Alabama on their left, these men from Texas pressed on up the hill farther than their previous two attempts, encouraged in their advance by what appeared to be the collapse of Vincent's right flank. Trouble had developed within the 16th Michigan, and that trouble threatened to unhinge Vincent's entire line.

During their advance up the hillside, the Texans and Alabamians worked their way around the exposed right of the Michigan regiment, and the bullets soon came crashing into the Michigan men from two directions. Then, for reasons that are not quite clear, an officer of the 16th ordered the color-bearer to fall back up the hillside, and with the flag went about one-third of the regiment. Vincent raced over to his crumbling right flank. While exhorting his men to rally and to hold firm, the brave, energetic young officer was struck down, mortally wounded.

For the moment, it seemed the Confederates would turn Vincent's right, but soon, Colonel O'Rorke and the hard-charging men of his 140th New York came sweeping into the whirlwind of battle that swirled on the hilltop, encountering a scene, said one New York officer, "very much like hell itself." The 140th charged down the hillside and directly toward the surging Texans and Alabamians, with O'Rorke leading the way, shouting, "Down this way, boys!" The New Yorkers ran into a murderous fire that felled almost a quarter of their men, but their entrance into the fight was too much for the winded Texans and Alabama men to bear. They fell back, driven from the slopes of Little Round Top for the final time. Very quickly, the tide had turned, and the right of Vincent's line was secured. But the cost was high. Vincent had already fallen with his mortal wound, and O'Rorke, first in his West Point class of 1861, had fallen dead, shot through the neck at the moment of his regiment's triumph. Yet even as affairs were settling down on Vincent's right, the matter had yet to be decided on the opposite end of the line, where the fighting still raged.

The 15th and 47th Alabama had been keeping up a steady pressure on the 20th Maine, though these men were well-nigh worn out. His ranks rapidly thinning, Colonel Oates increasingly found himself in a bad spot. His two regiments constituted the extreme right flank of the Confederate army, and they had nothing in the way of support. Because Benning's Brigade had followed behind Robertson and attacked Devil's Den, there was no one moving up behind Oates's Alabamians. Worse, following the repulse of their third attack, the soldiers of the 4th Alabama and 4th and 5th Texas began to withdraw from Oates's immediate left, leaving Oates and his Alabamians alone. But Oates was not yet ready to call it quits. Instead, the determined colonel began sidestepping the 15th Alabama to the right, seeking to turn the flank of the 20th Maine Infantry on the far left of the Union line.

Oates's counterpart, thirty-four-year-old Colonel Joshua Lawrence Chamberlain, a prewar professor of rhetoric at Bowdoin College in Maine, was having his own troubles. He, too, was losing men left and right, and his soldiers were running out of bullets. "The air seemed to be alive with lead," wrote one Maine soldier, as Oates's Alabamians repeatedly made their way up the hillside. "Again and again this mad rush repeated," said another of Chamberlain's men, "each time to be beaten off by the ever-thinning line that desperately clung to its ledge of rock." Admonished by Vincent to hold his ground to the last, Chamberlain was determined to do so, though it was increasingly becoming more difficult.

Chamberlain noticed as Oates's Alabamians worked their way around his left flank. In response, he stretched his line thin and turned it back on itself at a near ninety-degree angle so that his regiment came to resemble a "V," with the men on his left facing east while those on his right continued to face south. Once more, Oates's men surged up the hillside, getting to within a few dozen yards of Chamberlain's tenuous line. In some places, for a few brief moments, the combat was hand to hand. But, said Chamberlain, "the terrible effectiveness of our fire compelled them to break and take shelter." Nonetheless, Chamberlain believed that his men would not be able to withstand any more attacks. Never once considering falling back, Chamberlain yelled out the orders for his men to fix bayonets. Believing that it was his only option, Chamberlain then readied for a charge.

At this same time but at the base of the hill, Colonel Oates decided that enough was enough. The Union position was too strong, his men too tired and his casualties too heavy. Oates had sent to his left for help, only to learn that all the troops there had fallen back. Sensing his isolation and despairing of any support, Oates decided to retreat. It was not to be an orderly one, he told his officers; instead, every man should simply "run in the direction from whence we came." Then a shout was heard, and then came the hard-charging soldiers of the 20th Maine Infantry sweeping down the hill, through the trees and through the lifting clouds of smoke, their bayonets leveled forward.

Oates's men scattered before the charging tide, running, said Oates, "like a herd of wild cattle." Scores of Alabamians were rounded up and sent to the rear as prisoners of war, while those who were able scampered up the slopes of Big Round Top to safety. Drained by the exertions of the day, Colonel Oates fainted as he made his way back but was carried off before falling into enemy hands. Chamberlain called off the charge, and his men returned to their place while what remained of Oates's Alabamians continued on to safety. The struggle for Little Round Top was over.

The story of what Chamberlain and the men of his 20th Maine did on the slopes of Little Round Top has captured much popular attention, vying with if not surpassing Pickett's Charge as the best-remembered aspect of the three-day battle, and for good reason. It is, indeed, a compelling story, one fraught with many desperate moments, including the Maine men (on the far left flank of the Union line) beating back repeated attacks before running out of bullets and ultimately resorting to the bayonet in their defense of the hilltop. The thought that all would have been lost had the 20th faltered and the Alabama men gained the hilltop still remains strong. But it is extremely doubtful that a few hundred thoroughly exhausted Confederates, without any support, would have been able to achieve much.

Had the 20th Maine fallen back, Oates still would have had to contend with the rest of Vincent's brigade, and they would have found Little Round Top swarming with additional Union troops. Hazlett's guns were there, as was the 140th New York and the rest of Stephen Weed's brigade, for even as the action was concluding on the southern slopes of the hill, Weed was arriving and placing his remaining three regiments across the hilltop's western face. Samuel Crawford's Fifth Corps division arrived soon after on the northern shoulder of the hilltop, followed by the entirety of the army's Sixth Corps, thirteen thousand men strong. There were thus ample troops on hand to have regained the hill *if* it had been taken by Oates's Alabamians. Perhaps Oates said it best when after the war he wrote, "Had I succeeded in capturing Little Round Top isolated as I was I could not have held it ten minutes."

The tenacious defense and gallant charge of the 20th Maine was heroic. But Little Round Top was secured not by the actions of a single officer or those of a single regiment; it was, instead, a collective effort that began with Warren and continued with the likes of Vincent, Hazlett, O'Rorke, Chamberlain, Weed and the men of their various commands. Vincent and O'Rorke had given their lives in defense of the hilltop. So, too, would Hazlett and Weed. As the action subsided, a bullet tore through General Weed, and he fell to the ground, paralyzed from the neck down and mortally wounded. Hazlett was killed moments later when a bullet ripped through his head. The Union army lost a number of gifted and promising young officers, but their efforts had all helped to ensure that Little Round Top would remain firmly in Federal hands.

From start to finish, the battle for Little Round Top lasted about one hour. During all this time and continuing well afterward, combat was also raging with a fury in farmer John Rose's twenty-acre wheat field several hundred yards to the west. And while the attack and defense of Little Round Top ranks among the most famous episodes of the battle, the struggle in the Wheatfield remains the most complicated and complex. Variously and aptly described by both participants and historians alike as a whirlwind, a cauldron and a maelstrom, the fighting in the Wheatfield would ultimately involve the soldiers of at least *ten* different Union brigades from three different corps and those of six Confederate brigades, in all, more than twenty thousand men fighting back and forth for possession of just twenty acres of ground. In the end, that golden field of wheat would be trampled and stained red with the blood that flowed all too freely.

Soldiers from De Trobriand's brigade of Birney's Third Corps division, augmented by two regiments from Burling's brigade, had taken up positions in the Wheatfield and in front of Stony Hill, while Captain George Winslow unlimbered his Battery D, 1st New York Light Artillery, in the middle of the wheat, the barrels of his six guns aimed south, toward Rose's Woods. Support for these men would soon arrive in the form of Tilton's and Sweitzer's brigades, from Barnes's Fifth Corps division. De Trobriand's men were stretched out along the southern edge of the Wheatfield with the 17th Maine on the left of the line, taking up positions behind a three-foot-high stone wall along the Wheatfield's southern border, connecting loosely with the right of Ward's men on Houck's Ridge. From this position, the Maine men had fired into the left flank of the 3rd Arkansas as they pushed through Rose's Woods during the initial stages of the attack on Ward's line. With his men stymied in the trees, Confederate general Robertson called for help, and the four Georgia regiments of General George "Tige" Anderson's brigade soon came marching to his assistance.

Anderson had led his brigade forward from Seminary Ridge soon after Law and Robertson kicked off the assault. Crossing the Emmitsburg Road, Anderson led his men into Rose's Woods. The soldiers on the right of his line pushed straight ahead, bolstering the 3rd Arkansas in its attacks against Ward, while the regiments on his left angled to their left and began pushing northerly through the trees in order to contend with the Third and Fifth Corps soldiers in the Wheatfield and atop Stony Hill. The battle quickly intensified, and the Georgians suffered heavily. The commander of the 59th Georgia remembered that he "could hear bones crash like glass in a hail storm," and under heavy fire from the Union infantry and from Winslow's cannons, Anderson's men fell back through the trees, awaiting support before trying it again.

It was by now sometime around 5:30 p.m., and all of Hood's brigades had by this time been committed, slugging it out with various Third and Fifth Corps units on Devil's Den and Little Round Top and in the Wheatfield. Back on Seminary Ridge, General James Longstreet now decided that the time had arrived to unleash McLaws's Division. General Joseph Kershaw's 1,800 South Carolinians, on the right of McLaws's front line, advanced first, sweeping forward in parade-like precision while the Georgians of Paul Semmes's brigade moved out behind them in support. After scaling up and over the fences that lined the Emmitsburg Road, Kershaw's Brigade broke into two wings. The right wing, under Kershaw's direct command, continued straight ahead, marching toward the Rose house and barn in an effort to both connect with Tige Anderson's men in Rose's Woods and to strike at Tilton's and Sweitzer's men crowded on Stony Hill. At the same time, Kershaw's left wing—consisting of the 8th South Carolina, 3rd South Carolina Battalion and 2nd South Carolina—turned to the left and advanced in a northerly fashion directly toward a formidable line of Union cannons that had been wheeled into position along the Wheatfield Road.

One South Carolinian remembered that the Union shells "were cutting off the arms, legs and heads of our men, cutting them in two, and exploding in their bodies, tearing them to mincement." Yet in the face of this destructive fire, the three South Carolina units pressed on, drawing ever nearer to the largely unsupported line of Union guns. But just at the moment it seemed that these men might overrun the cannons, there occurred a tragic miscommunication

H.A. Ogden's dramatic rendering of General James Longstreet overseeing his divisions' attacks on July 2 at Gettysburg. *Library of Congress.*

of orders—all too common on both sides that day—that brought their attack to an abrupt and bloody end.

Kershaw had yelled out orders for the soldiers of his right wing to shift farther to their right in order to better close up with Anderson's men in Rose's Woods. Somehow, this order was also conveyed to the soldiers of his *left* wing, who then turned to their right and began bearing down easterly toward Stony Hill. This change in direction exposed their left flank to the devastating artillery fire, and the South Carolinians crumbled. As Kershaw later famously wrote, "[H]undreds of the bravest and best men of Carolina fell, victims of this fatal blunder." But this fatal blunder did have one unintended consequence, one that led to the unraveling of the Union line in the Wheatfield.

After Vincent's brigade had peeled away from the head of his division's column—going on to earn great glory on the slopes of Little Round Top—General James Barnes led Colonel William Tilton's and Colonel Jacob Sweitzer's brigades toward the Wheatfield. The 1,600 men of these two brigades arrived on Stony Hill just in time to help repulse Tige Anderson's first attack, but their position on that small, tree-covered rise of ground greatly troubled both Barnes and Colonel Tilton. There was a large gap between Tilton's right flank on Stony Hill and Graham's men in the Peach Orchard, covered only by a thin line of skirmishers and by those cannons lined up along the Wheatfield Road to their right-rear. Making matters worse for Tilton, following the repulse of Anderson's first attack, the 8th New Jersey and 115th Pennsylvania—two of Burling's regiments—withdrew from their positions in front of Stony Hill, mistakenly believing that they were being relieved, which, in turn, forced De Trobriand to spread his line ever thinner.

Then, surging forward once more through the trees came Tige Anderson's indefatigable Georgians, joined now by Kershaw's South Carolinians, advancing to their left, from around the Rose farm and toward Tilton's line on Stony Hill. "Shot and shell raged terrifically," recalled a soldier of the 118th Pennsylvania, while "[t]he familiar piercing rebel yell...dominated the uproar." The Georgians and South Carolinians struck hard, but De Trobriand's and Tilton's men held firm, and this second Confederate attack was brought to a standstill. Anderson's men limped back into the trees, while Kershaw's men fell back toward the Rose farm. Yet while Kershaw looked around for support, the situation to his front was about to change.

Tilton had watched with alarm as the left wing of Kershaw's Brigade swept across his right and toward the cannons on the Wheatfield Road and even more so when those three regiments then changed direction and began

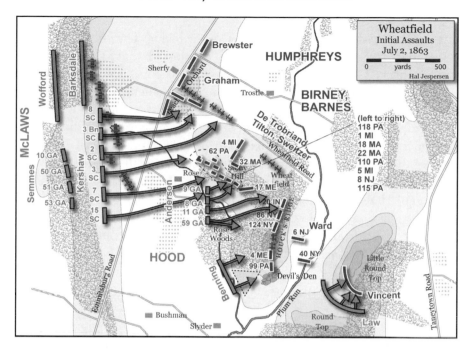

The opening struggle in the Wheatfield. *Map by Hal Jespersen.*

bearing down on his right and rear. Of course, Tilton could not know that this change in direction was due entirely to that false order—that "tragic blunder"—but having already expressed his concern about his right flank to Barnes and having already been told by his division commander to fall back if he felt threatened, the anxious colonel ordered his brigade to withdraw from Stony Hill. Sweitzer soon followed suit, and both brigades now made their way back several hundred yards to the relative safety of Trostle's Woods. Colonel De Trobriand could not believe what he was seeing: Tilton and Sweitzer were abandoning Stony Hill, leaving his three regiments alone to contend with the ever-growing number of Confederates gathering to his front. Believing his position now untenable, De Trobriand gave the order for his men to also fall back. They withdrew all the way back to the Wheatfield Road as the Confederates closed in.

With Devil's Den having by this time been secured, soldiers from Robertson's and Benning's Brigades began creeping their way up the tree-covered spine of Houck's Ridge while, to their left, Tige Anderson's men once more pushed through the trees of Rose's Woods and into the Wheatfield. At the same time, the 7th and the 3rd South Carolina from Kershaw's Brigade advanced toward Stony Top, now theirs for the taking. The only Union force remaining in the Wheatfield was Captain Winslow's Battery D, 1st New York Light Artillery. Winslow's gunners stood as long as possible in the wheat, but with their infantry support now gone and with Confederates closing in on them from three sides, Winslow called up his horses and ordered a retreat.

David Birney watched as the Union line crumbled and as the surging Confederates—"yelling," said one man, "like so many devils"—began making their way into the Wheatfield and onto Stony Hill. Birney knew that help for his beleaguered force was on its way, in the form of John Caldwell's division of Hancock's Second Corps, but until these men arrived, he needed to buy some time. Reining up in front of De Trobriand's fatigued men along the Wheatfield Road, the Third Corps division commander singled out Lieutenant Colonel Charles Merrill of the 17th Maine and ordered him to charge back into the wheat. Merrill's Mainers very quickly swept back into the cauldron. They were soon joined by the 5th Michigan on their right, and there developed yet another fierce firefight. The price paid was heavy but these two regiments did succeed in buying enough time for Caldwell's division to arrive, and yet again that ever-shifting, ever-changing tide of battle that defined the action in Gettysburg's bloody Wheatfield was about to turn.

Called on by Meade to send additional support to the army's wavering left flank, Winfield Scott Hancock gave the nod to John Caldwell, whose four brigades were stacked up on the left of the Second Corps line along Cemetery Ridge. Caldwell, a thirty-year-old former teacher and school principal, marched his 3,200 men south with Colonel Edward Cross's brigade leading the way, followed in turn by Colonel Patrick Kelly's famed Irish Brigade, then Brigadier General Samuel Zook's brigade and, finally, Colonel John Rutter Brooke's brigade bringing up the rear. When these men arrived and advanced into the Wheatfield, De Trobriand's stalwart regiments at last retired from the fight.

Cross's brigade was the first of Caldwell's division to enter the fray. All day, Colonel Cross had had a feeling that he would not survive the upcoming fight, and soon after his brigade set out, Hancock galloped up to the hard-fighting colonel, promising him that this day would earn him the star of a brigadier general. "No, General," replied Cross, "this is my last battle." Never one for stirring patriotic addresses, Cross simply told his men, "Boys, you know what's before you. Give them hell," and with that, Cross's four regiments advanced forward. The left of Cross's brigade swept into the trees that lined the eastern edge of the Wheatfield, while his right moved forward through the trampled field of wheat. Almost immediately, they came under fire from the Confederates

A September 1862 photograph of Brigadier General John C. Caldwell and staff. Caldwell, whose division suffered heavily in the Wheatfield, is standing in the center of the photograph. *Library of Congress.*

positioned in the trees and behind that stone wall on the southern edge of the field. Leading his old 5th New Hampshire, Cross was among those struck down, a bullet slamming into his stomach. Carried from the field and taken to the rear, Cross's premonition would soon come to fruition; his last words were, allegedly, "I think the boys will miss me. Say goodbye to all."

Cross's boys were keeping up a hot fire, gradually driving the Confederates back through the trees and at the same time securing the eastern half of the Wheatfield once more for the Union. At the same time but on the opposite or western edge of the field, Samuel Zook's New York and Pennsylvania men were just then coming to blows with Kershaw's men on Stony Hill. "[We] rushed at a double-quick boldly forward into the mouth of hell, into the jaws of death," wrote one of Zook's men, who added that the "firing became terrific and the slaughter frightful." Among those shot down early in this frightful slaughter was Samuel Zook, who, like Cross, caught a bullet in his stomach and slumped to the ground with a mortal wound.

Though their leaders were both down, Cross's and Zook's soldiers held strongly to their work, inflicting heavy losses among the gray ranks. Meanwhile, the gap that developed between these two brigades was soon filled by the hard-fighting, hard-charging soldiers of Colonel Patrick Kelly's Irish Brigade, distinguished on any battlefield by their emerald green flags and by their sheer heroics. Kelly's remarkably undersized brigade went into the Wheatfield at Gettysburg with a total of just 530 men in its five regiments, the result of the horrific losses they received attacking the Sunken Road at Antietam and Marye's Heights at Fredericksburg. Though small in number, the Irish Brigade nevertheless helped to end the impasse that had developed between Zook's and Kershaw's men on Stony Hill.

Kelly led his men into the wheat to the left of Zook and then swung them up the eastern side of Stony Hill in order to strike at Kershaw's exposed right flank. His men now pressured on front and flank, Kershaw galloped back to Semmes's Brigade, which was just then approaching the western edge of Rose's Woods. Kershaw spoke briefly to Semmes, who a short time later would topple with a mortal wound, seeking support. He then galloped back to his men, who were struggling in the face of mounting pressure to hold on to Stony Hill. With no help then in sight, Kershaw ordered them to withdraw once more toward the Rose farm.

Cross, Zook and Kelly had regained much of the lost ground in the Wheatfield and on Stony Hill, although they were fast running out of bullets. In the meantime, Caldwell's fourth brigade, commanded by twenty-five-year-old Colonel John Rutter Brooke, lined up along the Wheatfield Road and watched as the action swirled and raged and unfolded before them. Knowing that his men would soon be called on, Brooke, a Philadelphia native, made his way to his old 53rd Pennsylvania Volunteers, calling out to them, "Boys—Remember the enemy has invaded our soil. The eyes of the world…[are] upon us and we are expected to stand up bravely to our duty."

Like Kelly's, though not nearly as pronounced, Brooke's was a small brigade, with just nine hundred or so men in its five regiments. Receiving orders to move forward and relieve Cross's men, Brooke's brigade swept with a fury through the Wheatfield, under a murderous fire. The din, said one of Brooke's officers, "was almost deafening." Wishing not to get too long engaged in a stand-up fight, Brooke ordered his men to fix bayonets, and his men charged forward, through the wheat, up and over that stone wall and through the trees of Rose's Woods, driving Tige Anderson's thoroughly worn-out soldiers before them. But Brooke's attack came to a sudden halt when the men reached the western edge of Rose's Woods and ran head-on with Semmes's relatively unbloodied brigade. Some of Anderson's men, reforming to the right of Semmes, began firing into Brooke's left, forcing him to refuse his line. Advanced well beyond any immediate support, Brooke knew that he would not be able to hold on for long and thus sent back to Caldwell for help.

Caldwell was already desperately looking about for help. He first called on a wounded General Barnes, whose two brigades under Tilton and Sweitzer clung to their positions in Trostle's Woods. He told Barnes that Brooke's men were "driving the enemy like hell over yonder in the woods" and that they needed support. Barnes agreed to send in Sweitzer, and after delivering some stirring words of encouragement, Barnes ordered them forward into the wheat. Minutes later, Caldwell encountered General Romeyn Ayres, the thickly bearded career soldier commanding the Second Division of the Fifth Army Corps.

Ayres's three brigades had followed Barnes's division south toward the threatened Union left. Arriving by way of the Wheatfield Road, General Stephen Weed's brigade, at the head of Ayres's column, had broken away from the division and advanced up Little Round Top, arriving there in time to both turn back the final Confederate attack up its southwestern slopes and help render the hilltop secure. Weed's departure left Ayres with his remaining two brigades, commanded by Colonels Sidney Burbank and Hannibal Day, each consisting entirely of battle-hardened Regular Army troops. As Weed's men advanced up Little Round Top, Ayres deployed Burbank's and Day's brigades into lines of battle, with Burbank's men in front and Day's men behind them, in support. The Regulars then swept forward, across the Plum Run Valley and onward to the Wheatfield, all the while exposed to what one officer labeled as a "most destructive" fire poured into the blue columns from Confederates positioned around Devil's Den.

Caldwell and Ayres were discussing the situation when their conversation was interrupted by an uneasy officer on Ayres's staff by the name of William Powell. "General, you had better look out, the line in front of you is giving way," said Powell. "That is not so, sir; those are my troops being relieved," Caldwell snapped back. A few moments ticked by before Powell, unconvinced by Caldwell's report, again interrupted, addressing his commander directly: "General Ayres, you will have to look out for your command. I don't care what anyone says, those troops in front are running away." Peering through the smoke and into the Wheatfield, Caldwell and Ayres realized that the Union troops were, indeed, running. Once more, the Union line was broken, and the tide of battle in the Wheatfield had turned yet again.

Following Barnes's orders, Sweitzer had led his three regiments into the wheat and all the way across to that stone wall lining its southern border. Soon after arriving in position, Sweitzer saw Brooke's men now streaming back through the trees to his right. For twenty minutes, Brooke had done all he could to hold his ground on the western edge of the woodlot. He had sent for help, but before supports could get there, the time had come for the young warrior to order a retreat. His men fell back grudgingly. Brooke himself had to be helped to the rear after a bullet had slammed into his ankle. With Brooke's men giving way before them, Anderson's untiring Georgians and the Georgians of Semmes's Brigade then advanced through the trees and toward the Wheatfield, where they drew fire from Sweitzer's men, just then going into position. The situation quickly became dire for Jacob Sweitzer, for not only were Brooke's men falling back, but so, too, were Zook's and Kelly's brigades, falling back from Stony Hill in the face of yet another fresh, unbroken line of gray that was bearing down on them from the west.

As will be seen, Lafayette McLaws's remaining two brigades, under Barksdale and William Wofford, had by this time been thrown into the fight. Barksdale's men led the way, sweeping forward from Seminary Ridge

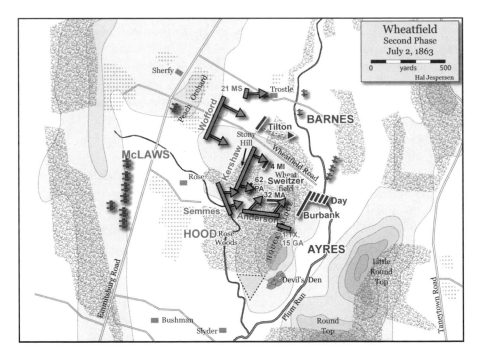

Confederates seize the Wheatfield. *Map by Hal Jespersen.*

"A Scene Very Much Like Hell Itself"

at about 6:00 p.m. After smashing through Graham's line in the Peach Orchard, several hundred yards west of Stony Hill, most of Barksdale's Brigade would then turn north and advance up the Emmitsburg Road, but Wofford's Brigade—1,400 men strong—would continue driving eastward, advancing along the axis of the Wheatfield Road. Seeing Wofford's serried ranks advancing breathed new life into Kershaw's men huddled up near the Rose farm, and they again moved forward to the attack, pressing toward Zook's and Kelly's men on Stony Hill. Taking fire again from the front and flank, and now with Wofford's men moving *behind* them, the soldiers of Zook's and Kelly's brigades abandoned Stony Hill, leaving Sweitzer, for the moment, alone in the Wheatfield.

Sweitzer's three regiments were facing south and firing at the Confederates, who were approaching through Rose's Woods, but when bullets began striking Sweitzer's men from the right and rear, fired by the Confederates who now occupied Stony Hill in force, the man carrying the brigade flag leaned over to Sweitzer and said, "Colonel, I'll be damned if I don't think we are faced the wrong way." Sweitzer sent back for help, but Tilton's brigade had by now also fallen back, and General Barnes was nowhere to be found. For Sweitzer, the grim realization set in that his men were about to be surrounded. To meet the threat on his right, Sweitzer turned his 62nd Pennsylvania and 4th Michigan to face west. The fighting "waxed hot and furious," said one of Sweitzer's men, and it was at very close quarters, complete with hand-to-hand combat. During the deadly melee, the flag of the 4th Michigan Infantry fell to the ground and was picked up by a Confederate soldier. Not wanting his regiment's flag captured, Colonel Harrison Jeffords, in what remains one of the most famous incidents of the Wheatfield fight, lunged forward and wrestled the colors back. He was shot and then, moments later, run through with a bayonet. Jeffords saved his flag, but it cost him his life. Sweitzer gave the orders for his men to retreat, and what remained of his shattered brigade raced their way back, their retreat covered in part by Ayres's Regulars, who were by that time just then advancing *into* the wheat.

Ayres had ordered his men into the maelstrom that was the Wheatfield to support both Caldwell and Sweitzer. Burbank's men, advancing with parade ground precision, led the way, sweeping into the corpse-strewn field and directly into disaster. Burbank's men were immediately struck in front, flank and rear by the soldiers of at least four Confederate brigades, converging from the south and west. Major Arthur Lee, whose 2nd U.S. Infantry held the right of Burbank's line, later wrote, "A fresh column of the enemy at this time appeared on our right, [and] we were ordered to retire. The word was scarcely given when three lines of the enemy, elevated one above the other on the slope to our right [on Stony Hill], poured in a most destructive fire, almost decimating my regiment."

Struck on two sides, Burbank's men retreated, falling back "as if on drill" as the bullets continued to tear into their ranks. Day's men, who had advanced behind Burbank, were also caught up in the storm. One of Stephen Weed's volunteers, watching the destruction of Burbank's and Day's brigades from atop Little Round Top, would never forget the scene and the heavy price paid by the Regulars. "[F]or two years the U.S. Regulars taught us how to be soldiers," this soldier remembered, while "in the Wheatfield at Gettysburg, they taught us how to die like soldiers." In just a few savage minutes, Burbank lost nearly half his men, his casualties totaling 447 of the 950 men he took into the fight; Day's losses were slightly fewer, with 382 of his men killed or wounded.

Flush with victory and now having smashed Ayres's Regulars, Confederate soldiers swept triumphantly into the Wheatfield. Of course, by this time, much of their strength had been sapped and their losses heavy, particularly in G.T. Anderson's Brigade, the only brigade on either side to have been involved throughout the entirety of the Wheatfield fight. Anderson had been wounded early in the struggle, while his brigade would lose nearly half of its 1,400 men. The 11th Georgia suffered the most, losing 201 of its 310 men, a staggering 65 percent loss, followed closely by the 8th and 9th Georgia Infantries, which each lost 55 percent of its men. Still, despite their losses, these men from Anderson's, Kershaw's and Semmes's Brigades would press on, sweeping through the wheat and on toward the northern slopes of Little Round Top, while to their left-rear Wofford's Brigade continued moving steadily on.

Farmer John Rose's Wheatfield had been transformed into a hellish place, its twenty acres trampled and made desolate by the fearful and murderous struggle that had raged there. Five decades later, an aging Robert Carter, who had served as a private in the 22nd Massachusetts, still vividly remembered the horrific scenes played out in that golden field of wheat and how those scenes stayed with him the rest of his life, describing the fighting there as "a perfect hell on earth, never, perhaps, to be equaled, certainly not to be surpassed, nor ever forgotten in a man's lifetime. It has never been effaced from my memory, day or night, for fifty years."

"A perfect hell on earth." An apt description, to be sure, and one that was no doubt also used by those who fought farther west, in and around the Peach Orchard, in describing their struggle there.

When Joseph Kershaw first led his brigade into the fight sometime around 5:30 p.m., he had expected that Barksdale's men, to his left, would also be

"A Scene Very Much Like Hell Itself"

Artist Edwin Forbes's depiction of Union Third Corps troops on the left of the Union line awaiting the onslaught. *Library of Congress.*

moving forward, but for whatever reason, they did not immediately come, and Kershaw's South Carolinians were thus forced to bear the brunt of the Union cannons posted both in the Peach Orchard and along the Wheatfield Road. This was through no fault of Barksdale's, for he was more than eager to enter the fray. Hearing the action unfold as Confederate troops assailed Devil's Den and Little Round and as Kershaw's men were catching hell in their advance toward Stony Hill and the Wheatfield beyond, Barksdale paced impatiently, awaiting his orders to advance. His four Mississippi regiments had been among the first to deploy that afternoon and had for far too long been suffering from the shot and shell fired from the Union guns posted just six to seven hundred yards to their front. At one point, spotting Longstreet, the restless Barksdale called out, "I wish you would let me go in, General; I will take that battery in five minutes!" "Wait a little," replied Longstreet, "we are all going in presently." Finally, just minutes before 6:00 p.m., the moment had at last arrived, and Barksdale was ordered to advance. With his long, silvery hair flowing and reportedly "radiant with joy," Barksdale led his Mississippi men forward.

Barksdale's 1,400 Mississippians emerged from the trees along Seminary Ridge and rushed straight ahead, their shrill yelps piercing the air. To their front, Charles Graham's Pennsylvanians, backed up by a few regiments from Burling's brigade, braced for the assault. Like Barksdale's men, these men, too, had suffered from the lengthy artillery barrage and had grown a bit weary, their nerves frayed while awaiting the attack. Now they rose to their feet, drew the hammers of their rifles back and waited for the Mississippians

Prewar photograph of William Barksdale as he appeared as a representative from Mississippi. *Library of Congress*.

to come within range. The gunners of Lieutenant John Bucklyn's Battery E, 1st Rhode Island, unloosed rounds of canister that "fairly peppered" Barksdale's gray tide, but there seemed to be no slowing the Mississippians, who charged forward, yelling "like devils incarnate," said one Union officer. They soon slammed head-on with the Federal troops manning Sickles's salient in the Peach Orchard.

Just as Barksdale had predicted, it only took a matter of minutes for his Mississippians to smash through the Union line. The 68th Pennsylvania, on the left of Graham's line, lost nearly half its strength, giving way under the weight of the 21st Mississippi, advancing on Barksdale's far right. Other regiments followed the 68th rearward, and the Union line quickly became unhinged. The batteries supporting Graham in the Peach Orchard and along the Emmitsburg Road began limbering up and galloped away, including Bucklyn's Rhode Islanders, but not before that battery lost twenty-nine men and forty horses. The 21st Mississippi swept through the splintered peach trees while, to its left, the soldiers of Barksdale's other three regiments crashed into Graham's regiments lined up along the Emmitsburg Road, rolling them up from left to right. The colorful Collis's Zouaves of the 114th Pennsylvania fell back after a desperate fight around the Sherfy house, soon followed by the 57th and 105th Pennsylvania.

Although Graham's men "fought like demons," they could do little to stem the tide. Casualties among Graham's regiments were heavy. The 141st Pennsylvania, for example, lost 149 of the 209 men it took into the fight, a

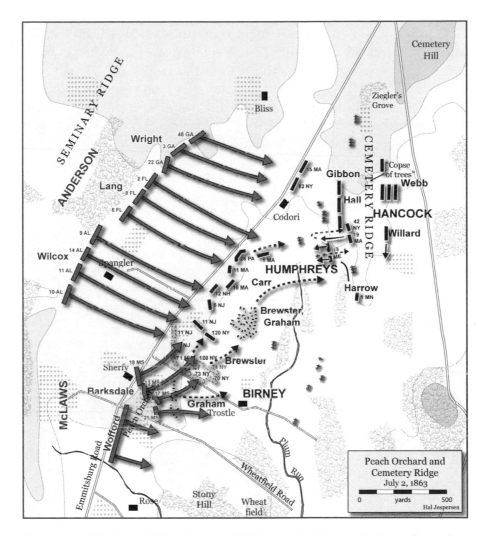

The attacks of Barksdale, Wilcox, Lang and Wright smashed through the Union line at the Peach Orchard and along the Emmitsburg Road. *Map by Hal Jespersen.*

staggering 70 percent loss. As the shattered remnants of the 141st raced back through the Trostle farm, General Daniel Sickles, witnessing the destruction of his line, called out to the regiment's commander Henry Madill, "Colonel! For God's sake, can't you hold on?" Madill looked up at Sickles and, with tears in his eyes, asked, "Where are my men?" In all, nearly half of Graham's brigade became casualties. Graham himself was among them. During the course of the fight, Graham had two horses shot from beneath him and was struck twice, once by a shell fragment and once by a bullet. Falling wounded, Graham would soon be swept up as a prisoner of war.

Watching the struggle from his headquarters near the Trostle barn, Sickles did his best to retain his composure. But soon after his encounter with Colonel Madill, a Confederate solid shot struck squarely into his right knee, nearly severing his leg. Helped from the saddle, the Third Corps commander was placed on a stretcher, and after a tourniquet was quickly applied to his mangled leg, he was carried from the field, coolly puffing on a cigar to assuage any fears some of his men may have had that he had been killed. Arriving at a field hospital later that evening, Sickles's right leg was amputated. With Sickles's wound, command of the Third Corps fell on

Generals Joseph Carr, Daniel Sickles and Charles Graham near the Trostle barn in 1886, at the spot where Sickles, twenty-three years earlier, lost his leg. *Library of Congress.*

the shoulders of David Birney, whose own division had already been cut to pieces at Devil's Den and in the Wheatfield.

Having smashed through Graham's line, Barksdale swung his 13th, 17th and 18th Mississippi to the left, advancing them northward toward the now exposed left flank of Andrew Humphreys's division, lined up along the Emmitsburg Road. Meanwhile, behind Barksdale advanced yet another solid line of gray: General William Wofford's brigade was moving out, no doubt an unnerving sight to the Federal soldiers still desperately trying to hold strong to their positions. But instead of advancing directly behind Barksdale's line, Wofford's four regiments moved forward astride the Millerstown/Wheatfield Road and, after crossing the Emmitsburg Road, continued on an easterly tact, bearing down toward the Stony Hill and the Wheatfield beyond. This advance caused Tilton's retreat from Trostle's Woods and the abandonment of Stony Hill by Zook's and Kelly's men.

With all of Hood's and McLaws's brigades now engaged, Longstreet rode forward with Wofford's men. The sight of their hard-fighting and much-respected corps commander leading them into the fight inspired Wofford's Georgians, who raised their caps to Longstreet and let out a round of cheers. In response, the taciturn Longstreet simply cried out, "Cheer less, men, and fight more!"

Ahead of Wofford's surging line, Colonel Benjamin Humphreys led the four hundred soldiers of his 21st Mississippi through the Peach Orchard, advancing east, while the rest of Barksdale's men continued to angle away in their advance up the Emmitsburg Road. The route of the 21st carried them directly toward the line of Union guns massed along the Wheatfield Road. With their infantry support now gone and with Humphreys's Mississippians bearing down on their exposed right, three of these batteries quickly limbered up and galloped away, leaving only Captain Charles Phillips's 5th Massachusetts Battery and Captain John Bigelow's 9th Massachusetts Battery, in battle for the first time that day, in position. Both of these batteries belonged to the army's Artillery Reserve and had been sent forward to help plug the gaps in and add support to Sickles's line. But with Sickles's line now smashed, it was time for them to go.

Lieutenant Colonel Freeman McGilvery, commanding the Artillery Reserve's First Volunteer Brigade, reined up behind Phillips's and Bigelow's pieces and ordered them to fall back. Phillips pulled out first followed shortly thereafter by Bigelow. With Confederate infantry fast approaching, Bigelow believed that there was not enough time to call forward his horses, so the young captain ordered his artillerists to make a fighting retreat, retiring by prolonge and withdrawing the cannons by hand, with each man grabbing on to the rope attached to each piece and dragging the cannons rearward, their efforts aided by the recoil every time the gun was fired. The sweating artillerists retired in this manner some four hundred yards all the way back to the Trostle house, all the while under a heavy fire from two sides.

Arriving at the Trostle house and believing that his gunners had made it safely through the storm, Captain Bigelow called for his horses, hoping to now use them for the final leg of the journey back to Cemetery Ridge. But Bigelow soon discovered that his men were not yet through for the day. Before he could limber up his guns, McGilvery arrived with new orders for Bigelow. Realizing that there were no organized troops back on Cemetery Ridge and that there existed a large gap in the Union line, McGilvery determined to plug it with artillery, but he would need time to do so. That's why he now called on Bigelow. "Captain, there is not an infantryman back of you," McGilvery hollered to the young Massachusetts captain. "You must remain where you are and hold your position at all hazards, and sacrifice your battery, if need be, until at least I can find some batteries to put in position and cover you." Bigelow summed up his new orders neatly when he wrote that "the sacrifice of the command was asked in order to save the line." It was a demanding task, particularly for soldiers engaged in their first battle, but the Massachusetts gunners would stand up well to their work. Bigelow wheeled his guns into position, ordered his caissons emptied and had rounds of canister piled up next to each piece, his gunners preparing to make one final stand.

Bigelow's artillerists blasted the advancing Confederates with canister. "They attacked furiously," related Bigelow, "but the battery men double-shotted every gun and swept them back." However, the determined Confederates rallied and began working their way around Bigelow's flanks. For thirty minutes, the gunners breathlessly went about their work, under an increasingly heavy fire. "[M]en and horses were falling like hail," reported Bigelow, "Sergeant after sergeant was struck down, horses were plunging and laying all around, bullets now came in on all sides…The air was dark with smoke…The enemy were yelling like demons, yet my men kept up a rapid fire." Nevertheless, they could not hold out forever. With his ammunition depleted and with the Confederates keeping up a hot fire, Bigelow at last gave the order to retreat. But not all of his pieces were able to get away, and four of his six cannons would fall, temporarily it turned out, into the hands of Humphreys's Mississippians. Bigelow was wounded during the retreat, while his 9th Massachusetts Battery lost twenty-eight men killed or wounded and

Captain John Bigelow. The guns he lost at the hands of the 21st Mississippi on the afternoon of July 2 would soon after be recaptured by Twelfth Corps soldiers sent south from Culp's Hill to stabilize the army's left. *National Archives.*

no fewer than forty-five of its horses. Despite the heavy price paid, Bigelow and his men had turned in a heroic performance and had bought precious time for McGilvery, who had, by this time, rounded up enough cannons on Cemetery Ridge to resist any further Confederate advance.

As McGilvery corralled and placed cannons on Cemetery Ridge, one of his counterparts in gray, Colonel E.P. Alexander, was dashing forward to the Peach Orchard. Seeing Barksdale's men smash the Union line, the young Confederate gunner, caught up in the moment, told his powder-stained gunners that the war would end that afternoon. He ordered six of his batteries forward, directing them to take up new positions in the Peach Orchard and along the Emmitsburg Road. More than twenty cannons came rushing forward in what Alexander described as "a general race and scramble to get there first." When Alexander got there, in the shot-torn and corpse-strewn Peach Orchard, his heart sank. He very quickly realized that the Union position in the Peach Orchard was *not* its main line of battle. Instead, its main line "loomed up near 1,000 yards beyond us" on Cemetery Ridge, where Alexander saw "batteries in abundance...and troops...marching and fighting everywhere." Perhaps the war would not end that afternoon after all. Still, as Alexander noted, "There was plenty to shoot at," and soon his gunners began hurling shot and shell toward that distant ridgeline, while others directed their fire north, into Humphreys's Third Corps troops in position along the Emmitsburg Road, trying desperately to fend off attacks from two different directions.

Humphreys had seen Barksdale's Mississippians run roughshod over Graham's men in the Peach Orchard, and he now gritted his teeth as three of Barksdale's regiments began bearing down on his division's exposed left flank. He had no soldiers in reserve since all of Burling's regiments had long since been parceled out to plug gaps in Birney's line. All Humphreys could do to meet Barksdale's hard-fighting Mississippians, then, was to turn his left-most regiments to face south, confronting them head-on. Yet even as these regiments were attempting to execute this change in front, Humphreys gazed off to the west and saw new waves of butternut and gray sweeping forward from Seminary Ridge, advancing directly toward his front.

These were the Alabamians of Cadmus Wilcox's brigade of Richard Anderson's Third Corps division. Continuing with the Confederate onslaught, Wilcox waited until Barksdale had stepped off. Then, a few minutes after 6:00 p.m., he ordered his 1,400 men forward. A soldier of the 9th Alabama remembered that when Wilcox "rode along down the line giving orders to charge, cheer after cheer filled the air almost drowning the sound of shells that were bursting above and around us." Wilcox's men would not

General Richard Anderson. *From* Battles and Leaders of the Civil War.

be advancing alone. To their left, two more of Anderson's brigades, under Colonel David Lang and General Ambrose Wright, would soon be entering the fray. Lang's was an undersized brigade, consisting of just three Florida regiments and totaling about seven hundred men, while Wright swept forward with twice as many men in his all-Georgia brigade.

Humphreys's men, now under pressure from two sides, were putting up a tough fight as the Confederates continued to bear down on them, while bursting artillery shells, fired from Alexander's guns in the Peach Orchard, continued to fill the air overhead. Humphreys had already directed his own artillery off the field. Then orders arrived from Birney: Humphreys was to fall back with his entire command. Humphreys later insisted that he could have held out and that he did not want to abandon his line. But, orders being orders, he directed his two brigades under Brewster and Carr to retreat. It was a fighting retreat, the men keeping up a steady fire as they retired eastward. The price Humphreys's division paid was a dear one, with 1,600 men, 40 percent of the division's total strength, becoming casualties.

Sickles's line had been crushed, and now the soldiers of four Confederate brigades—under Barksdale, Wilcox, Lang and Wright—pressed ahead toward an exceptionally thin Union line on Cemetery Ridge. Farther south, troops from Hood's and McLaws's Division, having cleared the Wheatfield, were now mustering strength for a push toward the northern slopes of Little Round Top. For George Meade and the Union army, these were some desperate moments indeed. But Meade's earlier efforts in confronting the crisis caused by Sickles's advance and his actions in responding to the vast Confederate onslaught were about to bear fruit, and it would not be long before the Confederate tide ebbed.

On the far Union left, two Fifth Corps brigades, under Vincent and Weed, had secured Little Round Top, while four others raced into the Wheatfield. Although these men along with those from Caldwell's Second Corps division—suffered heavily in the wheat, they had each severely sapped the Confederate strength. And as the thinned ranks of G.T. Anderson's, Kershaw's and Semmes's Brigades pushed eastward through the Wheatfield and continued toward the northern slopes of Little Round Top, they would soon encounter the Fifth Corps' final division under Samuel Crawford, just then arriving in position.

Crawford was a trained physician and a former army surgeon who happened to find himself stationed inside Fort Sumter when the first shots of the war were fired in April 1861. Trading in his scalpel for the sword, Crawford entered the infantry and proved himself a hard-fighting soldier.

When his two brigades of Pennsylvania Reserves arrived on the Union left that Thursday evening, Crawford, under Sykes's orders, immediately sent one of them to the support of Vincent's men on the southern slopes of Little Round Top, while aligning his remaining brigade, under Colonel William McCandless, on the hilltop's northern slopes, its line of battle stretching toward the Wheatfield Road.

To their left, Gibbs's Ohio battery and Hazlett's guns on the summit, commanded now by Lieutenant Benjamin Rittenhouse, kept up a lively fire, while to their front, Burbank's and Day's shattered U.S. Regulars came streaming back. Behind the retreating Regulars advanced "an irregular yelling line" of gray. Having been told by Sykes to do what he thought was best with McCandless, Crawford seized the moment and ordered a charge. Waiting for the Regulars to clear their front, the Pennsylvanians charged down the hillside, sweeping into the Plum Run Valley, with Crawford leading the way, hoisting aloft a flag he had taken from one of McCandless's regiments. With this surging line of blue heading straight for them and with their energies long since spent, the Confederates gave way and fell back through the Wheatfield, ultimately settling into positions in Rose's Woods and on Stony Hill.

Sensing that nothing more could be done and recognizing the "sturdy regular blow [that] tells a soldier instantly that he has encountered reserves or reinforcements," Longstreet had by this time also ordered Wofford to halt his advance. Wofford was angry at the order since his brigade had thus far suffered relatively few casualties and his men were still full of fight. But had they continued forward, they would have encountered not only Crawford's men but also much of the Union army's Sixth Corps—thirteen thousand men who were just then arriving on the field, having completed their marathon, nineteen-hour, thirty-mile march from Manchester. As Longstreet later noted, "To urge my men forward under these circumstances would have been madness."

After a three-hour slugfest, the fighting on the Union left at last tapered to a close; the Federal flank was secure. Fifth Corps soldiers strengthened their line on Little Round Top and also took up positions on Big Round Top, while Crawford's and Sedgwick's men, backed up by what remained of Ayres's and Barnes's divisions, took up a defensive line stretching north from Little Round Top and along lower Cemetery Ridge. What remained of Hood's and McLaws's Divisions settled in along the eastern base of Big Round Top and on Devil's Den, their line extending northwesterly from there along Houck's Ridge, through Rose's Woods and across Stony Hill to the Peach Orchard, where E.P. Alexander had established his line of guns.

Samuel Crawford led the Pennsylvanians of McCandless's Brigade down the Plum Run Valley, finally driving the Confederates back through the Wheatfield. *Library of Congress.*

As things were quieting down on the Union left, the final, dramatic moments of the battle were also playing out farther north, along Cemetery Ridge.

When he learned that Sickles had been wounded, Meade directed Hancock to take charge of what remained of the Third Corps, in place of Birney. It was by no means an easy assignment, for not only was Hancock given command of what was then a broken corps, but he also, more importantly, had to somehow piece together a line of defense on Cemetery Ridge, which had been stripped of most its troops. Caldwell's division had long since departed, while several of Gibbon's regiments and a number of batteries had been sent forward to the area around the Codori house along the Emmitsburg Road to provide support to the right of Humphreys's line. The departure of all these units had left Cemetery Ridge largely bereft of troops, and the Confederate soldiers under Barksdale, Wilcox, Lang and Wright were now driving directly toward it.

Needing troops—and fast—Hancock first called on Brigadier General Alexander Hays, whose division still held the northern end of Cemetery Ridge in strength. Responding to Hancock's call, Hays turned to Brigadier General George Willard, telling the New York–born, West Point–educated officer to move his brigade south and to "knock the hell out of the rebs." Willard dutifully set off with his four New York regiments. They were soon overtaken by Hancock, who led them into position north of the George Weikert farm and near McGilvery's line of cannons. Barksdale's men were just then advancing to their front. After helping to drive back Humphreys's men, Barksdale's regiments veered to their right and advanced east, sweeping down into the brush-covered and boulder-strewn bottomland known as the Plum Run swale.

Wasting little time, Willard led three of his regiments forward; his fourth, the famed Garibaldi Guards of the 39th New York, moved farther south to deal with the detached 21st Mississippi Infantry near the Trostle Woods. Barksdale's Mississippians poured in a deadly fire as Willard's men charged toward them, but there was no stopping the determined New Yorkers. "On we rushed with loud cries!" wrote one of Willard's men. "With shells screaming and cannon balls tearing the air, like so many fiends bent on destruction...on, on we rushed, through [the] storm of fire and death, thundering above and darting around us like the thunder and lightning of heaven." Barksdale's attack finally ran its course, grinding to a bloody halt in the marshy thickets of Plum Run. They had crushed Graham and battled with Humphreys, but Willard's attack proved too much for the Mississippians to bear. Their fragmented ranks fell back, but not before many Mississippians raised their hands in surrender. By this point, Barksdale was down, mortally wounded. Riddled by bullets, the fiery secessionist and fierce battlefield warrior was gathered up by Union soldiers and carried behind their lines, where, overnight, he drew his last breath.

Momentum carried Willard's men through and beyond the Plum Run swale and nearly all the way to the Emmitsburg Road, where they came under a heavy fire from Alexander's cannons in the Peach Orchard off to their left. Under this fire and with his mission fulfilled, Willard ordered his men to fall back. He had repulsed Barksdale, but Willard would have but little time to bask in his brigade's glory. As his men made their way back toward Cemetery Ridge, Willard was struck squarely in the face by a shell fragment and instantly killed.

Barksdale's men may have been driven back, but for Hancock, the crisis was far from over. Through the smoke and dust and with the sun fast setting behind South Mountain to the west, the indefatigable Hancock—truly superb that late afternoon and early evening—saw another line of infantry, Wilcox's Alabamians, heading straight toward Cemetery Ridge. Desperately needing

"A Scene Very Much Like Hell Itself"

General George Willard.
From Battles and Leaders
of the Civil War.

men to meet this new threat, Hancock happened upon a single regiment, the 1st Minnesota, lined up in support of Lieutenant Evan Thomas's thundering cannons of Battery C, 4th U.S. Artillery. "My God!" exclaimed Hancock. "Are these all of the men we have here?" Hancock singled out Colonel William Colvill, commanding the Minnesota regiment. "Do you see those colors?" asked Hancock, pointing to Wilcox's flags; Colvill nodded. "Then take them!" snapped Hancock. Colvill gave the order, and with bayonets fixed, the Minnesota men charged forward. "Every man realized in an instant what that order meant," later wrote a survivor of the attack, "death or wounds to us all, the sacrifice of the regiment to gain a few minutes' time and save the position."

The charge of the 1st Minnesota would forever afterward become enshrined in the great lore of Gettysburg, its actions rivaling in fame that which had been achieved by the 20th Maine on Little Round Top. This single regiment, just 262 men strong, was ordered to charge an entire brigade with four times its number. The men knew that they were being sacrificed, yet they charged forward anyway, directly toward Wilcox's line.

Wilcox's Brigade had already lost much of its momentum by the time the Minnesota men charged toward it. It had taken losses in its dealings with Humphreys's division along the Emmitsburg Road. Then, after crossing the roadway, those on the right of Wilcox's line came under fire from some

157

of Willard's New Yorkers, while those on the left were hit by a number of Humphreys's units that had rallied on Cemetery Ridge. All the while, Thomas's gunners continued to thunder away. Taken somewhat aback by the Minnesotans' impetuous charge, Wilcox's skirmishers fell back to the main line while Colvill's men swept all the way down to the Plum Run swale, where they settled in for a savage firefight with the Alabamians.

Unsupported on both sides and with no one advancing behind him, Wilcox realized that he was alone. To his right, Barksdale's men had already been driven back, while Lang had not kept up with his left. Without any help, Wilcox believed that there was nothing more his Alabamians could do and thus ordered them to fall back—"to prevent," as he later wrote, "their entire destruction or capture." At the same time, as if by common consent, a badly wounded Colonel Colvill directed his shattered regiment to retire as well. What was left of the 1st Minnesota rallied on Cemetery Ridge. The number of Minnesotans who fell during this famed dusk attack on July 2 at Gettysburg varies. Traditionally, sources place the number at 215, which out of the 262 men who made the charge, equated to an appalling 82 percent loss. More recent studies show that "only" 180 Minnesotans fell, a 68 percent loss. Whatever the exact figure, there can be no denying that the 1st Minnesota suffered heavily in its heroic feat, turning back Wilcox while buying Hancock a few precious minutes to further strengthen the Union line on Cemetery Ridge.

Not long after Wilcox's Alabamians fell back, so, too, did Lang's Floridians. This small brigade—just three regiments strong—began the assault with about seven hundred men, and like Wilcox's Brigade, it had also lost many men during its advance toward the Emmitsburg Road. After helping to drive back Humphreys's men, Lang's Floridians suffered from a deadly fire poured into them by the 19th Maine Infantry and from Lieutenant Gulian Weir's Battery C, 5th U.S. Artillery, whose cannons were peppering the advancing Confederate lines with canister. Both these units had taken up positions just south of the Codori barn and were in a good position to hammer Lang's left. Lang's ever-dwindling line crossed the Emmitsburg Road, but it would not be long before their advance stalled out. Like Wilcox, Lang also realized that he was in a bad spot, and he, too, ordered a retreat.

For the Union troops, Lang's withdrawal left only Wright's Brigade to contend with. Wright, a thirty-seven-year-old Georgia lawyer and politician, led his 1,400 men forward from Seminary Ridge around 6:30 p.m., from a point almost due west of the Codori house. "Shells around us tore our bleeding ranks with ghastly gaps," remembered one of Wright's men as the brigade neared the Emmitsburg Road. There, Wright's men crashed headlong into the 15th Massachusetts and 82nd New York, two of Gibbon's regiments that had been advanced to the roadway. It was a short but fierce fight. The commanders of both these Union regiments were killed before the Massachusetts and New York men beat a hasty retreat.

Wright's seemingly irresistible tide now brought them bearing down on the guns of Lieutenant T. Frederick Brown's Battery B, 1st Rhode Island Artillery, which had also been sent forward. Brown's men blasted the Georgians with a few rounds of canister, but before they could limber up and retreat, the Georgians were upon them. Brown, who had fallen wounded with a bullet through his neck, lost all but two of his pieces. At the same time, the soldiers on the right of Wright's line stormed across the Emmitsburg Road south of the Codori house and overran Gulian Weir's battery, capturing three of his six cannons. But Wright's men could not stop to haul away the captured pieces; they continued forward instead, charging directly toward the Union center on Cemetery Ridge.

Wright's strength faded with each step, yet the "mad Georgians" rushed onward, sweeping up the gentle western slope of Cemetery Ridge and piercing the Union line several hundred yards south of the soon-to-be-famous copse of trees, which the following day would serve as the supposed focal point of George Pickett's charge. "We were now complete masters of the field," Wright later romanticized, "having gained the key, as it were, of the enemy's whole line." But it proved only a momentary breakthrough. Soldiers of General Alexander Webb's Philadelphia Brigade, who in less than twenty-four hours would bear the brunt of Pickett's attack, poured a destructive fire into Wright's left flank, while the cannons of Lieutenant Alonzo Cushing's and Captain William Arnold's batteries, in position north of the copse, raked the Georgians' lines with canister. Under such a destructive fire and lacking any support, Wright ordered a retreat. "[W]ith painful hearts," wrote a distressed Wright, "we abandoned our captured guns, faced about and prepared to cut our way through the closing lines in our rear." The next day, in speaking with fellow Georgian E.P. Alexander about the prospects of Pickett's men gaining the same Union position on Cemetery Ridge, Wright said that the problem would not be in getting there but in *staying* there since the "whole infernal Yankee army is up there in a bunch."

As Wright's men fell back, soldiers from Webb's Philadelphia Brigade charged forward and recaptured Brown's guns, while those of the recently arrived 13th Vermont, a First Corps regiment, rushed ahead to retake Weir's pieces. The 106th Pennsylvania of Webb's brigade claimed also to have captured no fewer than two hundred Georgians in and around the Codori house and barn.

The tide had turned. Barksdale had been repulsed, as had Wilcox, Lang and Wright. The survivors of these battered brigades fell back to the trees that lined Seminary Ridge, where they caught their breaths and settled in for the night, mourning the dead and wondering how—and *why*—they had made it through. Where was their support? It was a question on the minds of many Confederate soldiers that night. On the opposite ridgeline, soldiers in blue reformed their lines. Despite many desperate moments, the Union line on Cemetery Ridge had held. Darkness quickly enveloped the fields as the smoke of battle began to lift. Behind his lines, a much-relieved George Gordon Meade took stock of the situation. One of his officers turned to him and said that things had gotten close—their lines had nearly crumbled and the day was nearly lost. "Yes," agreed the now calmed army commander, "but it is all right now. It is all right now."

Meade made his way back to the Leister house, and at 8:00 p.m., when the onslaught against his left and center at last subsided and as his lines there began to recover from the shock of the repeated blows, he wired Henry Halleck in Washington, reporting with not a little relief that "[t]he enemy attacked me about 4:00 p.m. this day, and, after one of the severest contests of the war, was repulsed at all points." But even at that late hour, the fighting was not yet over, and the contest had yet to be determined, for even as Meade composed these lines to Halleck, the soldiers on his right flank—on Culp's and Cemetery Hills—were engaged with Richard Ewell's men in a desperate struggle for possession of these hilltops.

Ewell's orders for the day were to make a demonstration against the Union right flank as soon as Longstreet began his assault on the opposite end of the line and to convert the demonstration into a full-fledged attack should the opportunity present itself. All throughout that hot day, he and his men had waited patiently while Longstreet marched, countermarched and maneuvered Hood and McLaws into position. For Johnson's and Early's men, positioned east of town, the wait was a particularly trying one, for there was little in the way of shade, and the sun was merciless. To their front loomed Culp's and Cemetery Hills. While both were strong positions to assail, Culp's Hill was especially formidable, as it was the steeper of the two, its slopes strewn with boulders and covered by trees. To make matters worse for the Confederates drawn up opposite Culp's Hill, as the hours ticked by that Thursday and as they waited in tense anticipation, they could hear Union soldiers felling trees and constructing earthworks on the hilltop, turning Culp's Hill into a fortress. One Confederate remembered hearing the Union troops on Culp's Hill "chopping away and working like beavers," while another recorded that "[g]reatly did the officers and men marvel as morning, noon, and afternoon passed in inaction—on our part, not on the enemy's, for, as we well knew, he was plying axe and pick and shovel in fortifying a position which was already sufficiently formidable."

The wooded, boulder-covered slopes of Culp's Hill actually consisted of two summits, or peaks. The taller of the two towered 180 feet above the waist-deep Rock Creek, while the lower summit rose some 80 feet about the creek's waters. A thin saddle of ground, cutting east–west across Culp's Hill, separated the higher and lower peaks. Union forces had occupied Culp's Hill since late on the afternoon of July 1 when elements of James Wadsworth's battered First Corps division took up positions there. It was the presence of these men that had deterred Allegheny Johnson from carrying out Ewell's wishes for seizing this important position late on July 1. The Union position on Culp's Hill only continued to get stronger when, early on the morning of July 2, the 9,800 men of the Twelfth Corps arrived, taking up a line of battle that stretched in a southerly fashion across the eastern face of the hillside and all the way down to McAllister's Woods at the hill's southern base. John Geary's division held the left of the Twelfth Corps line, with his own left—held by the 1,300 New Yorkers from George Greene's brigade—connecting to the right of and forming at right angles to Wadsworth's First Corps troops on the summit. Charles Candy's brigade formed to the right-rear of Greene, taking up a supporting line, while Thomas Kane's small brigade formed directly to Greene's right, its 700 men stretching across the saddle and along the crest of the lower summit. From there, the soldiers of Alpheus Williams's division took over, extending the Twelfth Corps line south, down the lower summit, across the marshy bottomlands near Spangler's Spring and on through McAllister's Woods on the far right of the Union line.

As soon as they arrived on Culp's Hill, Geary's men began to dig in, following the lead of Wadsworth's soldiers, who hastily threw up breastworks and fortifications the night before. Stacking their rifles, the men of Geary's division removed their jackets, rolled up their sleeves and, with spade and axe, started to entrench. Trees were chopped down, and dirt and stones were piled up high to form breastworks. An 1823 graduate of West Point and a gifted engineer, George Greene—who at age sixty-two was the oldest general in the Union army—recalled the sheer strength of his brigade's position on the hilltop and how his men improved upon it: "Our position and front were covered with a heavy growth of timber, free from undergrowth, with large ledges projecting above the surface. These rocks and trees offered good cover for marksmen. The surface was very steep on our left, diminishing to a gentle slope on our right…As soon as we were in position, we began to entrench ourselves and throw up breastworks of covering height, of logs, cordwood, stones and earth." Jesse Jones of Greene's 60th New York further explained that "Culp's Hill was covered with woods; so all the materials needful were at our disposal. Right and left the men felled trees, and blocked them up into a close log fence…The sticks, set slanting on end against the outer face of logs, made an excellent battening." By noon, Geary's men had completed a formidable—some would say impregnable—line of entrenchments and breastworks on Culp's Hill, complete with a traverse of logs, dirt and brush that Greene directed be built partially down the taller summit and running at right angles to his main line of entrenchments.

And all the while—as the Twelfth Corps men continued to dig in—Ewell and his soldiers continued to wait, idling away the day under that hot, merciless sun, expecting at every moment to hear the sounds of Longstreet's guns. Finally, at about 4:00 p.m., there came that long, low and familiar rumble, akin to distant thunder. It was the noise Ewell had long been waiting for: the sound of Longstreet's cannons. Longstreet's assault had finally commenced.

Instructed to launch his demonstration simultaneously with Longstreet's attack, Ewell dutifully did so—not by advancing his infantry, but by unleashing his artillery instead. Nineteen-year-old Major Joseph Latimer, commanding the artillery of Johnson's Division, wheeled four batteries into position on Benner's Hill, a gentle rise of ground east of Gettysburg. Latimer was a talented young gunner, but at Gettysburg, he drew a tough assignment. Unlimbering twenty-four cannons on Benner's Hill, Latimer was to blast the Union positions on Cemetery Hill in the hopes of weakening the lines there in preparation for an infantry advance. What made the assignment difficult was that Benner's Hill was an inherently poor position; it was lower in elevation than Cemetery Hill and could be easily dominated by the far more numerous Union guns posted there. But there was no other choice, for Benner's Hill offered the only viable platform artillery position east of town. With his guns quickly in position, Latimer opened fire, unleashing a torrent of shot and shell toward Cemetery Hill, some nine-tenths of a mile away.

"The shots came thick and fast, bursting, crushing and ploughing," remembered one Union soldier on Cemetery Hill; it was, he said, "a mighty storm of iron hail, a most determined and terrible effort of the enemy to cripple and destroy the guns upon the hill." The Union response was not long in coming. Cemetery Hill lit up with the combined fire of dozens of cannons, from both the First and Eleventh Corps, all trained on Latimer's outnumbered pieces on that vulnerable hilltop. During the course of the bombardment, John Geary also managed to get five cannons in position on the summit of Culp's Hill, and these guns soon added their fire to the fearful din. Benner's Hill, said one Confederate, became a "hell infernal." Caissons were struck, horses disemboweled and men fell right and left in the unequal contest.

Thomas Osborn, commanding the Eleventh Corps artillery, described the effect of the bombardment on Cemetery Hill: "[N]o impression was made on the artillery beyond the loss of a very few men killed or wounded, a few horses killed, and a caisson or two blown up. The batteries were in no way crippled or the men demoralized." Latimer and his artillerists stood nobly to their guns for nearly two full hours, but the price *they* paid was heavy. By the time the barrage was over, Latimer had lost fifty-one men and thirty horses. Believing that his men could take no more, at 5:45 p.m., Latimer rode off to find Johnson, requesting permission to withdraw what remained of his battalion from Benner's Hill. Johnson agreed but instructed Latimer to keep four pieces in position to support his infantry in their attack. Latimer rode back to Benner's Hill and withdrew most of his pieces. He remained with the four guns left behind on the hilltop, but a short time later, the nineteen-year-old gunner was struck down by a shell fragment and mortally wounded.

Although the artillery did not have the desired effect, Richard Ewell nevertheless believed that the time had arrived to launch his infantry. His plan called for Johnson to attack Culp's Hill and, once Johnson became fully engaged, for Jubal Early to then launch an attack up the eastern slopes of Cemetery Hill. Completing the attack would be Robert Rodes, whose division was to strike Cemetery Hill from the northwest as Early struck it from the east. It was by now after 6:00 p.m. Barksdale's men were just then striking at the Peach Orchard on the opposite end of the line when Richard Ewell issued the orders for his men to attack.

The soldiers of Allegheny Johnson's division stepped forward first, advancing in a southwesterly direction toward Culp's Hill. To protect his flank, Johnson was forced to leave the 1,300 men of the famed Stonewall Brigade behind, meaning that he went forward with only three of his brigades, some 4,700 men in all. John M. Jones's Virginians advanced on the right of Johnson's line, Jesse Williams's Louisianans were in the center and George "Maryland" Steuart's mixed brigade of Virginia, North Carolina and Maryland soldiers were on the left.

What the Confederates did not know when they stepped off to the attack was that the Union defenses on Culp's Hill had changed significantly.

Major General Edward "Allegheny" Johnson. *Library of Congress*.

Focused on his beleaguered left flank and with only the Confederate artillery just then pounding his right, George Meade had sent urgent pleas to Henry Slocum, telling him to send all the troops he could spare to the south. Believing that this might open the door for the Confederates to seize Culp's Hill and, more importantly, the Baltimore Pike beyond, Slocum suggested that at least one division remain behind on the hilltop. Willing to jeopardize his right to meet the crisis on the left, Meade told Slocum to keep just one brigade in place and send the rest southward. And so it was that by 6:00 p.m., just about the same time Johnson was preparing to advance, most of the Twelfth Corps—five of its six brigades—had marched away from Culp's Hill, leaving only the 1,300 men of Greene's brigade as the sole defenders of the hilltop. Instructed to hold Culp's Hill at all costs, Greene spread his five regiments thin, stretching them south down the hillside in order to occupy as much of the vacated entrenchments as possible while calling on nearby First and Eleventh Corps units for help.

Twilight had already descended when the two sides collided. Jones's and Williams's men, on Johnson's right and center, were the first to make contact. Coming under a pesky fire from Greene's skirmishers, the

"A Scene Very Much Like Hell Itself"

At age sixty-two, George Sears Greene was the oldest general in the Union army at Gettysburg. His brigade defended Culp's Hill against repeated attacks on July 2 and 3. *From* Battles and Leaders of the Civil War.

Confederates advanced through the brush and briar, returning fire and ultimately driving Greene's skirmishers back up the hillside to their main line of defense. The Virginia and Louisiana troops next waded across the waist-deep waters of Rock Creek before beginning the tough climb up the boulder-strewn slopes of Culp's Hill, drawing a lively fire from the New Yorkers above. The terrain disrupted alignments, and in the gathering darkness, with the hillside covered in smoke, it was not long before all became confusion, many of the men later writing that they could detect the enemy's position only by the flashes of their rifles. Greene's men, well protected behind their breastworks and entrenchments on the summit, blazed away as Confederates inched their way up the slopes. Despite their best efforts, there was little Jones's or Williams's men could do; the ground there was too difficult and Greene's position too strong. General John Jones fell with a nasty thigh wound, and it was not long before his men withdrew down the hillside toward Rock Creek. Williams's men, to Jones's immediate left, faced slightly less challenging ground and were able to work their way to within one hundred yards of Greene's line, but they, too, were unable to crack the Union position.

Edwin Forbes's depiction of the Confederate attack up Culp's Hill. *Library of Congress*.

The repulse of both Jones and Williams left only Steuart's Brigade on Johnson's left. When the attack began, the rough terrain they encountered caused Steuart's Brigade to break into two pieces. The 3rd North Carolina and 1st Maryland Battalion on the right of his line crossed Rock Creek alongside Williams's men, and like Williams's men, they also came under a destructive fire as they neared the Union line. These two regiments found themselves in a tight spot. Approaching the saddle of ground between the taller and lower summits, they were taking fire from Greene's men to their front and from the 137th New York on their left. The 137th, under Colonel David Ireland, had taken up position on the far right of Greene's line and in the trenches recently vacated by Kane's men on the hilltop's lower summit. From there, they poured a destructive fire into the left of Steuart's right-two regiments, and the Confederates, said one observer, "reeled and staggered like a drunken man."

"Men fell like autumn leaves," lamented William Goldsborough of the 1st Maryland Battalion, but the situation would soon change when the remaining four regiments of Steuart's Brigade caught up. Lurching forward in the gathering darkness after finally wading Rock Creek and seeking to reconnect with the rest of the brigade, their advance brought them bearing down directly on Ireland's exposed right flank. Ireland's men, holding the extreme right flank of the entire Union line, were in danger of being turned. Like Chamberlain earlier in the day, but now in the darkness, Ireland refused his line to meet the developing threat, but the Confederate line far overlapped his regiment. The 10th Virginia managed to work its way around the flank of the 137th, and coming under fire from two sides and having already lost more than one hundred men, Ireland ordered his regiment to fall back to the traverse that had been constructed partially up the slope of the taller summit.

Greene's right flank was being hard-pressed. Ireland and his 137th New York held on tight behind the traverse as Steuart's men continue to feel their way up the hillside. Then, sweeping down the hillside to the right of the 137th came the 6th Wisconsin and 14th Brooklyn—First Corps troops Wadsworth had sent in response to Greene's pleas for assistance. The arrival of these two regiments, combined with the lateness of the hour and the lack of any support, compelled Steuart's Confederates to fall back to the empty entrenchments on the lower summit.

At about 10:00 p.m., an uneasy quiet fell on Culp's Hill. Jones's Virginians settled in near Rock Creek, as did some of Williams's men. Many other Louisiana soldiers remained pinned down on the slopes less than one hundred yards from Greene's position, forcing them to speak that night in hushed tones and whispers. Steuart's advance had brought several of his regiments directly into the line of trenches vacated earlier that evening when most of the Twelfth Corps had shifted south. In these captured earthworks, Steuart's men settled in for what proved an edgy, tense night, clutching to their tenuous foothold on the lower summit of Culp's Hill. It would not be long before the Twelfth Corps began to return from their foray south, seeking to take up their previous positions on the hillside.

Johnson's attack on Culp's Hill had ended, but that was only one part of Ewell's equation, for the Confederate Second Corps commander also had his sights set on that keystone of the Union position, Cemetery Hill. The irascible Jubal Early waited until Johnson was fully engaged and then ordered his men forward, setting out sometime around 8:00 p.m. Like Johnson, Early went into the fight minus one of

General Jubal Early. *Library of Congress.*

his four brigades. To keep an eye eastward and to protect his left, Smith's Brigade had been kept in place on the York Pike, east of town. John Gordon's all-Georgia brigade was moved forward but was held back as a supporting force, ready to exploit any opportunity that might be gained by the soldiers of Early's remaining two brigades, a total of some 2,400 men under General Harry Hays and Colonel Isaac Avery, who were slated to lead the twilight assault.

The orders to advance came as welcome relief to many of Hays's and Avery's men. As Major James Beall of the 21st North Carolina later explained, "After lying all day under a July sun, suffering with intense heat, and continually annoyed by the enemy's sharpshooters from the heights, from sheer desperation, we hailed with delight the order to again meet the veteran foe." Early ordered the two brigades forward, with Hays's famed and ferocious Louisiana Tigers on his right and Avery's men to the left.

As soon as Early's men stepped forward, Cemetery Hill erupted with cannon fire. It was, said one Union officer, "as if a volcano had been let loose." At least fifteen guns on the hilltop hurled shot and shell at the advancing lines. So, too, did the six Napoleons of Captain Greenleaf Stevens's 5th Maine Battery, posted on McKnight's Knoll, which rose up from the saddle of ground between Cemetery and Culp's Hill. The artillery fire was terrific, but Early's men pressed on, quickly closing the gaps in their lines while continuing to bear down on the hilltop. Early's plan was to strike both the northeastern and eastern slopes of Cemetery Hill; thus, while the two regiments on the right of Hays's line advanced straight ahead from their positions along Winebrenner's Run on the southeastern limits of town, Hays's other three regiments pivoted in a southwesterly fashion, wrapping around the curve of the hill.

In order to strike the hill's eastern side, Avery's Brigade was forced to execute a broad, sweeping, right-wheel maneuver, so that the men went from advancing south to advancing west, all the while exposed to a torrent of exploding shells. They had a lot of ground to cover, and it was, said Colonel A.C. Godwin, a maneuver that "none but the steadiest veterans could have executed under the circumstances." And execute it they did, in textbook fashion. But the change in the direction of their march now exposed the North Carolinians' left flank to the Maine gunners on McKnight's Knoll, who now packed their guns with canister. The results were fearful. Godwin's regiment, the 57th North Carolina, on the left of Avery's line, was cut to shreds.

As Early's men drew nearer, the Eleventh Corps soldiers positioned either on or along the base of Cemetery Hill braced for the attack, many of them surprised that the Confederates were attacking at so late an hour. Theirs was a shattered and shaken force. The previous day, the Eleventh Corps had suffered frightful casualties north of town, and now, what was left of its three divisions was spread out across Cemetery Hill. Orland Smith's brigade, kept behind by Howard as a rallying force on Cemetery Hill, had been unbloodied on July 1 but had spent much of July 2 on the skirmish line, trading shots with Rodes's men in and on the outskirts of town. These men, along with the broken fragments of Charles Coster's brigade, occupied west Cemetery Hill. To their right and rear and occupying the crest of the hilltop were the remnants of Schurz's division, a total of just 1,500 men in the two brigades of Krzyanowski and Schimmelfennig, commanded that day by Colonel George von Amsberg, since Schimmelfennig, presumed either dead or captured, still remained crouched behind Anna Garlach's woodshed on Baltimore Street.

Schurz's line extended northeasterly toward the Baltimore Pike. On the other side of this critical roadway, occupying east Cemetery Hill, went the soldiers of the Eleventh Corp's final division, under twenty-eight-year-old Adelbert Ames, an 1861 graduate of West Point who had the previous day assumed command of Barlow's division, or at least what was left of it, after Barlow fell with his grievous wound. Just over 1,100 men composed the ranks of Ames's two brigades on July 2. The 25th Ohio had been so roughly handled on July 1 that the entire regiment numbered just sixty men on July 2. The losses in Colonel Leopold von Gilsa's brigade were so heavy that when the survivors of his four regiments rallied on Cemetery Hill late on the afternoon of July 1, one of his officers told him, "You can now command your brigade easily with the voice, my dear Colonel, this is all that is left."

Ames placed his severely thinned brigades at right angles to one another, in the shape of a backward "L." Colonel Andrew Harris's men—Ames's old brigade—found some shelter behind a stone wall that ran east from the Baltimore Pike and stretched across the northern face of the hilltop. The hill sloped down to the east to a narrow roadway, known as the Brickyard Lane, which ran south along the eastern base of the hill. Von Gilsa's men, constituting the long end of the "L," formed behind the stone walls that lined the roadway. Augmenting his line was the 33rd Massachusetts, sent over from Orland Smith's brigade, which went into position to the right of Von Gilsa and stretched toward Stevens's Maine gunners on McKnight's Knoll. Ames's men were stretched thin, especially along Harris's front, where, wrote Harris, his men had all the elbowroom they wanted. Hays's and Avery's men drew ever nearer, driving back the Union skirmishers while, said one man of the 25th Ohio, "yelling like demons with fixed bayonets."

Stevens's battery from atop McKnight's Knoll blasts Early's lines with a destructive fire. Alfred Waud sketch, *Library of Congress*.

Early's men had suffered considerably from the artillery during their advance, Avery's men especially. Then, hundreds of Union muskets lit up the gathering darkness, dropping scores of Louisiana and North Carolina soldiers. Major Beall of the 21st North Carolina did his best to describe the scene: "The hour was one of horror. Amid the incessant roar of cannon, the din of musketry, and the glare of bursting shells making the darkness intermittent—adding awfulness to the scene—the hoarse shouts of friend and foe, piteous cries of the wounded and dying, one could well imagine… that 'war is hell.'" But despite their losses, it was not long before the Confederates came crashing down on Ames's shaky position.

Hays's Tigers struck first, slamming into Harris's front and striking at the salient of the Union line. Desperate hand-to-hand combat broke out. "At that point and soon along the whole line," said Harris, "the fighting was obstinate and bloody. The bayonet, club-musket, and anything in fact that could be made available was used, by both the assailing and the assailers." Harris's line was too thin, and there were too few Union troops to stem the tide. They began to fall back, streaming up the hillside, closely followed by Hays's men, who, said one Federal soldier, "put their big feet on the stone wall and went over like deer." To the right and rear of Harris's line, Von Gilsa's line was also crumbling, its left struck by Hays and its center and right by Avery's North Carolinians.

Hays's and Avery's men advance up the eastern slopes of Cemetery Hill. *From* Battles and Leaders of the Civil War.

"[C]lubs, knives, stones, fists—anything calculated to inflict death of pain was resorted to," said one man in the 153rd Pennsylvania. Several Eleventh Corps regiments clung tenaciously to the stone walls, while others retreated.

Confederates filtered through the holes in the line and began climbing up both the northern and eastern slopes to the summit. But much of the Confederate strength had already been sapped. Colonel Godwin of the 57th North Carolina attested to this when he wrote that the men "charged up the hill with heroic determination, and drove the enemy from his last stone wall. In this charge, the command had become much separated, and, in the darkness it was now found impossible to concentrate more than 40 or 50 men at any point for further advance." Those North Carolinas who did hammer through the Union defenses and who now advanced to the hilltop did so without their commander. At some point early in the advance, Colonel Isaac Avery was struck down from the saddle, shot through the neck with what proved to be a mortal wound. No one had seen him fall, but when his body was later discovered, it was found with a note, stained red with blood. It read, "Tell my father I died with my face to the enemy."

Wild, confusing scenes were playing out on the hilltop, the men guided by the moonlight and by the rapid and frequent discharges of muskets and

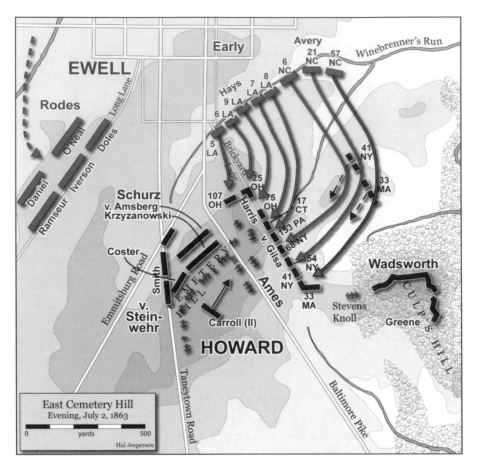

Hays and Avery attack East Cemetery Hill. *Map by Hal Jespersen.*

cannons. "For a time the opposing forces were much mixed up together," said an Ohioan, "and with the uncertainty of the light, in the dusk of evening it was difficult to distinguish friend from foe." Hays's and Avery's panting soldiers rushed directly toward the Union cannons that lined the hilltop. The powder-stained, sweating gunners of Michael Weidrich's Battery I, 1st New York Artillery, and R. Bruce Ricketts's Batteries F and G, 1st Pennsylvania Light Artillery, were able to fire off a few rounds of canister before being overrun. More hand-to-hand fighting broke out as the Union gunners stood manfully to their pieces, battling it out, said Captain Ricketts, "with pistols, handspikes and rammers."

Early's men had made it to the very summit of Cemetery Hill, where they held on desperately to their foothold there. Engaged in a hand-to-hand

Alfred Waud captured the intense action that flared up on the night of July 2 between Hays's Louisiana Tigers and Union artillerists and infantrymen on Cemetery Hill. *Library of Congress*.

struggle with Union infantry and artillerymen, these men looked to the rear, hoping to see reinforcements heading their way. Division commander Early also looked about for support, expecting at every minute to hear Rodes's attack unfolding on the opposite side of the hilltop. But Rodes never came.

Rodes had been ordered to "cooperate with the attacking force as soon as any opportunity of doing so with good effect was offered." He had expected that Dorsey Pender's division from A.P. Hill's Third Corps would form up to his right and add further support to the attack against Cemetery Hill, but Pender had been struck down by a shell fragment that afternoon—mortally wounded—and it seems no one had made any preparations for his division to participate in the attack. There would thus be no troops to Rodes's right to support his planned assault. The young Confederate division commander waited until *after* Early's attack commenced before extracting his brigades from town, misgauging or underestimating the time it would take to side-step them to the south before wheeling left to face west Cemetery Hill, and by the time his brigades were in position, Early's attack had already subsided. Because of this, and because Rodes and his subordinates believed that the Federal position on the hilltop to their front was much too strong, and with the lateness of the hour, Rodes aborted his assault, believing that it would have resulted "in a useless sacrifice of life."

Jubal Early would also use this same justification for not sending John Gordon's brigade into the fight; with Rodes not attacking to his right, Early wrote that it would have been "a useless sacrifice of life" to have done so. Hays's and Avery's men, their numbers rapidly dwindling, were thus left alone, abandoned on the hilltop as a fresh tidal wave of blue rushed into the hellish cauldron on east Cemetery Hill.

Following Howard's orders, Carl Schurz led portions of Krzyzanowski's and Coster's brigades into the fight. Charging across the Baltimore Pike, Schurz later described what these men then encountered. "Arriving at the batteries, we found an indescribable scene of melee. Some rebel infantry had scaled the breastworks and were taking possession of the guns. But the cannoneers defended themselves desperately. With rammers and fence rails, hand spikes and stones, they knocked down the intruders…Our infantry," said Schurz, the German-born abolitionist scholar turned warrior, "made a vigorous rush upon the invaders, and after a short but spirited hand-to-hand scuffle tumbled them down the embankment." Behind Schurz's men and to the rear of the tangled mass of men fighting for possession of the cannons came even more Federal reinforcements: Second Corps soldiers from Samuel Carroll's brigade.

Hearing the action erupt on Cemetery Hill and receiving a request for support from Howard, the indefatigable Hancock turned to John Gibbon and, in measured undertones, said, "We ought to send some help over there. Send a brigade; send Carroll." "Bricktop" Carroll moved quickly toward east Cemetery Hill with three of his four regiments, men from Indiana, Ohio and West Virginia. "We started…at the double-quick, which soon became a dead run," noted one man of the 4th Ohio, "many of our men throwing away their knapsacks and blankets in order to keep up with the mad dash." Passing among the graves of the Evergreen Cemetery, then through and around the arched gatehouse, Carroll's men charged toward Avery's small band of men clustered around Ricketts's battery, slamming into them and driving them down the hillside. Carroll's men followed, scooping up scores of prisoners along Brickyard Lane and in the open fields beyond. Overwhelmed by Krzyzanowski's and Coster's men, Hays had already ordered his Louisianans to retreat. For a brief moment, Confederate soldiers had gained the crest of Cemetery Hill but, unsupported, were forced back by timely arriving and hard-hitting Union reinforcements.

"The charge was a daring and a desperate one, and, although unsuccessful on account of the failure of our supports to come up, we gained great credit for it," wrote Hays's adjutant, who further added that "[t]his want of concert of action on the part of our Generals was the chief cause of the loss of the great battle of Gettysburg." Indeed, the fight for east Cemetery Hill was reflective of the overall Confederate offensive on July 2 at Gettysburg. The men had attacked with great gallantry and had punched through the Union defenses, but their gains were only temporary and never fully exploited, for they found their support to be lacking and the Union response swift. Writing more than ten years later, Lee's chief of staff Walter Taylor would echo the sentiments of Hays's adjutant, declaring that "[t]he whole affair [on July 2] was disjointed. There was an utter absence of accord in the movements of the several commands and no decisive results attended the operations."

For Robert E. Lee, July 2 had been a long and trying day. He wanted to strike early, but much of the morning had passed by the time he finally settled on a plan of attack. Longstreet's march and countermarch had consumed additional time, and once his men did reach their designated jumping-off point, they found the Union army occupying a position not at all what they had envisioned. After a last-minute change of plans, it was already after 4:00 p.m. before the battle finally commenced. As usual, Lee's men had fought boldly and gallantly that day, and they were able to secure some ground—namely on the Confederate right, at Devil's Den and the Peach Orchard, as well as a foothold, at least, on the left, on the lower summit of Culp's Hill. They had crushed the Union Third Corps and inflicted severe damage on portions of other Federal corps as well. Still, their gains were minimal and the cost of securing them heavy. Like many others in gray, Lee was also frustrated by the "lack of a proper concert of action" among his commands.

Despite all of the problems the Army of Northern Virginia encountered that day, Lee still believed that his men had come close—very close—to delivering a crushing, knock-out punch to their opponents, and that night, without meeting with any of his corps commanders, without a good understanding of the condition of his various commands and perhaps still with only a vague understanding of the strength of the Union positions, Lee decided that he would continue the fight early the following day, on Friday, July 3. As he later wrote of July 2, "The result of this day's operations induced the belief that with proper concert of action, and with the increased support that the positions gained on the right [at the Peach Orchard] would enable the artillery to render the assaulting columns, we should ultimately succeed, and it was determined to continue the attack. The general plan was unchanged."

As opposed to Lee, George Meade was everywhere along his line that day and had taken a very active role in the fight. Sickles's advance had unhinged his lines and had placed the army in jeopardy. But Meade responded well to the crisis, shifting Sykes's entire Fifth Corps and elements of most of his other corps south to meet the emergency. He was ably assisted by many of his subordinates, from the regimental level on up, and especially by Hancock, who turned in a heroic performance in repulsing the waves of Confederate assaults against the Union left-center and in reestablishing the line on Cemetery Ridge.

Meade's losses were numerically greater than Lee's, and there was many a desperate moment. But the boys in blue had demonstrated a remarkable tenacity, and by day's end, they had weathered the storm. By nightfall, the Union army still held much the same position it had occupied, or was *supposed* to occupy, that morning, with Big and Little Round Top also fully secured. What was more, John Sedgwick's big Sixth Corps had also arrived, helping to offset some of the losses incurred by the Second, Third and Fifth Corps on the southern end of the field. General John Newton may have summarized it best when, late on July 2, he told General Meade that he ought to be very much happy and satisfied with the day's results. "In the name of common sense, *why?*" asked Meade. Because, replied Newton, "they have hammered us into a solid position they cannot whip us out of."

Unlike Lee, Meade *would* meet with his subordinates that night, to discuss the condition of their commands and decide on their next course of action.

The entire top brass of the Army of the Potomac gathered at Meade's headquarters late on July 2 for a famed council of war. *Library of Congress.*

176

Sometime around 10:30 p.m., with the final shots of the struggle fading away on east Cemetery Hill, twelve Union generals—the entire top brass of the Army of the Potomac—gathered at army headquarters and crammed into the small, ten- by twelve-foot front parlor of Lydia Leister's home. Present were Meade, Hancock, Slocum and the commanders of all the army's infantry corps: Newton, Gibbon, Birney, Sykes, Sedgwick, Howard and Alpheus Williams. Chief of staff Daniel Butterfield was also present. So, too, was chief engineer Gouverneur Warren, who, exhausted by the day's exertions, huddled up in a corner and promptly fell asleep.

With the light of only a single candle, and in a room that must have been thick with cigar smoke, the generals discussed the day's action and reported their losses and positions. Then Meade got to the crux of the meeting, wanting to sound out his generals' thoughts on what the army should next do. Most likely, Meade had already made up his mind to stay, for in an earlier telegram to Halleck, he wrote that he would "remain in my present position to-morrow." Still, he had Butterfield draft up three questions. The first asked whether "under existing circumstances," it was "advisable for this army to remain in its present position or to retire to another nearer its base of supplies?" The response was unanimous: all agreed to stay there, at Gettysburg. The second question then asked whether they should assume the offensive and attack Lee "or wait the attack of the enemy?" Again, the reply was unanimous: hold their ground and await attack. Finally, how long should they wait? The answers to this one varied, but all agreed to wait at least another day. "Such then is the decision," said Meade. The army would, in the words of General Henry Slocum, "stay and fight it out!" on July 3.

Chapter Notes

For the best accounting of the second day's battle, see Pfanz's *Gettysburg: The Second Day*, and for the best history of the battle that raged that night against the Union right, see Pfanz's *Gettysburg: Culp's and Cemetery Hills*, which also includes the battle action that occurred on day three on Culp's Hill. These two works by Pfanz rank among the best battle studies in those vast annals of American Civil War historiography. For more on day two as a whole, see Coddington, chapters 13–17 (pages 323–464); Sears, chapters 9–11 (pages 245–355); Grimsley and Simpson (pages 54–130); Woodworth, chapters 6–7 (pages 105–160); and Trudeau, chapter 13 (pages 277–426). For more detailed studies focusing on specific aspects of the second day's battle, see

Twilight at Little Round (2005) by Glenn LaFantasie; *The Myth of Little Round Top* (2003) by Garry Adelman; *Devil's Den: A History and Guide* (1997) by Adelman and Timothy Smith; *Gettysburg's Bloody Wheatfield* (2002) by Jay Jorgensen; and John Archer's *"The Mountain Trembled": Culp's Hill at Gettysburg* (2011) and *"The Hour Was One of Horror": East Cemetery Hill at Gettysburg* (2002), both excellent, concise accounts of the fighting at these important locations. Dan Sickles and his controversial actions at Gettysburg have been the focus of several book-length studies, the best being *Sickles at Gettysburg* (2009) by James Hessler. For this same topic, see also *Gettysburg: The Meade-Sickles Controversy* by Richard Sauers (2003). Finally, for the actions of specific units during the battle on July 2, see *Pale Horse at Plum Run: The First Minnesota at Gettysburg* (2002) by Brain Leehan and *Struggle for the Round Tops: Law's Alabama Brigade at the Battle of Gettysburg* (1999) by Morris Penny and J. Gary Laine. See also *The Second Day at Gettysburg: Essays on Confederate and Union Leadership*, edited by Gary W. Gallagher.

Chapter 4

"None but Demons Can Delight in War"

The Third Day, July 3, 1863

DAY THREE OVERVIEW

The third day's battle at Gettysburg is best remembered for the grand Confederate attack launched directly against the center of the Union battle line along Cemetery Ridge. That afternoon, nearly thirteen thousand Confederate soldiers advanced steadily and valiantly across three-quarters of a mile of open ground into a veritable storm of iron and lead in what proved a vain effort to break through the Union position. Gallant though the effort was, the Confederates were turned back, repulsed with a near 50 percent loss, while only a few hundred of them were able to momentarily pierce the Union line.

Although most commonly known as Pickett's Charge, some students of the battle refer to it—rather clumsily—as the Pickett-Pettigrew-Trimble Charge in an effort to make clear that this attack involved much more than just the Virginians of Pickett's Division. Others refer to it much more simply as Longstreet's Assault, since Longstreet was tasked with overseeing it even though only one-third of the attacking columns—Pickett's three brigades—belonged to his First Corps and even though Longstreet himself felt that the attack was doomed to failure. But no matter how one refers to it, this attack remains the Civil War's most legendary charge and has naturally come to dominate the history of the third day's fight at Gettysburg. And even though some may argue that the Army of Northern Virginia might have actually come closest to achieving victory at Gettysburg on July 2, the attack on the afternoon of July 3

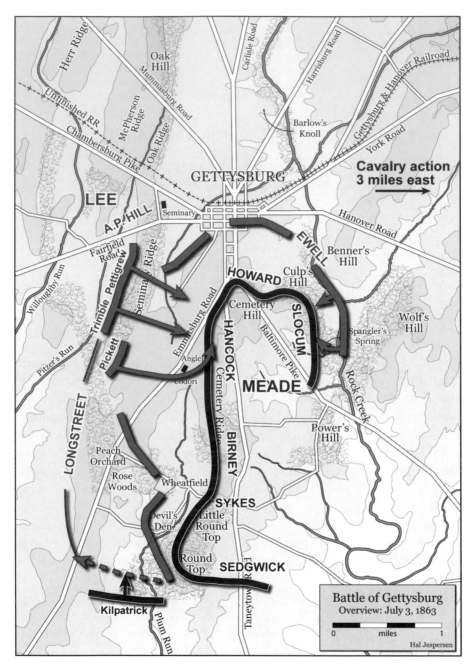

Overview of the Third Day's Battle at Gettysburg. *Map by Hal Jespersen.*

has come to symbolize the supposed "high-water mark" of the Confederacy, the point where so many believe Confederate fortunes crested, reaching their full tide before they began receding—the point, when looking back with hindsight mixed with nostalgia, where so many believe the Confederacy witnessed its last real chance at military triumph vanish.

After two days of terrific combat, Robert E. Lee remained determined, ever hopeful of achieving that crushing battlefield victory he had come north seeking. He believed that his army's assaults of the previous day had come very close to succeeding and thought that this attack, aimed at the Federal center, would smash the Federal lines and send them reeling. When this attack failed, Lee's hopes were shattered.

But this attack was not Lee's original plan for the day. Instead, the Confederate army commander wanted to simply pick up where the previous day had left off by renewing the attack at daybreak with a simultaneous advance by both Ewell and Longstreet. As was the case on July 2, however, things again went poorly for Lee.

The fighting did commence at daybreak, but it was the Federals who delivered the first punch. Determined to regain their entrenchments lost the night before on Culp's Hill and to drive the Confederates from this important position, the soldiers of the Twelfth Corps readied for a daybreak attack. The attack was planned to immediately follow a fifteen-minute artillery bombardment designed to soften the Confederate lines. The Federal cannons erupted at 4:30 a.m., but instead of the Federal troops then moving forward, the Confederates beat them to it, advancing in lines of battle seeking to drive the Federals entirely off Culp's Hill. Ewell, having received Lee's orders late the night before to renew the fight in the morning, stood poised to do so, his men ready to strike. The two sides went at it for nearly seven hours, slugging it out on Culp's Hill in what proved to be the most sustained combat of the entire three days at Gettysburg. The Union line would not budge, and after a series of desperate and costly attacks, the Confederates withdrew, leaving Culp's Hill firmly in Union hands.

Hearing the battle pick up at daybreak in front of Ewell's position, General Lee galloped south, hoping to see Longstreet's men advancing. Longstreet, whom Lee expected to be reinforced overnight by the arrival of Pickett's Division, was ordered to sweep forward at daybreak from his soldiers' hard-won positions of the previous day toward the Federal center, rolling up the Union line as they advanced. One can only imagine the surprise, disappointment and even anger Lee must have felt when instead he discovered that Longstreet was in no way prepared for an early morning attack; his men were not ready, and worse, Pickett's Division had yet to arrive. Longstreet greeted Lee by urging him—again—to move around the left of the Federal line, but just as in the previous two days, Lee would not hear of it. He would attack the enemy where they were, but Lee was now forced to develop a new plan. Believing it to be weakened, Lee would focus everything on an all-out attack against the Federal center, using Pickett's men when they arrived plus six of A.P. Hill's brigades. To command this assault, Lee called on a reluctant Longstreet, his "Old War Horse."

The third day's battle at Gettysburg was not confined solely to the open, undulating ground between the opposing ridgelines, the ground over which Pickett's men advanced along with the Third Corps soldiers under Pettigrew and Trimble, nor to the wooded, boulder-strewn slopes of Culp's Hill. July 3 also witnessed some intense cavalry actions at Gettysburg, with sabers clashing east and south of town. Excepting a forlorn and foolhardy cavalry attack late that afternoon at the base of Big Round Top ordered by General Judson Kilpatrick, the Federals were everywhere successful that day and the Confederates everywhere repulsed. Meade lost fewer than four thousand men—killed, wounded or captured—during the third day of combat; Lee lost two and a half times as many, with Confederate casualties exceeding ten thousand.

The third and final day of battle at Gettysburg ended late in the afternoon, following the repulse of the Confederate attack against the Federal center and after Kilpatrick's mad cavalry dash. It had begun twelve hours earlier, just at daybreak, when the heavily whiskered Alpheus Williams, commanding the Union's Twelfth Corps, directed his artillery to open fire on the Confederates occupying the entrenchments on Culp's Hill.

* * *

Late on the night of July 2, the soldiers of the Twelfth Corps who had been sent to the opposite end of the Union line trudged their way by moonlight back to their original positions on Culp's Hill. As they approached their previous positions on the lower summit, however, gunfire rang out, briefly lighting up the darkness. Believing that they had been mistakenly fired on by Greene's New Yorkers, who had been left alone on the hilltop, several Twelfth Corps officers continued to probe forward, triggering even more fire. It was not until a number of Union soldiers were either killed or wounded that they finally realized that their old entrenchments were now occupied by Confederate troops. This rather disconcerting news was reported to Alpheus Williams, who, in turn, reported it to Henry Slocum. "Well, drive them out at daylight!" was Slocum's simple reply, an order Williams rather wryly noted was easier said than done.

There would be little rest that night for Williams. In the darkness, and in an effort to reestablish contact with Greene and fashion a new line of battle, his weary Twelfth Corps troops stumbled over rocks and boulders, ducking and dodging every now and then from the sporadic fire of Steuart's nervous Confederates occupying the trenches on the lower summit. The Ohioans and Pennsylvanians composing the ranks of Kane's and Candy's brigades, both of Geary's division, formed up to the right of Greene, while Williams's own division, led by Brigadier General Thomas Ruger, connected to the right of these men and stretched the Twelfth Corps line farther south to McAllister's Woods. With his men thus going into position, Williams gathered his subordinates and explained his plan to drive the Confederates "out at daylight." "We will hold the position we now have until morning,"

Brigadier General Alpheus Starkey Williams. *Library of Congress.*

explained Williams. "Then, from these hills back of us, we will shell hell out of them." Following an artillery barrage, the infantry was to then advance. After placing some twenty-six cannons in position along the Baltimore Pike and on nearby Power's and McAllister's Hills, Williams finally lay down on a flat rock, under an apple tree, in the hopes of catching just a little sleep.

Williams and his Twelfth Corps soldiers were not the only ones preparing for an early morning offensive action on Culp's Hill. Having received orders from Lee to renew the fight at daylight, Richard Ewell, late on July 2, met with his subordinates and worked out a plan on how to best go about doing so. Several of Ewell's subordinates objected to a renewal of the attack, believing that the Federal positions on Culp's and Cemetery Hills were too strong. Ewell disagreed, convinced that it could be done; the only question was where. Harry Hays, whose Louisianans had suffered heavily in the twilight attack up the slopes of Cemetery Hill, argued that it would have been useless slaughter to try that again, and Ewell agreed. It would thus be on Johnson's front, against Culp's Hill, where at least some of his men had a foothold on the lower summit, where the fighting would be renewed.

In preparation for this attack, Ewell bolstered Johnson's line overnight with O'Neal's and Daniel's Brigades from Rodes's Division and with three of Billy Smith's regiments from Jubal Early's division. The Stonewall Brigade under James Walker would also be on hand by daybreak since Jeb Stuart and his cavalry had arrived by then to guard the army's far left flank. The addition of these units essentially doubled the number of troops Johnson would have at his disposal for the morning attack, but with the return of the Twelfth Corps late on July 2, the Confederates attacking Culp's Hill would now be confronting equal numbers, not just Greene's sole brigade. They would also be attacking what was still a dominant defensive position.

Alpheus Williams awoke after just a half hour's rest and, at 4:30 a.m., gave the command for his artillerists to open fire. The salvos of twenty-six cannons rent the still morning air, blasting the Confederates on the lower summit of Culp's Hill. The soldiers of Steuart's Brigade, on the left of Johnson's line and occupying the entrenchments, were particularly exposed to this fearful shelling. Lieutenant John Stone of the 1st Maryland (CSA) noted that "[a]t times one could feel the earth tremble, so fearful was the cannonading," while another Confederate remembered that the cannonballs "could be heard to strike the breastworks like hailstones upon the roof tops." The entrenchments did offer some protection, but not against the falling tree limbs that began to rain down on the sheltered Confederates. For fifteen minutes, the Union gunners kept up a relentless and one-sided artillery barrage since there were no Confederate guns in position to return fire. As the smoke cleared from the heated iron barrels of the Union guns, Williams expected his infantry to move out. Instead, it was Johnson's Confederates who first surged forward.

The Virginians of John M. Jones's brigade—commanded now by Colonel Robert Dungan in place of the wounded Jones—led off the attack on the far right of Johnson's line; to their left advanced the Louisianans

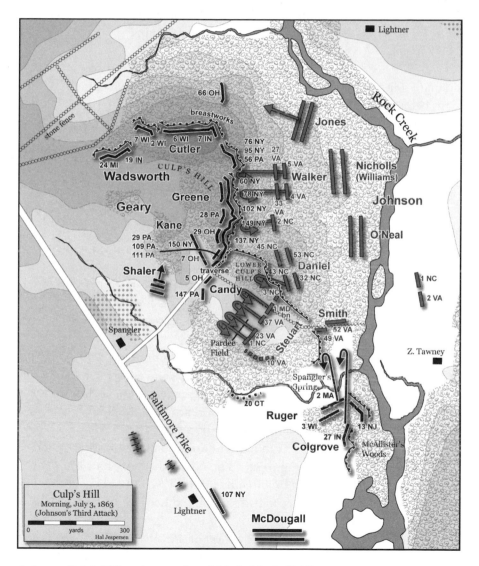

Action on Culp's Hill on the morning of July 3. *Map by Hal Jespersen.*

under Jesse Williams and the Alabamians from Edward O'Neal's brigade. They advanced, said Johnson, "with great determination" up the steep hillside, over ground that was strewn with their dead comrades from the previous night's battle and toward the same strong Union position they had unsuccessfully assailed just the night before. With their own planned attack necessarily canceled by the attacking Confederates, the soldiers of the Twelfth Corps were content to remain behind their formidable earthworks on the summit; leveling their muskets, they opened a murderous fire. Soon, as one Confederate remembered, "the whole hillside seemed enveloped in a blaze." The battle there would continue, without let up, for the next six and a half hours.

From his headquarters, Robert E. Lee could hear the noise of battle emanating from Culp's Hill. He had worked out his plan of attack late the night before and had sent out the necessary orders. As he later explained it, the "general plan was unchanged." Ewell was to renew the fight at daybreak against the Union right, while Longstreet, reinforced by George Pickett's small but fresh division, would pick up from where his attack had left off and, with his three divisions, roll up the Union position on Cemetery Ridge. With the din of battle drifting from Ewell's front early that Friday morning, Lee, satisfied that his Second Corps commander was faithfully carrying out his orders, mounted his horse and rode south toward Longstreet's position, expecting to see these troops attacking as well. His hope was that his orders would be better executed and that his army's attacks would be better coordinated than they had been the previous day. As he rode south along Seminary Ridge toward his army's right, however, Lee found this part of his line quiet. Hood's and McLaws's men were not in motion, and Pickett's Division was nowhere to be found.

The chagrined army commander soon found Longstreet, who explained that he was just then preparing to swing around the Federal left. "General, I have had my scouts out all night," said Longstreet, "and I find that you still have an excellent opportunity to move around...Meade's army and maneuver him into attacking us." His patience surely thin, Lee immediately canceled Longstreet's proposed movement and, pointing toward Cemetery Ridge, emphatically told Longstreet, "The enemy is there, and I am going to strike him." With the skies brightening and as Ewell's battle continued to rage, it was now apparent to a surely disappointed Lee that he had to fashion a new plan of attack.

Lee's first thought was to await the arrival of Pickett's Division, which was just then en route from its bivouac sites four miles away, and to have Longstreet advance with his entire corps once it arrived. Longstreet objected, correctly pointing out that Hood's and McLaws's Divisions had been severely cut up the day before, suffering more than four thousand casualties, and that if these two divisions advanced, it would simply expose the army's right flank and rear to Union troops posted on Little Round Top, offering an inviting target to Meade. Lee agreed but was still determined to attack. Looking eastward and scanning Cemetery Ridge as the sun continued to climb behind it, the army commander ultimately decided to strike directly at the Federal center, which, he believed, must be the weakest part of Meade's line. Pickett's three brigades, along with six others from A.P. Hill's corps, would make this assault—a total of perhaps fifteen thousand men, said Lee, who would advance across nearly three-quarters of a mile of open, undulating ground. To weaken the Federal lines on Cemetery Ridge, the attack would be preceded by a tremendous barrage of artillery, using all the army's available guns.

Longstreet listened patiently as the army commander explained the new plan. Feeling it his duty to express his convictions, Longstreet again voiced his objections, famously telling Lee, "General, I have been a soldier all my life. I have been with soldiers engaged in fights by couples, by squads, companies, regiments, divisions, and armies, and should know, as well as any one, what soldiers can do. It is my opinion that no fifteen thousand men ever arrayed for battle can take that position." But Lee would not be dissuaded. The attack would proceed, and Longstreet, despite his objections, would oversee it.

While Lee fashioned a new plan of attack against the Federal center and then set about preparing for it, Ewell's men continued to bleed on Culp's Hill. Johnson's first push up the steep slopes had been easily repulsed, and the two sides then settled in for a terrific firefight that enveloped Culp's Hill in a thick smoke. At 8:00 a.m., Johnson tried again, ordering another surge up the hillside. James "Bulldog" Walker's Stonewall Brigade led this effort, with Williams's Louisiana troops and O'Neal's Alabamians advancing to their left. It was not long before this attack, too, had foundered, the men falling back after just a few minutes and with much thinner ranks.

The well-protected Union troops kept up a relentless fire. Geary shifted several regiments from Candy's and Kane's brigades to the summit, and soon a brigade of Sixth Corps soldiers arrived to lend a hand. Several First Corps units were also present, adding the weight of their muskets to the brawl. The regiments on the hilltop worked out a methodical system of swapping positions on the front line. Once a regiment's ammunition was expended, the men would fall back to a sheltered ravine some fifty yards to the rear, where they would rest and refill their cartridge boxes, while fresh units advanced to the front.

Artist Edwin Forbes's depiction of Greene's New Yorkers holding strong behind their entrenchments and breastworks on Culp's Hill. *Library of Congress.*

This allowed the Union troops to maintain a constant fire. Because of their fortifications and their strong position, casualties among the Union defenders were comparatively light, although they, too, were exposed to a heavy musketry fire of many hours' duration. After the battle, the soldiers of the 149th New York, of Greene's brigade, took pride as they counted no fewer than eighty-one bullet holes in their flag. Their flagstaff had also been cut in two, although during the heat of battle, color-sergeant William Lilly spliced it back together with wood splints and leather haversack straps.

After more than five hours of intense action and perhaps at the urging of Lee, Richard Ewell ordered yet another attack. Allegheny Johnson objected, as did George Steuart and Junius Daniel, who believed that the Federal position was so strong that "it could not have been carried by any force." But the attack would go forward. Steuart's men were ordered to sweep forward from their entrenchments on the Confederate left, while Walker and Daniel, to the right of Steuart, prepared their men for yet another advance. Major William Goldsborough in Steuart's 1st Maryland Battalion later wrote that it was "nothing less than murder to send [the] men into that slaughter pen."

The Confederates steeled themselves for the attack and, at 10:00 a.m., swept forward into a storm of Yankee lead. Randolph McKim, serving on Steuart's staff, remembered it as the "most fearful fire I ever encountered and my heart sickened with the sight of so many gallant men sacrificed." This attack seemed the most determined of the three launched that morning against Culp's Hill, but as with the previous two, this one was also futile, and the Confederates again failed to break the Union line. Steuart wept when he saw the destruction of his brigade, sobbing, "My poor boys! My poor boys!"

"None but Demons Can Delight in War"

During this final assault on Culp's Hill, the soldiers of both sides watched as a dog raced frantically back and forth between the opposing lines of battle, caught up in this human destruction, before it was struck down and killed. After the battle, as the Union troops gathered the wounded and buried the dead, the body of this poor animal was discovered. Brigadier General Thomas Kane, whose Ohioans and Pennsylvanians manned this sector of the Twelfth Corps line and who was described by a peer as "the bravest little man that ever lived," directed that the dog receive a proper burial since, he said, it was "the only Christian being on either side."

Despite their valiant efforts, Ewell's men were unable to dent the Federal position on Culp's Hill; each of their attacks was easily turned back by the stubborn Union defenders. The only reversal to Federal arms on Culp's Hill that morning occurred early in the contest when, just before 7:00 a.m., General Slocum ordered an advance across the open meadow near Spangler's Spring on the hill's southern base. Believing the Confederate line there to be weak and wavering, Slocum instructed Thomas Ruger, commanding Williams's division, to advance a line of skirmishers and find out. Ruger then turned to Colonel Silas Colgrove, whose brigade anchored the far right flank of the Twelfth Corps line. Through some sort of miscommunication or through a simple bungling of orders, instead of advancing a skirmish force, Colgrove ordered the 2nd Massachusetts and 27th Indiana forward to the attack.

When Lieutenant Colonel Charles Mudge received Colgrove's instructions, he asked, "Are you *sure* that is the order?" When he was assured that it was, Mudge stared across the open meadow toward the Confederates, well protected behind the entrenchments on the hill's lower summit, and replied, "Well, it is murder, but it is the order." No skirmishers were sent forward to test the strength of the Confederate line, and the forlorn Union attack commenced. Mudge, a Harvard graduate, led his 2nd Massachusetts over a low stone wall, and with a yell, the Bay Staters advanced, joined a few minutes later by the Hoosiers to their right. They charged into a wall of musket fire, delivered by Steuart's men on the lower summit and by Billy Smith's Virginians positioned behind a stone wall directly on the exposed right flank of the attacking columns. The blue lines melted rapidly. Lieutenant Colonel Mudge was shot through the neck and killed, while five men carrying the regimental colors were struck down, either killed or wounded. By the time it was over, the 2nd Massachusetts had lost more than 40 percent of its men, while the Indianans suffered 32 percent casualties. The survivors limped back to the safety of their lines.

After nearly seven hours of sustained combat, the fighting on Culp's Hill at last subsided just after 11:00 a.m. Allegheny Johnson, believing the Union troops to be "too securely entrenched and in too great numbers to be dislodged by the force at my command," ordered his men to fall back. By noon, the battered and exhausted Confederate survivors were east of Rock Creek, and the Union army had maintained possession of Culp's Hill. At 12:20 that afternoon, Henry Slocum rather laconically reported to Meade, "I think I have gained a decided advantage." The right flank of the Union's fishhook line was secure, as was the vital Baltimore Pike, the army's main line of supply, just a few hundred yards behind Culp's Hill. In later summarizing the fighting, Alpheus Williams could only wonder why the Confederates had for so long "persisted in an attempt that the first half hour must have told them it was useless."

Although it is impossible to know with any degree of certainty, Confederate casualties that Friday morning on Culp's Hill totaled anywhere between 2,400 and 3,000 men, or nearly 30 percent of the 9,000 engaged; Federal casualties numbered about 1,000, or less than 10 percent of the total number engaged. Scanning the wreckage left in the wake of this action—at the devastated landscape, the lifeless forms and the hundreds of wounded men—a soldier in the 123rd New York later observed that "none but demons can delight in war." If true, then there would be much more fighting ahead that day to further delight those demons.

The action on Culp's Hill was still raging when the men of Pickett's Division arrived at a point west of Seminary Ridge, behind the center of the Confederate battle line. Pickett's Virginians were in good spirits that morning. "The usual jests and hilarity were indulged in," said one of Pickett's men, and "no gloomy forebodings hovered over our ranks." Captain John Dooley of the 1st Virginia later recorded that some of the men amused themselves that morning by pelting one another with green apples. "So frivolous men can be," said Dooley, "even in the hour of death." Pickett's men were eager to enter the fray and get a shot at glory. Held in reserve at Fredericksburg and detached from the army during the Chancellorsville Campaign, they had not been engaged in serious combat since Antietam, ten months earlier. During the current campaign, they had brought up the rear of the army as it moved north into Pennsylvania, guarding the wagon trains, and thus missed out on the first two days of battle. Pickett's Division was actually composed of five brigades, but two had been kept behind to man the defenses of Richmond while the other three—composed entirely of Virginia regiments—accompanied the army north. Halting on the west side of Seminary Ridge, the troops lounged in the tall grass and filled their canteens from the waters of Willoughby Run as their commander, thirty-eight-year-old George Pickett, rode on ahead to consult with Longstreet.

General George Pickett awaits the signal to advance his division in this sketch by Confederate staff officer Colonel Alexander Boteler. *National Park Service, Gettysburg National Military Park.*

The two had enjoyed a close and long-standing friendship. Like so many of the officers in both blue and gray, Longstreet and Pickett had fought alongside each other in Mexico, and like so many other officers, Pickett was a West Pointer, graduating last in the class of 1846, the same class in which George McClellan graduated second and Thomas Jonathan Jackson eighth. Personally brave, the dashing Virginian fell wounded at Gaines's Mill in June 1862 and, upon his return to the army that fall, was promoted to major general and given divisional command, much because of the influence of his friend Longstreet. Now, that Friday morning, with his men catching a break from the march, Pickett walked along the crest of Seminary Ridge and stared across the open field toward the Union position on Cemetery

Ridge, as Longstreet explained his orders. As Longstreet later recorded, Pickett "seemed to appreciate the severity of the contest upon which he was about to enter, but was quite hopeful of success."

His instructions now clear, Pickett then brought his three brigades forward through Spangler's Woods to a swale of ground immediately east of the trees. Pickett formed his division into two lines, with General James Kemper's brigade on the right of the front line and General Richard Garnett's on the left. General Lewis Armistead lined up his troops roughly two hundred yards behind Garnett's Brigade. Taking up these positions between 9:00 and 10:00 a.m., the men were next instructed to make themselves as comfortable as possible and await the orders to advance. Some of the more curious walked to the crest of the ridgeline to see what was expected of them that day. Very quickly the seriousness of the situation sank in to those who ventured forth. It was clear that deadly work lay ahead. "My heart almost failed me," wrote Private Samuel Pawlett of the 18th Virginia as he gazed across the open fields to the formidable Union position on Cemetery Ridge. Turning to a comrade, Pawlett called out, "This is going to be a heller! Prepare for the worst."

Pickett's 5,500 men constituted less than half the force Lee slated for the afternoon attack. Maneuvering into position and forming up in lines of battle to the left-rear of Pickett's Virginians were some 6,800 soldiers from A.P. Hill's Third Corps, composing the ranks of six brigades from two divisions. Heth's Division of four brigades, commanded by Johnston Pettigrew, went into line on the western slopes of Seminary Ridge, with Archer's Brigade—commanded since Archer's capture on July 1 by Colonel Birkett Fry—forming the division's right flank. To the left of Fry's men went Pettigrew's Brigade, which was now led by Colonel James Marshall because of Pettigrew's elevation to divisional command. Completing the division's deployment was Joseph Davis's brigade, which filed into line to the left of Marshall, and John Brockenbrough's Virginians, who formed up to the left of Davis. Forming several hundred yards behind the right of Pettigrew's line were two brigades from Dorsey Pender's division. Alfred Scales's battered brigade, led that day by Colonel William Lowrance, formed to the right of this supporting line, while James Lane's comparatively fresh troops went into line to the left of Lowrance. Since Pender had been struck down, mortally wounded, late the afternoon before, General Isaac Trimble was assigned command of these two brigades.

Excepting the North Carolinians under Lane, all of these Third Corps brigades were in rough shape, having suffered heavily during the first day's fight. Archer's Brigade, for example, lost one-third of its number on July 1, while casualties in Scales's now skeletal brigade neared 60 percent. In addition, while Lane and Fry were experienced and highly capable commanders, Marshall and Lowrance were entirely inexperienced in brigade command, and Davis and Brockenbrough were mediocre, uninspiring commanders at best. Lee's decision to use these battered and bloodied brigades for the attack against the Union center seems to have been based almost entirely on the fact that they had been kept out of the action on July 2 and were thus spared that day's brutal carnage. Lee might also have been simply unaware of the actual extent of their losses sustained during the first day's brawl or simply was still caught up in the faulty belief in the invincibility of his men. Either way, because of the battered condition of these troops, Longstreet later labeled it a mistake to have included them in such an important attack.

Longstreet also wrote that Lee should have placed someone other than himself in charge of overseeing the attack—someone who had more faith in it. "Never was I so depressed as upon that day," Longstreet later declared. "With my knowledge of the situation, I could see the desperate and hopeless nature of the charge and the cruel slaughter it would cause." But despite his objections, Longstreet was Lee's ablest lieutenant, his most trusted and longest-serving subordinate. There was no one else Lee could rely on more than Longstreet.

The Confederates were to advance east, toward the center of the Union line on Cemetery Ridge, the objective point, supposedly, being a small grove, or copse, of trees atop Cemetery Ridge, several hundred yards to the south of the much larger and more distinguishable Zeigler's Grove and roughly 1,400 yards east of where Pickett's, Pettigrew's and Trimble's men were forming. Birkett Fry's brigade, on the right of Pettigrew's line, was designated as the unit of advance, meaning all other brigades would conform or align to its movement as it marched straight ahead. Because there existed a large, yawning gap of some four hundred yards between Fry's right flank and the left flank of Pickett's Division, Pickett's men would be forced to execute a series of left-oblique maneuvers as they advanced, angling to the northeast in order to close the gap with Pettigrew's command while still driving toward Cemetery Ridge.

The fields over which these men were to advance rose and fell in a series of undulations, which would provide some cover, but a series of fence lines that crisscrossed these same fields threatened to disrupt their formations, most notably those that lined either side of the Emmitsburg Road, especially in front of Pettigrew's command. For support and to exploit any breakthrough, Lee had assigned Longstreet the brigades of R.H. Anderson's

Third Corps division, with Wilcox's and Lang's men already in position to the right of Pickett and the brigades of Ambrose Wright, William Mahone and Carnot Posey positioned to support Pettigrew, if needed.

While the infantry commanders worked out the specifics of the advance, and as their men settled into line under an increasingly broiling sun, sweating gray-coated artillerists galloped to and fro to their front, unlimbering and wheeling their cannons into position along the crest of the ridgeline, preparing for the tremendous bombardment that was to precede the infantry assault. To command his First Corps guns, Longstreet tabbed the gifted twenty-eight-year-old artillerist E.P. Alexander. Like Longstreet, he had serious doubts about the impending attack. "The point selected and the method of attack," wrote Alexander in his oft-quoted memoirs, "would certainly have been chosen for us by the enemy had they had the choice." Still, admitted the native Georgian and West Point graduate, "the fact is that like the rest of the army I believed it would come out right, because General Lee had planned it"—such was the profound faith the men had in their army commander. Alexander's instructions were simple: he was "to give the enemy the most effective cannonade possible. It was not meant simply to make a noise, but to try & cripple him—to tear him limbless, as it were, if possible."

With Pickett's infantry forming up behind his guns, Alexander positioned seventy-six cannons in a line that extended some 1,300 yards from the Peach Orchard on the right, northwesterly across the Emmitsburg Road, along the crest of Seminary Ridge. He also positioned nine guns south of the Peach Orchard to contend with the Union cannons on Little Round Top. Alexander instructed his men to fire slowly and methodically and to especially target the Union guns on Cemetery Ridge in order to soften the Union defenses and thus pave the way for the infantry. Naturally, it would be up to Alexander, the artillerist, to determine when the cannonade "had the desired effect." When he believed the guns had sufficiently pummeled the Union lines, he would give the word for the infantry to advance.

Artillery crews from the army's other two corps were also busy lining up their guns in preparation for the cannonade. To the left of Alexander's guns, Third Corps artillery chief R.L. Walker extended the line of cannons northward, stretching from in front of Pettigrew's command to the Lutheran Seminary Building and beyond toward the Railroad Cut. From there, ringing the high ground north and east of town, went a number of Second Corps batteries. In all, anywhere from 155 to 170 Confederate cannons were in position to batter the Union line. With their deployments complete by noon, the artillerists were instructed to await the signal and then let loose the fury of their guns.

Although the barrels of all these guns were aimed directly at them, the Union soldiers in position on Cemetery Hill, along Cemetery Ridge and even atop Little Round Top could not help but marvel at this martial display of artillery. Brigadier General Henry Hunt, the Army of the Potomac's chief gunner, was particularly impressed. "Our whole front for two miles was covered by batteries already in line or going into position," Hunt recalled. "Never before had such a sight been witnessed on this continent, and rarely, if ever, abroad."

Impressive though the sight was, Hunt knew that there was serious business ahead. He correctly deduced that Lee was setting the stage for a grand infantry charge, aimed directly at the center. Ordered that

Colonel Edward Porter Alexander, a master artillerist, oversaw the great cannonade on July 3. *National Archives.*

morning to make a thorough inspection of his artillery placements and the conditions of his batteries, Hunt made his way from one end of the Union line to the other, preparing his gunners for the anticipated bombardment. He met with Wainwright and Osborn, whose First and Eleventh Corps batteries ringed Cemetery Hill, facing east toward Benner's Hill, north toward Oak Hill and west toward Seminary Ridge. The men who worked the fifty-five cannons in position there, as well as the infantry who defended this hilltop, were in a particularly vulnerable spot, for they would be taking fire from three sides.

Hunt next rode south and examined the positions of the Second Corps guns along Cemetery Ridge. Captain John Hazard, commanding the Second Corps' artillery, had five batteries in position—a total of twenty-seven cannons—stretching from Zeigler's Grove on the right to a point several hundred yards south of the copse of trees. Lieutenant George Woodruff's

Brigadier General Henry Hunt, Meade's chief artillerist. *Library of Congress.*

Battery I, 1st U.S. Artillery, held a position just in front of the grove; to their left were Captain William Arnold's Rhode Island battery and Battery A, 4th U.S. Artillery, commanded by twenty-two-year-old Lieutenant Alonzo Cushing, whose six three-inch ordnance rifles extended south toward the copse. South of the copse and in position to the left of Cushing was Fred Brown's Battery B, 1st Rhode Island Artillery, commanded that day by Lieutenant Walter Perrin. Finally, completing the deployment of Hazard's guns was Captain James Rorty's 1st New York Light Artillery.

Holding positions atop Cemetery Ridge, directly in the center of the Union line, these batteries were fated to suffer heavily that afternoon, for they were especially targeted by Porter Alexander and other Confederate gunners across the way, on Seminary Ridge. To the left of Hazard's guns and extending south from Cemetery Ridge was a formidable array of Union artillery, numbering some thirty-seven pieces in all and commanded by the indefatigable Freeman McGilvery. And finally, farther south, also standing poised to contest the Confederate infantry, were the gunners of Gibbs's 1st Ohio Light Artillery and those of Rittenhouse's Battery D, 5th U.S., in position on the northern slopes and summit of Little Round Top.

In all, more than 110 Federal artillery pieces were lined up, with most of their now cold barrels facing west toward Seminary Ridge. Wanting to ensure that these guns would have enough ammunition left in their caissons for the anticipated infantry attack, Hunt instructed his artillerists to wait a full fifteen to twenty minutes after the Confederate guns opened before responding and to fire slowly, sparingly and methodically. He did not want to use up all of his long-range ammunition in counter-battery fire. Completing his inspection, Hunt was satisfied that when Lee's men stepped off for the attack, his gunners would be ready to greet them with a well-directed and murderous fire.

Hunt was certainly not alone in thinking that Lee was preparing to attack the Union center; army commander George Meade believed so as well. Indeed, late the night before, upon the adjournment of his famed council of war, Meade allegedly pulled aside General John Gibbon, whose Second Corps division held a position on Cemetery Ridge, left and right of that little copse of trees. "If Lee attacks tomorrow, it will be on your front," said Meade. Asked why, the army commander very quickly answered, "Because he has made attacks on both our flanks and failed, and if he concludes to try it again, it will be on our center." Like Hunt, Meade had also ridden the length of his line that morning, inspecting his army's positions. He liked what he saw; his men, after two days of terrific combat and enduring heavy losses, still held a formidable defensive position and were still full of fight. In a letter penned to his wife that Friday morning, Meade noted that "[t]he army [is] in fine spirits and every one [was] determined to do or die."

After a bite to eat and a round of cigars with a few of his subordinates, Meade returned to his headquarters at about 12:30 p.m. where he received Slocum's report that the army's right flank, on Culp's Hill, was secure. The din of battle there had subsided, and an eerie silence had descended across the battlefield. On Seminary Ridge, Confederate artillerists stood to their guns, waiting for the signal to open fire, while the gray-coated infantrymen under Pickett, Pettigrew and Trimble continued to lounge in the swales on either side of Spangler's Woods. Many soldiers in both blue and gray took advantage of the noonday lull—many of them, like Meade, no doubt writing letters home, while others played cards, boiled up some coffee, nibbled on some hardtack or simply caught up on some much-needed sleep. Things had become so still, so silent, that one Union soldier wrote that he could "distinctly hear the hum of honeybees working."

Then, at 1:07 p.m., two cannons of Louisiana's celebrated Washington Artillery, positioned near the Peach Orchard, opened fire in quick succession, shattering the afternoon silence. It was the signal the Confederate gunners had been waiting for; they were now to commence the barrage. For the next ninety minutes, the very earth trembled in what would prove to be the largest and most sustained artillery fire of the entire war. At first, it was only the Confederate guns that fired, throwing their shot and shell toward Cemetery Hill and especially Cemetery Ridge, where Union troops hugged the ground, keeping their heads down in this terrible storm of iron, while Union artillerymen stood by their guns, patiently waiting out those first fifteen or twenty minutes, as

Hunt as had directed. Yet before this time had elapsed, the Federal guns on Cemetery Ridge opened fire.

As his men bore the brunt of the Confederate fire for what must have seemed several very long minutes, Hancock could not imagine why his guns were quiet. He sought out Hazard, who told him of Hunt's instructions, but Hancock would have none of it and, declaring that he would take full responsibility, ordered his Second Corps artillery to respond. Whereas Hunt wanted to husband as much ammunition as possible for the anticipated infantry attack, Hancock, fearful that his men might break under so heavy a fire, wanted to show them that they were supported. With Hazard's guns now opening fire, Hancock next rode south, where he found the muted pieces along McGilvery's line. "Why the hell do you not fire with these batteries?" demanded Hancock. McGilvery, like Hazard, told the Second Corps commander of Hunt's instructions. Hancock insisted McGilvery open fire, and a few of his batteries did, but as soon as Hancock galloped away, McGilvery ordered them to cease fire and had his men take cover.

By this time, Cemetery Ridge was covered in smoke, as the gunners of Hazard's five batteries—from Zeigler's Grove to south of the copse of trees—returned shot for shot with the Confederate gunners on Seminary Ridge. Federal cannons on Little Round Top and Cemetery Hill had by now also added to the din. In all, perhaps as many as 250 cannons belched forth their fire and smoke that Friday afternoon, producing a continual and deafening roar. Most of the soldiers in blue and gray who fought at Gettysburg were seasoned veterans, many of them having already experienced two years of war, with all of its attendant horrors. But this cannonade at Gettysburg was something they had never experienced before. In letters home or in their memoirs, those who had survived the bloodshed did their best to describe it, but as John Moore of the 7th Tennessee Infantry wrote, "No imagination can adequately conceive of the magnitude of this artillery duel." It was an experience that would stay with them for the rest of their lives. Years afterward, referring to this great cannonade, John Dooley of the 1st Virginia Infantry recorded, "Never will I forget those scenes and sounds. The earth seemed unsteady beneath the furious cannonade, and the air might be said to be agitated by the wings of death."

The boys in blue left similar descriptions. One soldier of the 1st Delaware, positioned near Arnold's battery on Cemetery Ridge, wrote that the experience of having to endure the cannonade was "like some terrible night-mare where one was held spell-bound by the appalling grandeur of the storm." There was

Confederate soldiers wait out the artillery bombardment within the trees on Seminary Ridge. *From* Battles and Leaders of the Civil War.

little the infantry on either side could do but to wait it out. "All we had to do while undergoing the shelling was to chew tobacco, watch caissons explode, and wonder if the next shot would hit you," wrote one soldier of Brigadier General William Harrow's brigade, positioned just south of the copse of trees. Another soldier, one of the few survivors of the battered 1st Minnesota Infantry, recalled the scene vividly: "There was an incessant, discordant flight of shells, seemingly in and from all directions: howling, shrieking, striking, exploding, tearing, smashing and destroying. The ground was torn-up, fences and trees knocked to splinters, rocks and small stones were flying in the air, ammunition boxes and caissons were exploded; guns were dismounted and men and horses were torn to pieces. We commended our souls to God, shut our teeth *hard* and lay flat on the ground, expecting every minute to be blown to atoms."

If the experience was harrowing enough for the well-seasoned soldiers, for the people of town it must have been especially frightful. Professor Michael Jacobs remembered that the barrage of artillery "produced such a continuous succession of crashing sounds as to make us feel as if the very heavens had been rent asunder." Sarah Broadhead employed similar language and imagery when she wrote that it seemed "as if the heavens and earth were crashing together."

From his headquarters atop Cemetery Hill, Union Eleventh Corps commander Oliver Howard, whom one observer remembered as being "imperturbably cool" during this awesome conflagration, noted the effect of the Confederate artillery fire there. "Shells burst in the air, on the ground, at our right and left, and in front, killing men and horses, exploding caissons, overturning tombstones, and smashing fences. The troops hugged their cover, when they had any, as well as they could," said Howard, who also noted that men "fell while eating, or while the food was in their hands, and some with cigars in their mouths." But for all the damage done to the artillerists and infantrymen positioned on Cemetery Hill, it was the Union batteries positioned along Cemetery Ridge that suffered the most from the Confederates' iron storm.

Hazard's guns were especially targeted during the bombardment since they would pose the greatest threat to the advancing infantry. Particularly hard hit were the batteries positioned near the copse of trees. Twenty-six-year-old James Rorty, a native of Ireland who had immigrated to the United States in 1857, was struck by a piece of shell and killed while tending to his guns. More than two dozen other men of Rorty's battery also fell either dead or wounded, while two of the battery's four guns were destroyed. Casualties in Perrin's Battery B, 1st Rhode Island, were also heavy and the battery so severely wrecked that Hunt would order it to be withdrawn. Alonzo Cushing lost so many of his men during the bombardment that by the time it was over only enough men remained to operate two of his six cannons. Cushing was himself struck twice by shell fragments, but he refused to leave his guns; with pistol drawn, he threatened to blow the brains out of anyone who showed any inclination to do so.

But few if any of the veteran artillerists in either blue or gray so much as flinched during this tempest of shot and shell; they instead kept gallantly to their guns, loading and firing their pieces while iron rained down on them or covered them with dirt and sod. An artillerist in Cushing's thrashed battery recalled that "[e]very few seconds a shell would strike right in among our guns, but we could not stop for anything. We could not even close our eyes when death seemed to be coming." Confederate gunner John Marye of Virginia's Fredericksburg Artillery left a vibrant account of the intensity of the action on smoke-covered Seminary Ridge: "The air was alive with screaming, bursting shells and flying fragments...Cannoneers with jackets off and perspiration streaming down their faces, blackened with powder,

A September 1862 photograph of Union artillery officers, including Lieutenant Evan Thomas (seated, front row, left); Lieutenant Alonzo Cushing (standing, back row, center), killed during Pickett's Charge; and Lieutenant James McKay Rorty (seated, front row, right), killed during the bombardment preceding Pickett's Charge. *Library of Congress.*

kept the guns cool by plunging the spongeheads in buckets of water, and as fast as a man fell another took his place; guns were dismounted, limbers and caissons blown up and horses ripped open and disemboweled."

And while the artillerists kept busy, infantry officers on both ridgelines made their presences known, hoping to calm the nerves and strengthen the resolve of their men, who were forced to endure the storm while unable to do anything but hug the earth and wait it out. Hancock rode slowly behind his lines. When told that he was exposing himself too greatly, Hancock replied simply that "[t]here are times when a corps commander's life doesn't count." Two of Hancock's three divisions manned the center of the Union line, their five thousand men spread out across nearly half a mile of largely open ground. Alexander Hays's troops were positioned near Zeigler's Grove, many of them behind a stone fence that extended south from the deserted home of Abraham Bryan, a black man, who fled with his family upon the Confederates' advance into Pennsylvania. Continuing the Second Corps line south were Gibbon's three brigades, which took up positions in front of the copse of trees. Like Hancock, both Hays (a tough, combative soldier whom one man said "seemed happiest when in the thickest of the fight") and Gibbon (that "[t]ower of strength...cool as a steel knife") paced coolly, calmly, back and forth behind their men, telling the men to keep still. Expecting an infantry attack to follow in the wake of the bombardment, Hays instructed his men to stack up rifles and pile cartridges up high next to them.

Such gallant displays of leadership were very much evident on Seminary Ridge as well. During the midst of the bombardment, one of Kemper's Virginians remembered seeing Longstreet, his thoughts no doubt heavy, riding slowly along the lines, "as quiet as an old farmer riding over his plantation on a Sunday morning," while General Armistead, walking among his troops in Spangler's Woods, exhorted his anxious soldiers to be still and to keep calm even as shells burst overhead and showered them with falling leaves and branches.

The Confederates, positioned behind the lines of cannons, waiting patiently for the orders to advance, suffered the worst during the bombardment. Scores, perhaps hundreds, of men in Pickett's and Pettigrew's Brigades were struck with shell fragments, killed or wounded even before stepping off for the attack. One Confederate spoke to the devastating effect of the Federal shells when he wrote, "There were to be seen at almost every moment of time, guns, swords, haversacks, human flesh flying above the earth, which now trembled beneath us as shaken by an earthquake." Indeed, such was the loss sustained during the bombardment that another Confederate remembered that when the order to attack at last arrived, "it appeared that as many men were left dead and wounded as got up."

For all the noise and smoke it created, and excepting the devastation done to the Union Second Corps batteries atop Cemetery Ridge, the effect of the Confederate artillery was not nearly as destructive as they had hoped. The dense smoke and rolling terrain made it difficult for the Southern gunners to accurately gauge distance, and they suffered from many a defective fuse. The result was that many of their shells simply sailed over the Union troops positioned on the ridgeline. And while these shells struck heavy behind them—tearing up the ground on the eastern slope of Cemetery Ridge, near Meade's headquarters and along the Taneytown Road—the pummeling of the Union defenses on the ridgeline was not nearly as great as the Confederates had envisioned. One Federal gunner wrote that the Confederate bombardment was a brilliant fireworks display, "but as a military demonstration it was the biggest humbug of the season." Sergeant Frederick Fuger, who served under Cushing, concurred while seemingly

Meade's headquarters, the Leister house along the Taneytown Road. The destruction done by the artillery bombardment on July 3 is apparent in this post-battle photograph. *Library of Congress.*

ignoring the heavy casualties within his own battery. "As a demonstration, or rather as a spectacle, it was superb," wrote Fuger, "but as a military operation it was not effective, because its destructiveness was not such as to impair the power of our Infantry to resist and repulse the great charge for which it was designed to pave the way, nor did it cripple our own artillery."

As one who respected the power of artillery, Brigadier General Henry Hunt described the cannonade as "incredibly grand," but he, along with many other officers in blue, realized that this great show of guns was but a prelude to a major infantry attack. Hunt was on Cemetery Hill sometime before 2:30 p.m. as the barrage raged the hottest, discussing the situation with Oliver Howard and others of the Eleventh Corps. Thomas Osborn, commanding the corps' artillery, stated that if the Confederates were, indeed, preparing to charge, would it not be a good idea for Hunt to order the Union guns to cease fire, giving the false impression that they had been driven off and ensuring that they would have enough ammunition on hand to greet the infantry? Essentially, to lure the Confederates out? Hunt thought it a grand idea. Riding south from the hilltop, Hunt ordered his artillerists to cease fire, and the Union guns, one by one, went quiet. The shroud of smoke, which had enveloped the cannons and their crews, began to lift, and as it did so, Hunt also ordered some of the battered guns out of position and sent for new, fresh batteries to take their place.

On Seminary Ridge, E.P. Alexander noted this slackening of fire, and through his field glasses he could see Union guns being wheeled away. The bombardment had gone on much longer than he had expected. Now, with the cessation of Union fire, Alexander believed that he had at last succeeded in driving off the Union guns. With his own supply of ammunition dwindling, he believed that the time had now come for the infantry to advance. Sometime around 2:45 p.m., Alexander scribbled off a quick note to General Pickett, telling him the Union guns have been driven off and pleading, "For God's sake come on quick or we cannot support you; ammunition nearly out." It was the summons for which Pickett had been waiting. Still confident of success, but perhaps with less enthusiasm, Pickett passed the note along to Longstreet, asking, "General, shall I advance?" Words failing him, Longstreet could only nod his assent. "I shall lead my division forward," said Pickett before riding off to ready his men.

The orders went out, and the Confederate infantrymen fated to make the attack rose to their feet, stretched their legs and filed into line. With his men dressing ranks and gritting their teeth for the long-awaited advance, Pickett rode to the front of his division and yelled out to those within earshot, "Up men! Up and to your posts and don't forget today that you are from old Virginia!" After conversing briefly with Kemper, Pickett next rode to General Richard Garnett. With no flowery rhetoric, Pickett simply instructed Garnett to "get across those fields as quick as you can, for in my opinion you are going to catch hell." Behind Garnett's line, Armistead was doing his best to inspire his troops. "Men, remember what you are fighting for. Remember your homes and your friends, your wives, mothers, sisters, and your sweethearts."

John Dooley of the 1st Virginia best captured the thoughts racing through the men's minds as they prepared to go forward. "I tell you there is no romance in making one of these charges," wrote the Virginia captain. "When you rise to your feet...I tell you the enthusiasm of ardent breasts in many cases *ain't there*, and instead of burning to avenge the insults of our country, families and altars and firesides, the thought is most frequently, *oh*, if I could just come out of this charge safely how thankful *would I be!*"

To the left of Pickett's men, the brigades under Pettigrew and Trimble also readied for the charge. Although all were aware of the deadly work that lay ahead, and though many of the men sensed that this would be their final attack, the orders to advance came as welcome relief to the men who had endured and survived the ninety-minute cannonade. "After lying inactive under that deadly storm of hissing and exploding shells, it seemed a relief to go forward to the desperate assault," admitted Colonel Birkett Fry. "At the command the men sprang up with cheerful alacrity." Ordered to advance, Fry's small, battered brigade of Tennesseans and Alabamians moved forward. With Fry's Brigade in motion, Johnston Pettigrew galloped over to Colonel James Marshall, commanding his old brigade of North Carolinians: "Now, colonel, for the honor of the good old North State, forward."

Brigadier General J. Johnston Pettigrew was wounded while leading Heth's Division on July 3 and mortally wounded eleven days later at Falling Waters during the Confederate retreat from Gettysburg. *From* Battles and Leaders of the Civil War.

The attack thus commenced. The advancing lines—fifty regiments strong and composed of men from six states—moved forward with almost parade-like precision sometime just after 3:00 p.m. Pickett's and Pettigrew's men were cheered on loudly by the exhausted artillerists as they passed through the rows of cannons and over the scarred ground. It was a grand, magnificent sight. Those who viewed it were swept up in its majesty. One of Robert Rodes's men wrote that "never did men move in better lines—never did a flag wave over a braver set of men." Even the Union troops on Cemetery Ridge could not help but admire the martial display—and marvel at the audacity of the attack. These long lines of butternut and gray were heading directly toward them, across nearly three-quarters of a mile of open, rolling ground.

In eloquent prose, Frank Haskell, an officer on General John Gibbon's staff, captured the moment brilliantly:

Edwin Forbes's depiction of Pickett's men moving out to the attack. *Library of Congress.*

Every eye could see his legions, an overwhelming resistless tide of an ocean of armed men sweeping upon us! Regiment after regiment, and brigade after brigade, move from the woods and rapidly take their places in the lines forming the assault…More than half a mile their front extends; more than a thousand yards the dull gray masses deploy, man touching man, rank pressing rank, and line supporting line. The red flags wave; their horsemen gallop up and down; the arms of eighteen thousand men [sic], barrel and bayonet, gleam in the sun, a sloping forest of flashing steel. Right on they move, as with one soul, in perfect order, without impediment of ditch, or wall or stream, over ridge and slope, through orchard and meadow, and cornfield, magnificent, grim, irresistible.

But this military pageantry was short-lived. As soon as the Confederates came into view, Union artillery erupted, tearing holes in the marching columns. Rittenhouse's and Gibbs's guns on Little Round Top and those along McGilvery's line, which survived the cannonade relatively unscathed, proved especially destructive to Kemper's and Garnett's men of Pickett's Division, while First and Eleventh Corps cannons, positioned on Cemetery Hill, began to blast Pettigrew's lines. Major Osborn recorded that "[f]rom the very first minute," his Eleventh Corps batteries "created sad havoc" in the Confederate ranks. So destructive was the fire endured by Kemper's Brigade that within less than fifteen minutes, seven men carrying the flag of the 7th Virginia Infantry fell either killed or wounded. Men dropped at almost every step, yet the Confederates pressed onward, continuing to dress ranks and fill the gaps that were torn in their lines.

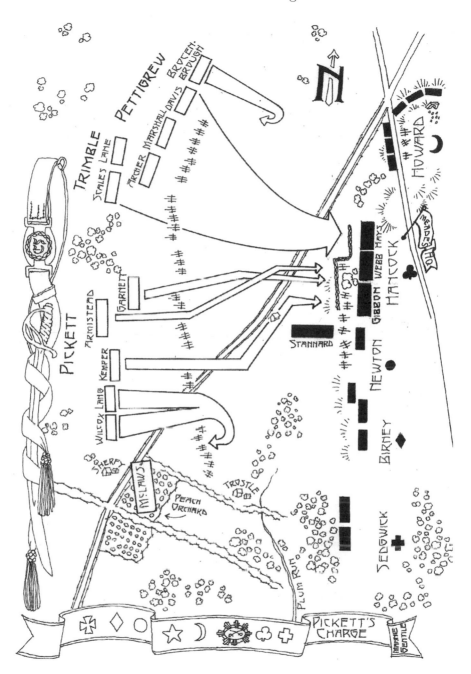

Pickett's Charge. *Map by Mannie Gentile.*

On the far left of the Confederate line, things went poorly from the start. For whatever reason, the Virginians of Brockenbrough's Brigade did not move when the rest of Pettigrew's line advanced. Now they were forced to run in order to catch up. As they crested the ridgeline, they came under fire from the Union cannons on Cemetery Hill. Exposed to this fearful shelling, many of Brockenbrough's men bolted back to the rear. Then, just as soon as the rest of these panting Virginians caught up to the left flank of Davis's Brigade, they came under an unexpected and destructive musket fire delivered at less than one hundred yards by the soldiers of the 8th Ohio Infantry. These Buckeye State soldiers were positioned along the Emmitsburg Road, well to the front of Hays's division, as a skirmish force.

When Brockenbrough's men came into view, Colonel Franklin Sawyer advanced his men westward and then swung them to the left, so that they now faced south, directly on the left flank of the Virginians. The Ohioans opened fire, and at once, said Colonel Sawyer, the Confederates "were enveloped in a dense cloud of smoke and dust. Arms, heads, blankets, guns, and knapsacks thrown and tossed into the clear air." One of Brockenbrough's men wrote, "Hell could never be so bad." This unexpected fire destroyed Brockenbrough's formations. Panicked, most of those not struck down fled to the rear. The exit of Brockenbrough's Brigade then exposed the left flank of Davis's Brigade to the Ohio troops, who continued to blaze away. "[O]ur blood was up," reported Sawyer, "and the men loaded and yelled and howled at the passing column." Seeing Brockenbrough's Brigade disintegrate, Longstreet sent orders for Isaac Trimble to help cover Pettigrew's left. At the same time, he called on Richard Anderson to prepare the brigades of Wright, Posey and Mahone for action.

Even though its far left was crumbling, the rest of the Confederate line continued to move forward. Thus far in the advance, Pickett's and Pettigrew's men—excepting those of Brockenbrough's Brigade—had been exposed solely to long-range artillery fire and to some sporadic musketry fire delivered by Union skirmishers posted in front of their main line of defense. Although these rounds had been deadly enough, as the gray and butternut lines approached the Emmitsburg Road, they came under a much more intense and savage fire as Second Corps cannons positioned on Cemetery Ridge erupted. True, these batteries had suffered heavily during the cannonade, and their gunners had used up all of their long-range ammunition, but Henry Hunt had ordered up fresh guns to bolster this line and all the batteries had plenty of short-range ammunition.

With the Confederates now within just two hundred yards, the Second Corps guns lit up, as did several pieces from the artillery reserve, unleashing devastating rounds of canister into the massed Confederate ranks. The Confederates were also now within easy range of Union muskets. Gibbon's and Hays's men, who had been waiting in anxious anticipation as the gray ranks drew ever nearer, opened fire, delivering a steady and well-aimed fire. The effect of all this fire was fearful. Scores of Confederates fell as they scrambled up and over the post-and-rail fences that lined both sides of the Emmitsburg Road. Pickett's men crossed the roadway left and right of the Codori farm buildings. Because many of the fences that lined the roadway there had been toppled during the previous day's action, they were less of an impediment to Pickett's men than they were to Pettigrew's much-reduced ranks farther north, where the fences, for the most part, remained intact. The canister and small arms fire was so intense and the carnage so fearful along the length of the line that many Confederates refused to advance any farther beyond the roadway.

The Federal fire was "raining death upon us," remembered one Virginian as Pickett's men began ascending the gentle western slope of Cemetery Ridge. After crossing the Emmitsburg Road, Garnett's men drove straight forward; Kemper's Brigade, which had crossed the road south of the Codori farm, angled once more to the left, executing yet another oblique maneuver as it continued toward the Federal center. Kemper's men were now moving at right angles to the Union line, and while Gibbon's Second Corps soldiers under Alexander Webb, Norman Hall and William Harrow continued to pound away at the front of the Confederate line, General George Stannard, commanding a brigade of Vermonters to the left of Gibbon and roughly five hundred yards south of the copse of trees, sensed an opportunity. Stannard's regiments belonged to Doubleday's division of the First Corps but had not arrived in time to participate in any of the action on July 1. They were also nine-month men whose terms of service were about to expire. Stannard advanced his Vermonters and then turned them to face north so that they were now squarely on the right flank of Kemper's line.

Captain Henry Owen of the 18th Virginia remembered the moment he saw Stannard's troops approaching: "[T]here appeared in the open field a line of men at right angle with our own, a long, dark mass, dressed in blue, and coming down at a 'double-quick' upon the unprotected right flank of Pickett's men, with their muskets 'upon the right shoulder shift,' their battle flags dancing and fluttering in the breeze created by their own rapid motion and their burnished bayonets glistening above their heads like forest twigs covered with sheets of sparkling ice when shaken by a blast." The Vermonters opened fire, and the effect was appalling. "[W]e took deliberate aim and with a simultaneous flash and roar fired into the compact ranks of the desperate foe and again and again in quick succession until a dozen or more volleys had been discharged," said Private Ralph Sturtevant of the 13th Vermont. "We saw at every volley the grey uniforms fall quick and fast and the front line hesitated, moved slowly and melted away."

Caught up in this deadly fire, what remained of Kemper's Brigade crowded to its left, merging together with Garnett's men; all formations were lost, the fire relentless. "We…bowled them over like nine pins, picking out the colors first," remarked Major Henry Abbott of the 20th Massachusetts rather casually. Yet somehow the mass of Confederates continued to surge forward into the maelstrom. One Federal gunner later wrote, "I remember distinctly that they pulled their caps down over their eyes and bowed their heads as men do in a hail storm." Brigadier General James Kemper was knocked from his horse, severely wounded by a musket ball that lodged at the base of his spine. Carried to the rear, Kemper would recover from the wound that many believed to be fatal. Garnett was struck down as well, shot through the head and instantly killed. On his famed mount Red Eye, Garnett galloped among his men, encouraging them with shouts of "Faster men! Faster!" Captain Owen of the 18th Virginia remembered the moment when Garnett was killed, for "his clarion voice was no more heard above the roar of battle."

To the left of Pickett's disordered Virginians, the Tennesseans, North Carolinians, Mississippians and Alabamians from Pettigrew's division, having scaled the fences along the Emmitsburg Road, continued to push forward toward Hays's dense line of blue, stacked many ranks deep behind the stone wall that ran south from the Bryan farm. Hays's men unloosed a terrific storm of musketry, while Woodruff's artillery pieces in Zeigler's Grove belched forth deadly rounds of canister. As was true of Pickett's Division, the price paid by Pettigrew's was incredibly high. Brigadier General Isaac Trimble, riding behind Pettigrew's line, wrote that Pettigrew's men "seemed to sink into the earth under the tempest of fire poured into them." Among the wounded was Colonel Birkett Fry, commanding Archer's Brigade, who fell near the Emmitsburg Road, shot through the left thigh. He lay in the meadow just east of the roadway, yelling for his men to press on. General Johnston Pettigrew had been wounded as well, a shell fragment shattering his hand and wrist. Fallen, too, was young twenty-four-year-old Colonel James Marshall, a graduate of the Virginia Military Institute and a grandson of John Marshall, the long-serving and highly influential chief justice of the U.S. Supreme

Colonel James Marshall (back row, left) was killed while leading Pettigrew's Brigade toward the Union center on Cemetery Ridge. *Virginia Military Institute Archives.*

Court. Advancing on horseback, Marshall, who commanded the four North Carolina regiments of Pettigrew's Brigade, made it to within sixty yards of the Union position before being struck simultaneously by two bullets in the head and instantly killed.

As Pettigrew's lines continued to disintegrate under this terrific fire, Alexander Hays ordered two of his regiments—the 108th and 126th New York—as well as two guns from George Woodruff's Battery I, 1st U.S. Artillery, to swing to the right and take up position along the Bryan farm lane, which ran westward to the Emmitsburg Road. Woodruff fell mortally wounded while wheeling his pieces into this new position, but soon his gunners, along with the infantrymen of the 108th and 126th New York, began raking Pettigrew's ranks with a devastating enfilading fire. Taking fire from front and left, Pettigrew's force finally crumbled, unable to breach Hays's position. Some stood valiantly, loading and firing their muskets, before finally falling back or raising their arms in surrender.

Few of the troops supporting Pettigrew, under Lowrance and Lane, advanced farther than the Emmitsburg Road, where they, too, came under a withering fire from Hays's men to their front and from the flanking column along the Bryan farm lane. Viewing the destruction ahead, many of these North Carolinians simply turned back toward Seminary Ridge. Even the aggressive Isaac Trimble realized the futility of any further advance. The sixty-one-year-old general was struck from the saddle with a wound that would later require the amputation of his left leg. As Trimble writhed in pain, and as Confederates fled past him, one of his officers asked if he ought to try and rally the men. Trimble said no. "It's all over! Let the men go back."

Watching the attack unfold from Seminary Ridge, General James Longstreet also came to the realization that it would do no good to send more men into that fiery cauldron. Upon the collapse of Brockenbrough's Brigade earlier in the assault, Longstreet had directed Richard Anderson to prepare three of his brigades to move forward. Now he sent orders for Anderson to stay where he was, telling the division commander that any further advance "was useless, and would only involve unnecessary loss," for not only had Pettigrew's men been repulsed on those blood-soaked slopes of Cemetery Ridge, but so too had Pickett's, near the copse of trees.

Thousands of Virginians from all three of Pickett's brigades crowded together in one dense, confused mass, taking fire from Gibbon's men to their front and from Stannard's Vermonters to their right. Their advance had lost its momentum, many of the men doing their best to stand their ground while trading shots with the Union soldiers now less than one hundred yards away. Others kept pushing forward. "[A]ll knew the purpose [was] to carry the heights in front," wrote Captain Owen of the 18th Virginia in a vivid, firsthand account of the attack, "and the mingled mass from fifteen to thirty deep, rushed toward the stone wall…over ground covered with dead and dying men, where the earth seemed to be on fire, and the smoke dense and suffocating, the sun shut out, flames blazing on every side, friend could hardly be distinguished from foe, but the division, in the shape of an inverted V…pushed forward, fighting, falling and melting away."

At the forefront of this "mingled mass" was Brigadier General Lewis Armistead, a fierce fighter with a distinguished military ancestry. His father was a general in the United States Army, while his uncle, Lieutenant Colonel George Armistead, held command of Fort McHenry during the War of 1812. Armistead's Brigade had advanced behind Garnett's, but once across the Emmitsburg Road, he led his men forward, his black slouch hat perched atop his sword, shouting, "Come on, boys, give them the cold steel! Who will follow me?" Like a wave rippling toward shore, several hundred of Armistead's men, joined by others from Garnett and Kemper, surged forward in one final, determined push.

Brigadier General Lewis Armistead.
From Battles and Leaders of the
Civil War.

The soldiers of Gibbon's division, stretching out in front of the copse of trees, held a less formidable defensive position than did Hays's men, eighty yards to their right-rear and farther up the slope of the ridgeline. Soldiers from Webb's Philadelphia Brigade held the right of Gibbon's line, with Hall's and Harrow's brigades continuing the line south. Lieutenant Alonzo Cushing, wounded twice during the cannonade, brought two of his guns to the front, positioning them next to soldiers of the 71st and 69th Pennsylvania of Webb's brigade while, farther south, Captain Andrew Cowan of 1st New York Independent Battery, positioned his cannons on the same ground previously held by Perrin's wrecked Rhode Island battery. These guns showered the advancing Confederates with canister while the infantry kept up a steady fire. Still, Armistead and his men continued driving ahead.

The Union line began to buckle. General John Gibbon was struck down, painfully wounded by a bullet that tore through his left arm and shoulder, while brave Alonzo Cushing fell dead beside his guns, a bullet entering his open mouth as he shouted out orders. Cracking under the pressure, Union soldiers along some portions of the line broke for the rear. After putting up a tough fight, a portion of the 59th New York fell back, thus uncovering Cowan's battery. Sensing an opportunity, members of the 9th and 14th Virginia dashed for the guns, but the artillerists acted quickly and unleashed rounds of canister that, in the words of Captain Cowan, "literally swept the enemy from my front."

Farther north, Armistead led roughly two hundred determined Virginians up and over the low stone wall held by Webb's brigade, crashing right into the soldiers of the 69th and 71st Pennsylvania. "The damned red flags of the Rebellion began to thicken and flaunt," said Frank Haskell, as a fierce, hand-to-hand melee ensued around Cushing's now muted guns. Private Robert Tyler Jones, grandson of the United States' tenth president, fell wounded while bearing the flag of the 53rd Virginia over the wall, while Captain Alexander McCuen of the 71st Pennsylvania severed the head of the man carrying the colors of the 3rd Virginia Infantry with one quick swoop of his sword. The 69th Pennsylvania held firm, but to its right, the four companies of the 71st Pennsylvania manning the angle of the stone wall fell back. Seeing this, General Webb tried desperately to mount a counterattack with soldiers from his 72nd Pennsylvania, but after advancing to the crest of Cemetery Ridge, they would move no farther, preferring instead to fire volleys from their positions farther back, on the crest of the ridgeline. The Union line was pierced, but it proved only a momentary breakthrough, as soldiers from elsewhere along the Union line rushed forward to plug the gap and stem the Confederate tide.

His men having beaten back the Confederate threat to their front, Colonel Arthur Devereaux of the 19th Massachusetts flagged down General Hancock, who was riding behind the lines, asking whether he ought to lead his men toward the angle. Yes, was Hancock's reply, telling Devereaux to get there "pretty God damned quick!" Devereaux led his Massachusetts men toward the copse of trees, followed closely by the 42nd New York and other regiments from both Hall's and Harrow's brigades. Colonel Francis Heath of the 19th Maine wrote that "[e]veryone wanted to be first and the men of the various commands were all mixed up. We went up more like a mob than a disciplined force." These Union troops crashed into the fight. The struggle inside the angle reached a fever pitch, the men locked in deadly combat, firing their weapons at point-blank range, wielding their muskets as clubs or simply using their fists as if in a street brawl.

Devereaux described the action best when he wrote, "Foot to foot, body to body and man to man they struggled, pushed and strived and killed. The mass of wounded and heaps of dead entangled the feet of

Artist Peter Rothermel's dramatic depiction of Pickett's Charge. *Library of Congress.*

the contestants, and underneath the trampling mass, wounded men who could no longer stand, struggled, fought, shouted and killed—hatless, coatless, drowned in sweat, black with powder, red with blood, with fiendish yells and strange oaths they blindly plied the work of slaughter." In the face of so many Union troops, the Confederates were quickly overwhelmed. Within a matter of minutes, nearly every single soldier who followed Armistead across the wall was either wounded, captured or killed. Armistead was himself gunned down, struck by several bullets as he reached for the barrel of one of Cushing's guns; he died two days later.

All the while, during the fury of the fight in front of the stone wall and inside the angle, Pickett's Virginians looked vainly to the rear for support, asking, "Why don't they come?" Indeed, some support was on its way, but by then it was far too little and far too late. As his men first advanced across the Emmitsburg Road, Pickett called on Longstreet for reinforcements. Longstreet authorized Pickett to call on the brigades of Wilcox and Lang, reduced to just 1,200 men following their attacks of the previous day. These two small brigades moved forward to the right of Pickett's Division, across the Emmitsburg Road south of the Codori farm and into the Plum Run Valley. They marched directly into the face of McGilvery's line of cannons, which opened a destructive fire. The Alabamians and Floridians sought shelter behind a fence that skirted a narrow tree line and from there opened a weak fire. By the time they arrived in this position, Pickett's attack had been bloodily repulsed, and it was not long before the soldiers of the 16th Vermont, from Stannard's brigade, about faced, fired a few deadly volleys and then charged this new Confederate line.

"The men were by this time so badly scattered in the bushes and among the rocks," said Colonel Lang, "that it was impossible to make any movement to meet or check the enemy's advance." Lang ordered a retreat but not before scores of his men were rounded up and captured. Wilcox ordered his men to fall back as well. It was a forlorn, belated attack; E.P. Alexander, who had moved up some of his cannons to help cover the retreat, described it as "both absurd and tragic," resulting only in five hundred additional Confederate casualties, or 40 percent of the number Wilcox and Lang led into the fray.

The grand Confederate charge took less than one hour, from the time Pickett's, Pettigrew's and Trimble's men stepped forward from Seminary Ridge until their shattered ranks came limping back. Their losses were simply staggering. Numbers vary, but of the nearly 13,000 men who made the attack, at least 5,300 became casualties; some sources place the number closer to 6,000. Pickett lost nearly half his division, including all three of his brigade commanders—Garnett killed, Armistead mortally wounded and Kemper severely wounded. Of the fifteen regimental commanders in the division, eight were either killed or mortally wounded, while five others sustained nonfatal wounds.

Some units were almost entirely wiped out. Company H of the 56th Virginia began the attack with 37 men; by the time it was over, only 1 remained. Losses in Pettigrew's division exceeded 40 percent, with Pettigrew's old brigade under Marshall suffering the highest losses, followed closely by Archer's Brigade, under Fry, and Joe Davis's Mississippians and North Carolinians. Losses in Brockenbrough's Brigade were not nearly as high. Pettigrew had been wounded during the attack, as had Trimble, commanding the supporting brigades under Lowrance and Lane, which, combined, lost another 600 men. Birkett Fry was wounded and captured, and Colonel James Marshall was dead. The 11th Mississippi of Davis's Brigade suffered an incredible 90 percent loss, including every single member of Company A, the University Greys. The 26th North Carolina, which suffered more than 500 casualties during the first day's action, lost another 130 that afternoon. Twenty-eight regiments, more than half that made the attack, lost their flags, captured by the victorious Union troops on Cemetery Ridge. "We gained nothing but glory," wrote a Virginia lieutenant in later summarizing the charge, "and lost our bravest men."

Union losses along Cemetery Ridge numbered somewhere between 1,700 and 2,000 men, with Webb's brigade, positioned at the angle and near the copse of trees, suffering by far the highest casualties of all the units engaged. Among the Union wounded was Winfield Scott Hancock. After directing Devereaux to take his 19th Massachusetts toward the copse of trees, the Second Corps commander galloped south to a position behind Stannard's Vermonters. There he was struck in the upper thigh by a bullet that had shattered the pommel of his saddle and carried wooden splinters and even a ten-penny nail into the wound. Helped from his horse, Hancock bled profusely. A tourniquet was quickly applied, but Hancock insisted that he not be moved until the battle was decided.

As the fighting subsided, hearty cheers rent the air along the length of the Union battle line, replacing the sharp crack of musket fire and the deep boom of artillery. As Pickett's and Pettigrew's survivors streamed back to Seminary Ridge, Union troops advanced forward toward the Emmitsburg Road, gathering up hundreds of Confederates either unable or simply too tired to make their escape. As many as eight hundred unwounded Confederates were now heading to the rear as prisoners of war. On their way rearward, many no doubt saw a victory-flushed Alexander Hays galloping back and forth, dragging captured Confederate flags on the ground.

Many Federals were simply overwhelmed by the carnage now spread out before them, across the smoldering, bloodstained fields. "The havoc upon the field in our front was appalling," wrote one New York officer. "The dead lay at intervals one upon the other, torn and mangled; and were strewn over the field in every conceivable condition. From among the slain arose the wounded, who struggled to reach our line; some in their vain endeavor, fell to rise no more."

George Meade galloped forward to the crest of Cemetery Ridge just as the Southern tide receded from its supposed high-water mark. There he found Gibbon's adjutant Haskell. "How's it going here?" asked Meade. "I believe, General, the enemy's attack is repulsed," was Haskell's reply. With a quick "Thank God," Meade then rode away to take stock of the condition of his men. Any thought of a counterattack was very quickly dismissed. His troops were too tired and too badly bruised in their repulse of Pickett and Pettigrew to undertake an immediate advance, and it would take too long to bring fresher units to the front, such as those from the Sixth Corps. He had held the defensive for the past two days and would not abandon so strong and so formidable a position by now launching a rash offensive action. Meade returned to his headquarters at the now shot-torn Leister house, where, at about 8:30 p.m., one hour after sunset and as an army band struck up "Hail Columbia" in the front yard, the army commander wired

General in Chief Henry Halleck in Washington. "At the present hour all is quiet," reported Meade, adding that the army "is in fine spirits…I do not think Lee will attack me again."

Because of its grand nature and its tremendous losses, and because it would later come to be regarded by so many as the Confederacy's high-water mark, Pickett's Charge has come to dominate the history of the third day's battle at Gettysburg. But there were other actions that Friday, each involving the mounted arms of both armies.

When Jeb Stuart at last returned to the army on the afternoon of July 2—and after what must have been an awkward, tense meeting—Lee directed him to take up positions east of town, with instructions to protect the army's far left flank while at the same time menacing the Union right and rear. Arriving in position later that evening, Stuart observed infantry of the Stonewall Brigade battling it out with Federal horsemen of David Gregg's division along Brinkerhoff's Ridge. On July 3, Stuart, with nearly six thousand horsemen in four brigades of cavalry, determined to drive the Federal cavalry from this area and to perhaps wreak havoc on the Federal rear, threatening its main supply line along the Baltimore Pike. The result was a three-hour-long struggle that swayed back and forth across John Rummel's farm, near the intersection of the Hanover and Low Dutch Roads. It was a magnificent clash of sabers and one of the largest cavalry actions of the war.

Several times, Stuart's troopers galloped forward, each time checked by hard-charging Union cavalry. The fighting ebbed and flowed across the Rummel farm, with troopers fighting both dismounted and on horseback. At last, Gregg unleashed a furious attack that smashed into the front and flanks of the Confederate horsemen, driving them back. At about 4:00 p.m., at just about the same time Pickett's and Pettigrew's attacks reached their bloody climax several miles to the west, Stuart brought an end to the engagement by ordering his men to withdraw, having lost 200 men killed and wounded. Among his casualties was Brigadier General Wade Hampton, who fell with a saber wound to his head. David Gregg, with his two brigades plus a brigade of Michigan cavalrymen under George Custer, borrowed from Kilpatrick's division, in all, some 4,500 men had sustained 250 casualties but had stymied all of Stuart's attacks, rendering the army's right flank and rear secure.

The final action at Gettysburg played out several miles south of town, on the wooded and boulder-strewn fields at the base of Big Round Top. There, the aggressive Union cavalry commander Hugh Judson Kilpatrick lived up well to his nickname "Kill Cavalry" by ordering a senseless charge against the soldiers of Evander Law's brigade on the far right of the Confederate line. Having learned of the Confederate repulse in the center of the line, Kilpatrick believed that he could create further chaos by launching an attack against the Confederate right flank and rear. He called on Brigadier General Elon Farnsworth, who objected to the order, saying that it was sheer madness to attack so strong an infantry position on horseback and over such rough ground. Kilpatrick ordered it anyway, and the result was predictable. The 1st West Virginia and 18th Pennsylvania Cavalry were very quickly turned back. The 1st Vermont Cavalry, with Farnsworth at the helm, was able to momentarily penetrate the Confederate line, but it was not long before the Confederates rallied and poured a devastating fire into the mounted ranks. Farnsworth fell dead, riddled with bullets, while the rest of his command raced and cut their way back to safety.

It seemed an unfitting end to the three days of horrific battle at Gettysburg.

CHAPTER NOTES

The best account of the battle of July 3 at Gettysburg is Jeffry Wert's *Gettysburg: Day Three* (2001); any study of this third and decisive day of battle at Gettysburg must begin with this book. See also Coddington, chapters 18–19 (pages 465–534); Sears, chapters 11–13 (pages 353–450); Trudeau, chapter 14 (pages 427–529); Woodworth, chapters 8–9 (pages 161–207); and Grimsley and Simpson (pages 132–179). Of course, Pickett's Charge has dominated the historiography of the third day's battle at Gettysburg, and many books focus on this most famous of attacks. The best include *Pickett's Charge: The Last Attack at Gettysburg* (2001) by Earl Hess; *Pickett's Charge: A Microhistory of the Final Attack at Gettysburg* by George Stewart (1959); *Nothing But Glory: Pickett's Division at Gettysburg* (1987) by Kathleen Georg and John W. Busey; and *Pickett's Charge in History and Memory* (1997) by Carol Reardon. For more on the various cavalry actions during the battle, see Eric Wittenberg's *Gettysburg's Forgotten Cavalry Actions* (2012).

Chapter 5

Roads South from Gettysburg

A heavy rain began to fall late on the evening of July 3, as though the heavens had opened to rinse the blood from the now crimson-colored fields surrounding Gettysburg and to help wash away the stains of war. With the ever-darkening shades of night stretching across the southern Pennsylvania skies, the soldiers of both armies, those who had somehow survived the storm of battle, began to settle in. Few in the ranks could have then predicted that there would be no more fighting at Gettysburg —no more thunderous cavalry charges, no more flank attacks, no more grand assaults. For the surgeons, of course, and for the hundreds of others helping to care for the wounded, their work continued well into the night and it would continue, unabated, for weeks ahead.

Following the repulse of the afternoon attack against the Union center, Generals Lee and Longstreet, fearing a counterattack, had worked feverishly to rally the troops and fashion a defensive line on Seminary Ridge. But as darkness continued to fall, it became clear that Meade was not advancing. Satisfied that the fighting had thus ended, a weary General Lee rode along his shattered ranks on Seminary Ridge. He had staked everything on the attack that day, and now that it had failed, he came to the painful realization that his defeated army could no longer remain in enemy country. His campaign—his bold gamble north—was over, and he must now order a retreat. Already the soldiers of McLaws's and Hood's Divisions were falling back from their hard-earned positions on the army's right flank, abandoning the Peach Orchard and the rocky ground west of the Round Tops, while

Ewell's Second Corps slipped away from its positions in front of Culp's and Cemetery Hills and from the town itself, having been ordered to fall back to the bloodstained fields north and west of Gettysburg, where much of the first day's fight played out and where the carnage of that day's actions was very much still in evidence.

Lee's spirits were naturally down. Late that afternoon, as he rode along his army's thinned and broken lines, and even as the scattered survivors of the attack came limping back, the army commander happened upon the British officer Arthur Fremantle. "This has been a sad day to us, Colonel, a sad day," remarked Lee, "but we can't always expect to win victories." The army commander also allegedly counseled a shaken George Pickett, who, with tears streaming down his face, reported that his division had been destroyed. "Come, General Pickett, this has been my fight," Lee replied, "and upon my shoulders rests the blame."

Arriving at his headquarters around 1:00 a.m. on July 4, an exhausted Lee met with Brigadier General John Imboden, who commanded a brigade of cavalry. Summoned to headquarters several hours earlier, Imboden had since waited for the army commander's return. According to the cavalryman, General Lee's face "revealed an expression of sadness" that he had never seen before. Helping Lee dismount, Imboden tried to offer some consolation.

"General, this has been a hard day for you."

"Yes, it has been a sad, sad day to us," replied Lee, "Too bad, *too bad!* Oh, too bad."

Despite the pall that had fallen on Lee, there still remained much work to be done. Lee explained to Imboden that his brigade of some 2,200 relatively fresh horsemen would be tasked with escorting the army's wagon train of wounded back to Virginia. It promised to be an arduous journey, said Lee, and one that had to be carried out with vigilance. The army commander instructed Imboden to conduct the wagons westward and across South Mountain through Cashtown Pass; once he reached the village of Greenwood, he was to then turn south and make his way to Williamsport, Maryland, where he was to cross the Potomac before continuing south to Winchester.

While Imboden moved west and then south, Lee's main body—his three infantry corps and his artillery—would follow a more direct route, moving westerly through Fairfield and across South Mountain via Monterrey Pass. A journey of more than forty miles lay ahead for the Army of Northern Virginia before it would reach the Potomac. Lee was anxious to get moving, but he would need time to gather in as many of the wounded as possible

Roads South from Gettysburg

Brigadier General John Imboden was given the difficult task of escorting the Confederate wagon train of wounded from Gettysburg. *From* Miller's Photographic History of the Civil War.

and prepare for the long trip home. Until then, it would be necessary to prepare for an attack, in case George Meade decided to abandon his lines and launch an offensive action. That possibility, however, would remain to be seen on the morrow.

The rain let up some overnight, but it began to pick up once more around daybreak on July 4. That afternoon, thunderstorms rolled in and the rain fell heavily, flooding the creeks and waterways and making the already grim task of burying the dead that much more somber. For the many seriously wounded who still lay about the fields or outside hospital tents painfully awaiting treatment, the rain only added to their misery. The irony of it being Independence Day was not lost on the soldiers in either army. But even in the Army of the Potomac there would be no widespread celebrations that day, just a few small observances and the scattered playing of some national airs, which were at times drowned out by the rain and thunder and by the pitiful cries of the wounded. As one New York soldier rather matter-of-factly wrote to his mother that day, "[W]hile you were celebrating, we were busy burying the dead."

Early that Saturday morning, Union soldiers noticed that Lee's position had changed and that the Confederates had abandoned much of the ground they had occupied the day before. Reports of this came trickling into Union army headquarters, and Meade forwarded the information to Halleck, further notifying him that he was just then advancing pickets to "ascertain the nature and extent of the enemy's movement." Twelfth Corps soldiers probed into town from the east, while Eleventh Corps men crept in from the south. On the other end of the Union line, soldiers of the Fifth and Sixth Corps moved west from the Round Tops, advancing as far as the Emmitsburg Road, where they at last spotted the Confederate line further to their front and where they came under fire from a few Confederate batteries. At 11:00 a.m., Meade again wired Halleck, this time informing him that Lee had "thrown back his left, and placed guns and troops in position in rear of Gettysburg, which we now hold."

Meade was soon satisfied that Lee had taken up a defensive posture, correctly discerning that his opponent did not intend to attack that day. Meade also had no intention to launch an offensive action—a prudent decision considering the condition of his army, as well as what was still Lee's formidable position along Seminary Ridge. Having withstood a series of determined Confederate assaults over the previous two days, Meade was not about to abandon his strong defensive positions and attack across the same ground that had caused Lee so much grief. Instead, the day would be spent resting and refitting. As the fatigued army commander told Halleck, he needed some time "to get up supplies, ammunition, &c, [and to] rest the army, worn out by long marches and three days' hard fighting."

Many soldiers in both blue and gray had expected a renewal of hostilities that day; indeed, many in the Confederate army—still full of fight and believing themselves by no means "whipped"—were hoping that Meade would advance, expecting that they could easily repulse any Union attack, but Meade would not oblige. Except for some sporadic and sometimes deadly skirmish firing, the day was spent quietly, with the soldiers resting and writing letters home. Many helped to gather and care for the wounded, while others buried the dead.

Even for the veteran soldiers well accustomed to the wreckage and carnage of battle, the scarred landscape around Gettysburg presented a horrid spectacle. Sergeant Thomas Marbecker of the 11th New Jersey, a regiment that suffered more than 150 casualties in intense action on July 2, left a striking account of the battle's ghastly aftermath:

> *Upon the open fields, like sheaves bound by the reaper, in crevices of the rocks, behind fences, trees and buildings; in thickets; where they had crept*

for safety only to die in agony; by stream or wall or hedge, wherever the battle had raged or their weakening steps could carry them, lay the dead. Some, with faces bloated and blackened beyond recognition, lay with glassy eyes staring up at the blazing summer sun; others, with faces downward and clenched hands filled with grass or earth, which told of the agony of the last moments...All around was the wreck the battle-storm leaves in its wake—broken caissons, dismounted guns, small arms bent and twisted by the storm or dropped or scattered by disabled hands; dead and bloated horses, torn and ragged equipments, and all the sorrowful wreck that the waves of battle leave at their ebb; and over all, hugging the earth like a fog, poisoning every breath, the pestilential stench of decaying humanity.

The horrors of battle were especially evident on the fields of the first day's fight, where for three days the dead had lain, exposed to the hot July sun. Confederates from Ewell's corps spent that sullen July 4 on these same corpse-strewn fields. Robert Stiles, one of Ewell's artillerists, noted that he and his comrades were "sickened" by the sight and by the stench and that

A Timothy O'Sullivan photograph showing the wreckage and destruction at the Trostle barn, where Captain John Bigelow's 9th Massachusetts Battery made its heroic stand. *Library of Congress.*

The grim work of burying the dead began as soon as the guns fell silent. *Library of Congress*.

Union soldiers, killed in action on July 1, littered the fields west and north of town. It was a true "harvest of death." *Library of Congress*.

they spent the day "lying with our mouths close to the ground, most of us vomiting profusely."

The burying of the dead was a grim and immense undertaking, one that would continue for some time to come. One Ohio soldier told his family that he was a "pallbearer to the largest funeral I ever attended," as he helped to bury more than two hundred Confederates on Culp's Hill. "[T]he ground here is very hard," explained another Union solider, "full of rocks and stones, the digging is very laborious work, the dead are many, the time is short, so they got but very shallow graves." Some effort was made to identify the dead, particularly slain officers. Those who could be identified were typically given individual graves with makeshift headboards, inscribed with the soldier's name and regiment. Because the Union army ultimately held the field, a greater attempt was made at identifying the remains of its fallen comrades than those of its fallen foes. Those who could not be identified—the thousands of "unknowns"—were gathered and placed rather unceremoniously in long trenches, two or three feet deep.

"[T]he dead are laid out in long rows, with their naked faces turned up to the sun, their clothes stiff with the dried blood, and their features retaining in death the agony and pain which they died with," wrote a wounded and captured Confederate soldier, who watched as a Union burial party went about its work while awaiting treatment for his injury. The dead were

Confederate dead gathered for burial near Rose's Woods. *Library of Congress.*

"dragged forth and thrust into a shallow pit, with, perhaps, the coarse jest of a vulgar soldier for their requiem, and bloody blankets for their winding sheets. What a blessing it is," concluded the reflective warrior, "that the gentle and tender loved ones at homes are spared the sight of the last moments of their torn and mangled soldiers!"

The Army of Northern Virginia spent much of that Saturday, July 4, gathering as many of its wounded as possible and loading them on the wagons, which were being lined up for the long journey south. Some 4,500 of the more seriously wounded—those deemed too unfit to endure the rigors of the retreat—would be left behind, later falling into Union hands and treated for their wounds while prisoners of war.

Late that afternoon, the Confederate retreat from Gettysburg at last commenced when General Imboden set the army's wagon train of wounded in motion. As Lee had warned, Imboden did face a demanding mission. In a driving rain, which turned the roads into quagmires and the fields into swamps, Imboden and his troopers escorted hundreds of wagons westward, across South Mountain and then south toward Williamsport. Imboden later claimed that the wagon train, laden with more than eight thousand wounded men, stretched no less than seventeen miles in length, from the head of the column to its end. Along the route, many of the wagons got stuck in the mud and were abandoned. One of Imboden's troopers later recalled that it was the "saddest" of all the nights he spent in the war. "We were already sad and disheartened by our misfortune," stated the cavalryman, "and this mental condition was made worse by the thunder and lightning, and the great torrents of rain that came down, augmented by the horrible groans of the wounded and dying." Imboden agreed, later writing, "During this one night I realized more of the horrors of war than I had in all the preceding years." Many of the wounded Confederates being borne home died along the way. Their bodies were either left along the roadside or buried in unmarked graves.

Near sunset and just several hours after Imboden set off with the vast procession of wagons, the Confederate army began its march away from Gettysburg. A.P. Hill's men—those who had precipitated the brawl three days earlier—led the retreat, followed by Longstreet's thinned ranks and finally Ewell's men, who had seen more of central Pennsylvania than any other force of Lee's army during the campaign. Also marching with the column were thousands of Union prisoners, being guarded by the soldiers of Pickett's shattered division. Lee had hoped to unload this burden earlier that day when he proposed, under flag of truce, an exchange of prisoners, but Meade turned down Lee's request.

Roads South from Gettysburg

As Lee's men turned their backs on Gettysburg, many tried to make sense of the fight and come to grips with the defeat. A few placed the blame on Lee, especially for ordering the July 3 attack against the Federal center. One Confederate wrote that "it was the worst piece of generalship I ever knew General Lee to exercise, in undertaking to storm the enemy's fortifications." Another commented on Lee's faulty belief in the invincibility of his men and how it contributed to the defeat: "It will learn Gen Lee a lesson[;] he had too much confidence in his army [and] he thought there was no place but he could take." Yet an air of defiance still hovered over Lee's army, with many men refusing to believe that they had been whipped by their contemptuous Yankee foes. Even those who would admit to being defeated believed that they were bested not because of the fighting prowess of their opponents or even the exertions of the Federal brass but rather by the strong defensive positions they had held.

As Lee's men slipped away on their weary trek from Gettysburg, General George Meade met with his subordinates for another consultation. Earlier in the day, the Union army commander had issued a congratulatory order to his men, praising their hard work but also reminding them that there was still work to be done. "Our task is not yet accomplished," wrote Meade, "and the commanding general looks to the army for greater efforts to drive from our soil every vestige of the presence of the enemy." Meeting with his subordinates, Meade now sought their advice on how to best go about doing this. When the question was asked whether the Union army should hold its position the following day, all but three of Meade's generals answered affirmatively. When asked whether they should assume the offensive if Lee was discovered to still be holding his line, the answer was a unanimous "no."

If it was discovered that Lee was retreating—as Meade and others believed would be the case—the question then became how best to pursue. Of all those gathered, only David Birney, once more commanding the Third Corps in place of the wounded Sickles, wanted to directly follow on the heels of Lee's retreating columns; the others thought it more advisable to move south toward Frederick, Maryland, and then cut westward across South Mountain, with the hope of intercepting Lee's army before it could reach the Potomac. Only the cavalry, they agreed, should shadow Lee's movement. Although this would force the Army of the Potomac to cover much more ground than Lee's men, who now had the inside track to the Potomac, it would place the Union army between Lee and Washington, thus allowing Meade to cover the Federal capital in accordance with his instructions as army commander. Following Lee's army directly might also be dangerous,

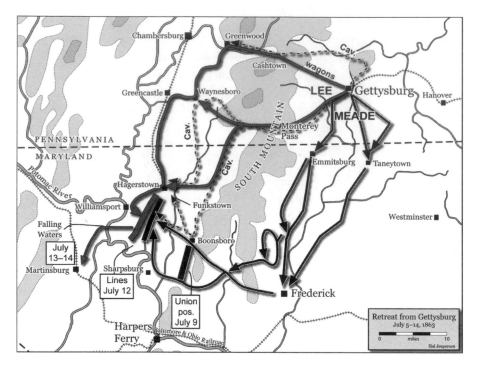

The roads south from Gettysburg. *Map by Hal Jespersen.*

the generals agreed, since it would allow Lee the opportunity to set up strong defensive positions at the South Mountain gaps. Meade would ultimately concur with the majority sentiment and adopt this course of action. First, though, he had to make sure that Lee was, in fact, retreating.

General John Sedgwick and the soldiers of his Sixth Corps conducted a reconnaissance in force early the following morning, July 5, which revealed that Lee had indeed fallen back. When he learned of this, Meade began preparing for the pursuit. He instructed Sedgwick to continue pushing on toward Fairfield to find out how far Lee's army had gone. Meanwhile, in an effort to better expedite the pursuit, Meade divided the army into three wings, naming Generals Sedgwick, Slocum and Howard as the wing commanders. Meade also directed General Alfred Pleasonton to put his horsemen in motion, with orders to "harass and annoy" the Confederates as much as possible during their retreat.

Various detachments of Union cavalry had already been annoying and harassing Imboden's wagon train of wounded. Imboden had hoped to move quickly to avoid any encounters, but on the morning of July 5, as the head of his train reached Greencastle, Pennsylvania, just a few miles north of the Mason-Dixon Line, a portion of his column was struck by a small force of Federal cavalrymen—one hundred men strong—under the command of Captain Ulric Dahlgren. A wild scene played out as Dahlgren's troopers came thundering along. The Union horsemen were assisted in their endeavor by a group of civilians that came out wielding axes, seeking to liberate some of the African Americans who had been rounded up by Lee's men in Pennsylvania and who were now being forced south to be sold into slavery. Between thirty and forty captured African American men and women did manage to flee, and some 130 Confederate wagons were damaged before two companies of 18th Virginia Cavalry appeared to drive Dahlgren and his civilian allies away.

Dahlgren's clash at Greencastle was not the only encounter with blue-clad horsemen that Imboden's column dealt with that day. Several hours later, at Cunningham's Crossroads just south of the Mason-Dixon Line in Maryland, a combined force of two hundred troopers of the 1st New York and 12th Pennsylvania Cavalry drove into the train, capturing more than 130 wagons, six hundred horses and mules, two cannons and nearly seven hundred Confederates, all at a loss of just three men killed or wounded.

Finally, on the afternoon of July 5, after a thoroughly exhausting ordeal, Imboden and the wagon train of wounded arrived in Williamsport. For the weary cavalryman, though, the situation only worsened once he got there. Surveying the river crossings, Imboden discovered that the heavy rains of the past few days had flooded the Potomac, thus making it impossible to cross. Imdoden further learned that the pontoon bridge that had stretched across the river several miles to the south had been destroyed. The previous morning, a detachment of Federal cavalry sent west from Frederick had driven off the Confederate defenders and set the pontoon bridge on fire. This meant that until the water receded or until a new pontoon could be constructed, the Confederates would not be able to cross the Potomac and were trapped on the Maryland side of the river. Realizing that Union cavalry was fast on his heels, Imboden immediately began preparing for a line of defense, organizing his horsemen and appealing to those of the wounded who felt capable of lending a hand.

The likelihood that the Potomac would be flooded because of the incessant rain was a thought on most everyone's mind and one that must have weighed particularly heavily on Robert E. Lee as his infantry continued to wind their way toward Williamsport. Meade considered this as well, knowing that it might force Lee to remain in Maryland longer than he would have liked.

As Meade's infantry readied for the pursuit, his horsemen were riding hard after Lee's retiring columns, following Pleasonton's instructions to annoy and harass the Confederates as much as possible. As far as the cavalry was concerned, what followed in the wake of Gettysburg was a weeklong series of skirmishes and sharp clashes, which one of Jeb Stuart's Confederate horsemen aptly labeled as "one continuous fight." During the overnight hours of July 5–6, in a driving rain and tremendous lightning storm, Kilpatrick's troopers attacked a portion of Lee's train at Monterrey Pass, during which the aggressive Union cavalier claimed to have captured 1,300 Confederates and hundreds of wagon at a cost of fewer than 50 casualties. Kilpatrick struck again on July 6, this time at Smithsburg and then later at Hagerstown, where he encountered a large force of Stuart's cavalry and even some Confederate infantry. After a desperate and deadly six-hour struggle, which included some street combat through the city, Kilpatrick ordered a retreat, directing his troopers south to link up with the three brigades of John Buford's division, which were just then engaged with Confederate horsemen from Imboden's and Grumble Jones's commands—plus some 700 of the Confederate wounded—near Williamsport itself. Soon after Kilpatrick's tired command arrived to augment Buford's force, however, a larger column of Confederate cavalry under Fitzhugh Lee reached the scene, galloping

The hard-charging Judson Kilpatrick. *Library of Congress.*

hard toward the Union right flank and rear. Kilpatrick pulled his men back, as did Buford; Williamsport was safe for the moment.

There would be even more action between the opposing cavalry forces in the days ahead, some quite spirited affairs, such as at Boonsboro on July 8 and at Funkstown on July 10, a battle that also involved some infantry forces on both sides. Through it all, and although the Army of Northern Virginia suffered a considerable number of casualties during its retreat from Gettysburg, Jeb Stuart and his horsemen turned in superb performances in both protecting Lee's infantry while they marched toward the Potomac and allowing the army commander time to construct a strong line of defense near Williamsport.

The main body of the Army of Northern Virginia had arrived in the area of Hagerstown and Williamsport on July 7–8. With the river flooded, Lee's immediate attention was naturally focused on establishing a strong defensive perimeter, as some of his men labored to complete a new pontoon bridge. And while Lee's men began taking up a new line of battle east of Williamsport, waiting for the waters of the Potomac to recede, the Army of the Potomac began its pursuit in earnest.

One Confederate cavalryman described the retreat from Gettysburg as "one continuous fight," marked by frequent encounters between Union and Confederate horsemen, as seen here in this drawing by Edwin Forbes. *Library of Congress.*

Artist Edwin Forbes's depiction of Union forces moving out in pursuit of Lee's retreating army in a driving rain. *Library of Congress.*

Meade's men had at last departed from Gettysburg, the army now divided into three columns, with each ordered to converge near Middletown, Maryland. They covered a lot of ground in a short time, marching much of the way through heavy rainstorms and over washed-out roadways nearly ankle-deep with mud. During the first few days of the pursuit, some elements of the Army of the Potomac covered more than twenty miles per day, others nearly thirty. Meade was marching his men hard, hoping to strike again before Lee could get across the river. Despite the wretched weather conditions, many in the Army of the Potomac marched with heads held high in the expectation that they would be able to deliver yet another blow to Lee's once seemingly invincible army and maybe even destroy the Army of Northern Virginia before it could get away.

Meade's superiors in Washington, both civilian and military, were hoping for as much. On July 7, Halleck wired the Union army commander with news that his "brilliant victory" at Gettysburg had earned him a promotion to the rank of brigadier general in the U.S. Regular Army. "You have given the enemy a stunning blow at Gettysburg," declared Halleck, who then urged him to "[f]ollow it up, and give him another before he can reach the Potomac." Lincoln was also hopeful that Meade would strike again, and after the president learned that Confederate forces under John Pemberton had surrendered, unconditionally, to Ulysses S. Grant on July 4 at Vicksburg, he was reportedly "beaming with joy." If Meade attacked again, thought Lincoln, the rebellion would finally be crushed.

Roads South from Gettysburg

George Meade arrived in Frederick on July 7, and he continued to receive dispatches from Washington, urging him not to let Lee get away. But Meade, more than anyone else, realized that this was something much easier said than done, particularly by those in the capital far removed from the front. The roads were in poor condition, and his soldiers were weary; plus, there were still two mountains to cross—the Catoctin and South Mountain ranges. Meade himself was thoroughly exhausted. His patience was wearing thin with the administration, believing that Lincoln, Halleck and Secretary of War Stanton did not understand the realities of the situation and may have been expecting too much from his much-reduced and worn-out army. In a letter penned on July 8 to his wife, Meade made known his mental and physical fatigue: "From the time I took command till today, now over ten days, I have not changed my clothes, have not had a regular night's rest and many nights not a wink of sleep, and for several days did not even wash my face and hands, no regular food, and all the time in a great state of mental anxiety." In that same letter, however, Meade predicted another fight "before Lee can cross the river."

The Army of the Potomac continued its pursuit of Lee. By July 9, most of it was across South Mountain and was gathering near the small village of Boonsboro. Pushing westward over the next few days, a part of the Union army passed the old battlegrounds near Sharpsburg on the west side of Antietam Creek as it continued to close in on the Confederates, still trapped by the river near Williamsport. The armies, it seemed, were set on yet another collision course, and both army commanders anticipated another great struggle. On July 9, Meade predicted to Halleck that "the decisive battle of the war will be fought in a few days."

Lee, too, anticipated a most "vigorous battle." With the Union army closing in—and as word of Pemberton's surrender and the loss of Vicksburg quickly spread through the ranks—Lee attempted to strengthen his soldiers' spirits and resolve. "Let every soldier remember that on his courage and fidelity depends all that makes life worth having—the freedom of his country, the honor of his people, and the security of his home," proclaimed the army commander. "Soldiers! Your old enemy is before you! Win from him honors worthy of your righteous cause—worthy of your comrades on so many illustrious fields." But these battle-hardened veterans needed little motivation; indeed, in their formidable defensive line, they were still full of fight and perhaps looking to reverse the tide from the defeat at Gettysburg one week earlier. Many of Lee's men hoped that Meade would attack, such as artillerist E. Porter Alexander, who later wrote, "Oh! how we all did wish that the enemy would come out in the open & attack us, as we had done them at Gettysburg."

The Army of the Potomac arrived opposite Lee's lines on July 12, and what the Union soldiers now saw confronting them dashed much of their eagerness for battle. Having had time to prepare, Lee's army was stretched out in an excellent defensive position running nearly six miles in length, north–south, with the army's left flank near Conococheague Creek, north of Williamsport, and its right near the Potomac River crossings at Falling Waters. The soldiers faced east across open plains and were positioned on a series of high ridges lined with artillery. Along some parts of the line, Confederates had dug trenches and erected parapets. Henry Abbott of the 20th Massachusetts recorded that the Confederate position "became identically that of ours at Gettysburg, & their ours," while another Union officer declared that Lee's defenses "were by far the strongest I have yet seen, evidently laid out by engineers, and built as if they meant to stand a month's siege." In such a formidable position, it is no wonder why so many of Lee's men were hoping that Meade would come out in the open and attack.

Meade wanted to attack, but after finding Lee in what he described as "a very strong position," he hesitated, rightly deciding to conduct a thorough examination of the Confederate line and its approaches. Still, he predicted battle. "[I]t is my intention to attack them tomorrow," the Union army commander declared to Halleck that Sunday night, "unless something intervenes to prevent it."

After wiring this message to Halleck, Meade summoned his chief lieutenants to headquarters for another consultation. The harried army commander, pressured by Washington to attack, admitted to his subordinates that he was not entirely sure of the layout of the Confederate lines but nevertheless made it known that he wanted to assume offensive actions the following day, with a reconnaissance in force, to be converted into a full-scale assault should a weakness in Lee's lines be detected. He had some supporters, including James Wadsworth, representing the First Corps; Oliver Howard, commanding the Eleventh Corps; cavalry chief Pleasonton; and Gouverneur Warren, the army's chief engineer. The commanders of Meade's four other corps, however—John Sedgwick, George Sykes, Henry Slocum and William Hays, commanding the Second Corps in place of the wounded Hancock and Gibbon—opposed such an action. From the looks of it, they argued, Lee had a formidable position and to attack without a firm understanding of the Confederate lines might result in disaster and jeopardize all that had been gained at Gettysburg. Having heard out the thoughts of his chief lieutenants, Meade conceded to those who argued against an attack the following day. Any offensive action would be delayed, Meade decided, until further reconnaissance can be conducted and until he can gain a better understanding of Lee's lines.

There was some light skirmishing on July 13, but things were otherwise quiet. Yet with each passing hour, as the Union army probed toward Lee's positions, the waters of the Potomac lowered while work was at last completed on a hastily constructed pontoon bridge at Falling Waters, which stretched some eight hundred feet across the river. If Meade wanted to strike again before the Confederate army escaped across the Potomac, time was quickly running out. On the other side of the lines, and despite being literally backed up to a river, Lee was so confident in the impregnable nature of his defensive position that he held out hope that the Army of the Potomac might still attack and that he could gain something from this campaign to help offset the disaster at Gettysburg. When no assault materialized, an irritated Lee allegedly snapped, "They have no courage!"

George Meade notified Washington of his consultation of the night before and his decision to delay the attack. Henry Halleck, anticipating an offensive action, could hardly disguise his frustration, famously wiring back to the army commander, "You are strong enough to attack and defeat the enemy before he can effect a crossing. Act upon your own judgment and make your generals execute your orders. Call no councils of war. It is proverbial that councils of war never fight." That night, Meade decided to follow through with his original intention and attack, sending out orders to his commanders to move forward at 7:00 a.m. the next day, July 14. But as Meade and the Army of the Potomac would discover, by then it would be too late.

While Meade prepared for an attack, the soldiers of Lee's bruised army slipped quietly across the Potomac. Ewell's men crossed at the ford near Williamsport, while Longstreet's command hobbled across the shaky pontoon bridge; by daybreak, Lee's cavalry and A.P. Hill's infantry were making their way across. It was a difficult and at times hazardous crossing, especially for those who waded through the waist-deep water by torchlight during the overnight hours. Still, by the morning of July 14, most of Lee's army was across.

On the southern end of the Confederate line, opposite Falling Waters, however, a portion of Lee's army—soldiers from Heth's and Pender's Divisions—remained on the Maryland side of the river, waiting for their turn to cross. Discovering this, Union cavalry general Buford planned an attack, but before he could carry it out, portions of Kilpatrick's command

Alfred Waud sketch of the July 14, 1863 Battle of Falling Waters, the final bloodletting of the Gettysburg Campaign. *Library of Congress*.

went galloping forward and struck the Confederates unawares. A South Carolina soldier recorded the riotous scene that followed as Union horsemen came crashing into the largely disorganized Confederate ranks: "The wildest excitement ensued. There was no time for arrangement, but every man must depend…on his own instincts. The enemy dashed in, firing pistols and sabering everything in their way…The din was horrible, the confusion inextricable. There was fighting, flying, shouting, robbing of dead men all at once."

Kilpatrick's forces, fed into the fight piecemeal, were repulsed with considerable loss. Buford's men next entered the fray, striking hard at portions of the isolated Confederate forces. Heth's and Pender's men were ultimately driven back to the river but not before scores of them had been killed or wounded and hundreds more captured. Among those struck down was General J. Johnston Pettigrew, shot through the stomach and fatally wounded. Under cover of artillery fire lining the west bank of the river, the Confederates scurried across the pontoon and by noon were fully across the Potomac. This sharp clash at Falling Waters was the final bloodletting of the Gettysburg Campaign.

Union soldiers advancing elsewhere found Lee's lines vacated—in places, their campfires were still burning. As was the case following Antietam ten months earlier, many of the boys in blue could not believe that Lee was able to slip away. Surgeon Henry van Aernam of the 154th New York could hardly contain his disgust, speaking for many when he reflected on the pursuit of Lee's army from Gettysburg:

When we were chasing the rebs, the boys, although barefooted and ragged and half-fed, were cheerful on their forced marches, but today they feel chagrined and humbugged. They are silent and morose and what little they say is damning the foolishness and shortsightedness of their officers. They are right, for they have endured everything, braved everything for the sake of success, and success beautiful and lasting was within their grasp—but lost by the imbecility of commandery. Our army is an anomaly, it is an army of Lions commanded by jackasses!

Another Union officer, frustrated that Lee had escaped and realizing that the war would continue, shouted to his men, "Another campaign along the Rappahannock, boys!"

Meade would face harsh criticisms in the days ahead, especially from newspaper editors and politicians in Washington. President Lincoln was "deeply grieved" when he learned of Lee's escape. To his personal secretary, Lincoln dejectedly stated, "We had them within our grasp. We had only to stretch forth our hands and they were ours." Halleck wired Meade, making known the president's dissatisfaction. Feeling unappreciated and angered over the criticisms from Washington, the army commander had had enough. To George McClellan, who led the Army of the Potomac to victory at Antietam only to be similarly criticized afterward for not attacking Lee before he could escape across the Potomac, Meade wrote on July 14, "Already I am beginning to feel the reaction, Lee having crossed the river last night without waiting for me to attack him in one of the strongest positions he had ever occupied."

Straddled with army command just two weeks earlier in the very midst of a campaign, with a Confederate army invading deep in Union territory and having just won one of the largest battles of the war, outgeneraling the renowned Robert E. Lee no less, a chagrined George Meade tendered his resignation. Halleck refused to accept it, and Meade would retain command of the Army of the Potomac for the duration of the war.

President Lincoln vented his disappointment in a letter addressed to Meade and written on the night of July 14. "I have just seen your dispatch to General Halleck, asking to be relieved of your command, because of some supposed censure of mine," wrote a more reflective Lincoln. "I am very—very—grateful to you for the magnificent success you gave the cause of the country at Gettysburg; and I am sorry now to be the author of the slightest pain to you." Still, the president lamented, "I do not believe you appreciate the magnitude of the misfortune involved in Lee's escape. He was

Photograph taken two months after Gettysburg of the Army of the Potomac's top brass. *From left to right*: Gouverneur K. Warren, William French, George Meade, Henry Hunt, Andrew Humphreys and George Sykes. *Library of Congress*.

within your easy grasp, and to have closed upon him would, in connection with our late successes [in Vicksburg], have ended the war. As is it the war will be prolonged indefinitely...Your golden opportunity is gone, and I am distressed immeasurably because of it." Finishing up his thoughts, Lincoln folded the letter, sealed it in an envelope and tucked it away in his desk. He never sent it.

For politicians and newspapermen, far removed from the front—and for historians, far removed from the time—commanding armies and fighting battles sometimes seem easy things to do. The truth of the matter was that there was no guarantee of victory had the Union army attacked at Williamsport, and the opportunity may not have been as golden as Lincoln assumed. And for every critic of George Meade, there were those who defended the general's decision to at least delay the attack, especially after having had time to survey Lee's now abandoned position. Many drew parallels between Lee's defenses there and those at Fredericksburg, where, seven months earlier, the Army of the Potomac had suffered heavily in a series of ill-fated assaults against a strongly entrenched Confederate army, with nothing to show for all the bloodshed. General Andrew Humphreys, Meade's new chief of staff, declared that Lee's Fredericksburg defenses "were not more formidable than those at Williamsport," while artillerist Henry Hunt concluded that "[a] careful survey of the enemy's intrenched line after it was abandoned justified the opinion of the corps commanders against an attack, as it showed that an assault would have been disastrous to us."

Meade's opponent, Robert E. Lee, would also face criticism in the wake of Gettysburg, though not nearly as heavily. Indeed, in that late summer of 1863, as the Confederacy reeled from its twin defeats at Gettysburg and at Vicksburg, most Southerners pointed to the latter as more devastating to their cause, and with good reason. The defeat of Lee's army at Gettysburg was dispiriting, but it was not nearly as crushing and important as the loss of Vicksburg.

The third week of July found Lee's army near Culpeper, Virginia, licking its wounds and preparing for the next campaign. To Jefferson Davis, Lee did his best at mitigating the damage. He allowed that he could be blamed "in perhaps expecting too much of [his soldiers'] prowess and valor," but the losses his army sustained at Gettysburg—which, he admitted, were heavy—were nevertheless not any higher than what he would have sustained had he never undertaken the campaign in the first place and had the two opposing armies remained battling it out in Virginia. Even though it met with defeat, the campaign, Lee reasoned, was one well worth taking and his strategy sound; it was just in the execution of his plans where his army came up short. Ever since the battle—in efforts at holding Lee blameless for the defeat—fingers have been pointed at almost all of his generals, placing blame on their shoulders for a long list of supposed failures and shortcomings: at Longstreet for dragging his heels; at Stuart for leaving Lee blind; at Ewell for not pressing the attack on Cemetery Hill on July 1; and at A.P. Hill and his generals for going against Lee's wishes and instigating the battle. And while fault may perhaps be found with the actions of these men, still, in the end, it was Lee's campaign and it was his battle; the defeat was his as well.

Like George Meade but for different reasons, Robert E. Lee also tendered his resignation in the wake of Gettysburg, citing declining health and believing that someone younger could better fill his position. But Jefferson Davis would hear none of it. "To ask me to substitute you by some one in my judgment more fit to command, or who would possess more of the confidence of the army, or of the reflecting men of the country," assuaged the Confederate president, "is to demand an impossibility." Lee would thus remain at the helm of the Army of Northern Virginia, as the hopes of the Confederacy continued to rest ever so heavily upon his shoulders and on those of his men.

CHAPTER NOTES

For further study of the retreat from Gettysburg, see Kent Masterson Brown's *Retreat from Gettysburg: Lee, Logistics, & the Pennsylvania Campaign* (2005) and *One Continuous Fight: The Retreat from Gettysburg and the Pursuit of Lee's Army of Northern Virginia, July 4–14, 1863* by Eric Wittenberg, J.D. Petruzzi and Mike Nugent. Also see Sears, chapter 14 (pages 459–514); Trudeau, chapters 15–17 (pages 530–55); and Coddington, chapter 20 (pages 535–74). For examinations of the grisly aftermath of the Battle of Gettysburg and the experiences endured by the people of town, see *A Strange and Blighted Land: Gettysburg: The Aftermath of a Battle* (1995) by Gregory Coco; *Debris of Battle: The Wounded of Gettysburg* (1997) by Gerard Patterson; *When the Smoke Cleared at Gettysburg: The Tragic Aftermath of the Bloodiest Battle of the Civil War* (2003) by George Sheldon; *The Colors of Courage: Gettysburg's Forgotten History: Immigrants, Women, and African-Americans in the Civil War's Defining Battle* (2005) by Margaret Creighton; *Days of "Uncertainty and Dread": The Ordeal Endured by the Citizens of Gettysburg* (1997) by Gerald Bennett; *African-Americans in the Gettysburg Campaign* (2005) by James Paradis; and *Gettysburg: A Journey in Time* (1975) by William A. Frassanito.

Order of Battle

FIRST CORPS
Maj. Gen. John Reynolds (k)
Maj. Gen. Abner Doubleday
Maj. Gen. John Newton

First Division
Brig. Gen. James Wadsworth

First Brigade
   Brig. Gen. Solomon Meredith (w)
   Col. William Robinson

   19th Indiana
   24th Michigan
   2nd Wisconsin
   6th Wisconsin
   7th Wisconsin

Second Brigade
   Brig. Gen. Lysander Cutler

   7th Indiana
   76th New York
   84th New York
   95th New York
   147th New York
   56th Pennsylvania

Second Division
Brig. Gen. John C. Robinson

First Brigade
    Brig. Gen. Gabriel Paul (w)
    Col. Samuel Leonard (w)
    Col. Adrian Root (w)
    Col. Richard Coulter
    Col. Peter Lyle

    16th Maine
    13th Massachusetts
    94th New York
    104th New York
    107th Pennsylvania

Second Brigade
    Brig. Gen. Henry Baxter

    12th Massachusetts
    83rd New York
    97th New York
    11th Pennsylvania
    88th Pennsylvania
    90th Pennsylvania

Third Division
Maj. Gen. Abner Doubleday
Brig. Gen. Thomas Rowley

First Brigade
    Brig. Gen. Thomas Rowley
    Col. Chapman Biddle

    80th New York
    121st Pennsylvania
    142nd Pennsylvania
    151st Pennsylvania

Second Brigade
    Col. Roy Stone (w)
    Col. Langhorne Wister (w)
    Col. Edmund Dana

    143rd Pennsylvania
    149th Pennsylvania
    150th Pennsylvania

Third Brigade
    Brig. Gen. George Stannard

    12th Vermont
    13th Vermont
    14th Vermont
    15th Vermont
    16th Vermont

First Corps Artillery Brigade
Col. Charles S. Wainwright

2nd Maine Light Artillery, Battery B: Capt. James Hall
5th Maine Light Artillery, Battery E: Capt. Greenleaf Stevens (w)
1st New York Light Artillery Batteries L and E: Capt. Gilbert Reynolds (w)
1st Pennsylvania Light Artillery: Battery B: Capt. James Cooper
4th U.S. Light Artillery, Battery B: Lt. James Stewart

SECOND CORPS
Maj. Gen. Winfield Scott Hancock (w)
Brig. Gen. John Gibbon (w)
Brig. Gen. John Caldwell

First Division
Brig. Gen. John Caldwell

First Brigade
    Col. Edward Cross (k)
    Col. H. Boyd McKeen

    5th New Hampshire
    61st New York
    81st Pennsylvania
    148th Pennsylvania

Second Brigade
    Col. Patrick Kelly

    28th Massachusetts
    63rd New York
    69th New York
    88th New York
    116th Pennsylvania

Third Brigade
    Col. Samuel Zook (k)
    Lt. Col. John Fraser

    52nd New York
    57th New York
    66th New York
    140th Pennsylvania

Fourth Brigade
    Col. John R. Brooke

    27th Connecticut
    2nd Delaware
    64th New York
    53rd Pennsylvania
    145th Pennsylvania

Second Division
Brig. Gen. John Gibbon (w)
Brig. Gen. William Harrow

First Brigade
    Brig. Gen. William Harrow
    Col. Francis Heath

    19th Maine
    15th Massachusetts
    1st Minnesota
    82nd New York

Second Brigade
    Brig. Gen. Alexander Webb

    69th Pennsylvania
    71st Pennsylvania
    72nd Pennsylvania
    106th Pennsylvania

Third Brigade
    Col. Norman Hall

    19th Massachusetts
    20th Massachusetts
    7th Michigan
    42nd New York
    59th New York

Third Division
Brig. Gen. Alexander Hays

First Brigade
    Col. Samuel S. Carroll

    14th Indiana
    4th Ohio
    8th Ohio
    7th West Virginia

Second Brigade
    Col. Thomas Smyth (w)
    Lt. Col. Francis Pierce

    14th Connecticut
    1st Delaware
    12th New Jersey
    10th New York Battalion
    108th New York

Third Brigade
    Col. George Willard (k)
    Col. Eliakim Sherrill (k)
    Col. Clinton McDougall (w)
    Lt. Col. James Bull

39th New York
111th New York
125th New York
126th New York

Second Corps Artillery Brigade
Capt. John Hazard

1st New York Light Artillery Battery B and 14th New York Light Artillery:
    Capt. James McKay Rorty (k)
1st Rhode Island Light Artillery, Battery A: Capt. William Arnold
1st Rhode Island Light Artillery, Battery B: Lt. T. Fred Brown (w)
1st U.S. Light Artillery, Battery I: Lt. George Woodruff (mw)
4th U.S. Light Artillery, Battery A: Lt. Alonzo Cushing (k)

THIRD CORPS
Maj. Gen. Daniel Sickles (w)
Maj. Gen. David B. Birney

First Division
Maj. Gen. David B. Birney
Brig. Gen. J.H. Hobart Ward (w)

First Brigade
    Brig. Gen. Charles Graham (c)
    Col. Andrew Tippin

    57th Pennsylvania
    63rd Pennsylvania
    68th Pennsylvania
    105th Pennsylvania
    114th Pennsylvania
    141st Pennsylvania

Second Brigade
    Brig. Gen. J.H.H. Ward (w)
    Col. Hiram Berdan

    20th Indiana
    3rd Maine
    4th Maine
    86th New York
    124th New York
    99th Pennsylvania
    1st U.S. Sharpshooters
    2nd U.S. Sharpshooters

Third Brigade
    Col. P. Regis de Trobriand

    17th Maine
    3rd Michigan
    5th Michigan
    40th New York
    110th Pennsylvania

Second Division
Brig. Gen. Andrew Humphreys

First Brigade
    Brig. Gen. Joseph Carr

    1st Massachusetts
    11th Massachusetts
    16th Massachusetts
    12th New Hampshire
    11th New Jersey
    26th Pennsylvania
    84th Pennsylvania

Second Brigade
    Col. William Brewster

    70th New York
    71st New York
    72nd New York
    73rd New York
    74th New York
    120th New York

Third Brigade
    Col. George Burling

    2nd New Hampshire
    5th New Jersey
    6th New Jersey
    7th New Jersey
    8th New Jersey
    115th Pennsylvania

Third Corps Artillery Brigade
    Captain George Randolph

    1st New Jersey Light Artillery, 2nd Battery B: Capt. Judson Clark
    1st New York Light Artillery Battery D: Capt. George Winslow
    New York Light Artillery, 4th Battery: Capt. James Smith
    1st Rhode Island Light Artillery, Battery E: Lt. John Bucklyn (w)
    4th U.S. Light Artillery, Battery K: Lt. Francis Seeley (w)

FIFTH CORPS
Maj. Gen. George Sykes

First Division
Brig. Gen. James Barnes

First Brigade
   Col. William Tilton

   18th Massachusetts
   22nd Massachusetts
   1st Michigan
   118th Pennsylvania

Second Brigade
   Col. Jacob Sweitzer

   9th Massachusetts
   32nd Massachusetts
   4th Michigan
   62nd Pennsylvania

Third Brigade
   Col. Strong Vincent (mw)
   Col. James Rice

   20th Maine
   16th Michigan
   44th New York
   83rd Pennsylvania

Second Division
Brig. Gen. Romeyn Ayres

First Brigade
   Col. Hannibal Day

   3rd United States
   4th United States
   6th United States
   12th United States
   14th United States

Second Brigade
   Col. Sidney Burbank

   2nd United States
   7th United States
   10th United States
   11th United States
   17th United States

Third Brigade
   Brig. Gen. Stephen Weed (k)
   Col. Kenner Garrard

   140th New York
   146th New York
   91st Pennsylvania
   155th Pennsylvania

Third Division
Brig. Gen. Samuel W. Crawford

First Brigade
   Col. William McCandless

   1st Pennsylvania Reserves
   2nd Pennsylvania Reserves
   6th Pennsylvania Reserves
   13th Pennsylvania Reserves

Third Brigade
   Col. Joseph Fisher

   5th Pennsylvania Reserves
   9th Pennsylvania Reserves
   10th Pennsylvania Reserves
   11th Pennsylvania Reserves
   12th Pennsylvania Reserves

Fifth Corps Artillery Brigade
   Captain Augustus Martin

   Massachusetts Light Artillery, 3rd Battery C: Lt. Aaron Walcott
   1st New York Light Artillery, Battery C: Capt. Almont Barnes
   1st Ohio Light Artillery, Battery L: Capt. Frank Gibbs
   5th U.S. Light Artillery, Battery D: Lt. Charles Hazlett (k)
   5th U.S. Light Artillery, Battery I: Lt. Malbone Watson (w)

SIXTH CORPS
Maj. Gen. John Sedgwick

First Division
Brig. Gen. Horatio Wright

First Brigade
   Brig. Gen. Alfred Torbert

   1st New Jersey
   2nd New Jersey
   3rd New Jersey
   15th New Jersey

Second Brigade
   Brig. Gen. Joseph Bartlett

   5th Maine
   121st New York
   95th Pennsylvania
   96th Pennsylvania

Third Brigade
   Brig. Gen. David Russell

   6th Maine
   49th Pennsylvania
   119th Pennsylvania
   5th Wisconsin

Second Division
Brig. Gen. Albion Howe

First Brigade
  Col. Lewis Grant

    2nd Vermont
    3rd Vermont
    4th Vermont
    5th Vermont
    6th Vermont

Second Brigade
  Brig. Gen. Thomas Neill

    7th Maine
    33rd New York
    43rd New York
    49th New York
    77th New York
    61st Pennsylvania

Third Division
Maj. Gen. John Newton
Brig. Gen. Frank Wheaton

First Brigade
  Brig. Gen. Alexander Shaler

    65th New York
    67th New York
    122nd New York
    23rd Pennsylvania
    82nd Pennsylvania

Second Brigade
  Col. Henry Eustis

    7th Massachusetts
    10th Massachusetts
    37th Massachusetts
    2nd Rhode Island

Third Brigade
  Brig. Gen. Frank Wheaton
  Col. David Nevin

    62nd New York
    93rd Pennsylvania
    98th Pennsylvania
    102nd Pennsylvania
    139th Pennsylvania

Sixth Corps Artillery Brigade
Col. Charles H. Tompkins

Massachusetts Light Artillery, 1st Battery A: Capt. William McCartney
New York Light Artillery, 1st Battery: Capt. Andrew Cowan
New York Light Artillery, 3rd Battery: Capt. William Harn
1st Rhode Island Light Artillery, Battery C: Capt. Richard Waterman
1st Rhode Island Light Artillery, Battery G: Capt. George W. Adams
2nd U.S. Light Artillery, Battery D: Lt. Edward Williston
2nd U.S. Light Artillery, Battery G: Lt. John Butler
5th U.S. Light Artillery, Battery F: Lt. Leonard Martin

ELEVENTH CORPS
Maj. Gen. Oliver Howard
Maj. Gen. Carl Schurz

First Division
Brig. Gen. Francis Barlow (w)
Brig. Gen. Adelbert Ames

First Brigade
 Col. Leopold von Gilsa

  41st New York
  54th New York
  68th New York
  153rd Pennsylvania

Second Brigade
 Brig. Gen. Adelbert Ames
 Col. Andrew Harris

  17th Connecticut
  25th Ohio
  75th Ohio
  107th Ohio

Second Division
Brig. Gen. Adolph von Steinwehr

First Brigade
 Col. Charles Coster

  134th New York
  154th New York
  27th Pennsylvania
  73rd Pennsylvania

Second Brigade
 Col. Orland Smith

  33rd Massachusetts
  136th New York
  55th Ohio
  73rd Ohio

Third Division
Maj. Gen. Carl Schurz
Brig. Gen. Alexander Schimmelfennig

First Brigade | Second Brigade
Brig. Gen. Alexander Schimmelfennig | Col. Wladimir Krzyzanowski
Col. George von Amsberg

82nd Illinois   58th New York

45th New York   119th New York

157th New York   82nd Ohio

61st Ohio   75th Pennsylvania

74th Pennsylvania   26th Wisconsin

Eleventh Corps Artillery Brigade
Maj. Thomas W. Osborn

1st New York Light Artillery, Battery I: Capt. Michael Wiedrich
New York Light Artillery, 13th Battery: Lt. William Wheeler
1st Ohio Light Artillery, Battery I: Capt. Hubert Dilger
1st Ohio Light Artillery, Battery K: Capt. Lewis Heckman
4th U.S. Light Artillery, Battery G: Lt. Bayard Wilkeson (mw)

TWELFTH CORPS
Maj. Gen. Henry Slocum
Brig. Gen. Alpheus Williams

First Division
Brig. Gen. Alpheus Williams
Brig. Gen. Thomas Ruger

First Brigade | Second Brigade
Col. Archibald McDougall | Brig. Gen. Henry Lockwood

5th Connecticut   1st Maryland (Eastern Shore)

20th Connecticut   1st Maryland (Potomac Home Brig)

3rd Maryland   150th New York

123rd New York

145th New York

46th Pennsylvania

Third Brigade
  Brig. Gen. Thomas Ruger
  Col. Silas Colgrove

  27th Indiana
  2nd Massachusetts
  13th New Jersey
  107th New York
  3rd Wisconsin

Second Division
Brig. Gen. John W. Geary

First Brigade
  Col. Charles Candy

  5th Ohio
  7th Ohio
  29th Ohio
  66th Ohio
  28th Pennsylvania
  147th Pennsylvania

Second Brigade
  Col. George Cobham Jr.
  Brig. Gen. Thomas Kane

  29th Pennsylvania
  109th Pennsylvania
  111th Pennsylvania

Third Brigade
  Brig. Gen. George Greene

  60th New York
  78th New York
  102nd New York
  137th New York
  149th New York

Twelfth Corps Artillery Brigade
  Lt. Edward Muhlenberg

  1st New York Light Artillery Battery M: Lt. Charles Winegar
  Pennsylvania Light Artillery, Battery E: Lt. Charles Atwell
  4th U.S. Light Artillery, Battery F: Lt. Sylvanus Rugg
  5th U.S. Light Artillery, Battery K: Lt. David Kinzie

ARMY OF THE POTOMAC ARTILLERY RESERVE
Brig. Gen. Robert O. Tyler
Capt. James Robertson

First Regular Brigade
  Capt. Dunbar Ransom

  1st U.S. Light Artillery, Battery H: Lt. Chandler Eakin (w)
  3rd U.S. Light Artillery, Batteries F and K: Lt. John Turnbull
  4th U.S. Light Artillery, Battery C: Lt. Evan Thomas
  5th U.S. Light Artillery, Battery C: Lt. Gulian Weir

First Volunteer Brigade
  Lt. Col. Freeman McGilvery

  Massachusetts Light Artillery, 5th Battery E: Capt. Charles Phillips
  Massachusetts Light Artillery, 9th Battery: Capt. John Bigelow (w)
  New York Light Artillery, 15th Battery: Capt. Patrick Hart (w)
  1st Pennsylvania Light Artillery, Batteries C and F: Capt. James Thompson

Second Volunteer Brigade
  Capt. Elijah Taft

  1st Connecticut Heavy Artillery, Battery B: Capt. Albert Brooker
  1st Connecticut Heavy Artillery, Battery M: Capt. Franklin Pratt
  Connecticut Light Artillery, 2nd Battery: Capt. John Sterling
  New York Light Artillery, 5th Battery: Capt. Elijah Taft

Third Volunteer Brigade
  Capt. James F. Huntington

  New Hampshire Light Artillery, 1st Battery: Capt. Frederick Edgell
  1st Ohio Light Artillery, Battery H: Lt. George W. Norton
  1st Pennsylvania Light Artillery, Batteries F and G: Capt. R. Bruce Ricketts
  West Virginia Light Artillery, Battery C: Capt. Wallace Hill

Fourth Volunteer Brigade
Capt. Robert Fitzhugh

Maine Light Artillery, 6th Battery F: Lt. Edwin Dow
Maryland Light Artillery, Battery A: Capt. James Rigby
1st New Jersey Light Artillery, Battery A: Lt. Augustus Parsons
1st New York Light Artillery, Battery G: Capt. Nelson Ames
1st New York Light Artillery Battery K/11th Battery: Capt. Robert Fitzhugh

CAVALRY CORPS
Maj. Gen. Alfred Pleasonton

First Division
Brig. Gen. John Buford

First Brigade
  Col. William Gamble

  8th Illinois Cavalry
  12th Illinois Cavalry
  3rd Indiana Cavalry
  8th New York Cavalry

Second Brigade
  Col. Thomas Devin

  6th New York Cavalry
  9th New York Cavalry
  17th Pennsylvania Cavalry
  3rd West Virginia Cavalry

Third Brigade
  Brig. Gen. Wesley Merritt

  6th Pennsylvania Cavalry
  1st U.S. Cavalry
  2nd U.S. Cavalry
  5th U.S. Cavalry
  6th U.S. Cavalry

Second Division
Brig. Gen. David Gregg

First Brigade
  Col. John McIntosh

  1st Maryland Cavalry
  Purnell (Maryland) Legion (Company A)
  1st Massachusetts Cavalry
  1st New Jersey Cavalry

Second Brigade
  Col. Pennock Huey

  2nd New York Cavalry
  4th New York Cavalry
  6th Ohio Cavalry
  8th Pennsylvania Cavalry

1st Pennsylvania Cavalry
3rd Pennsylvania Cavalry
3rd Pennsylvania Heavy Artillery, Battery H

Third Brigade
  Col. J. Irvin Gregg

  1st Maine Cavalry
  10th New York Cavalry
  4th Pennsylvania Cavalry
  16th Pennsylvania Cavalry

Third Division
Brig. Gen. Judson Kilpatrick

First Brigade
  Brig. Gen. Elon Farnsworth (k)
  Col. Nathaniel Richmond

  5th New York Cavalry
  18th Pennsylvania Cavalry
  1st Vermont Cavalry
  1st West Virginia Cavalry

Second Brigade
  Brig. Gen. George Custer

  1st Michigan Cavalry
  5th Michigan Cavalry
  6th Michigan Cavalry
  7th Michigan Cavalry

First Horse Artillery Brigade
  Capt. James Robertson

  9th Michigan Light Artillery
  6th New York Light Artillery
  2nd U.S. Light Artillery, Batteries B and L
  2nd U.S. Light Artillery, Battery M
  4th U.S. Light Artillery, Battery E

Second Horse Artillery Brigade
  Capt. John Tidball

  1st U.S. Light Artillery, Batteries E and G
  1st U.S. Light Artillery, Battery K
  2nd U.S. Light Artillery, Battery A
  3rd U.S. Light Artillery, Battery C

ORDER OF BATTLE

Army of Northern Virginia
Gen. Robert E. Lee

First Corps
Lt. Gen. James Longstreet

McLaws's Division
Maj. Gen. Lafayette McLaws

Kershaw's Brigade
  Brig. Gen. Joseph Kershaw

    2nd South Carolina
    3rd South Carolina
    3rd South Carolina Battalion
    7th South Carolina
    8th South Carolina
    15th South Carolina

Semmes's Brigade
  Brig. Gen. Paul Semmes (mw)
  Col. Goode Bryan

    10th Georgia
    50th Georgia
    51st Georgia
    53rd Georgia

Barksdale's Brigade
  Brig. Gen. William Barksdale (mw)
  Col. Benjamin Humphreys

    13th Mississippi
    17th Mississippi
    18th Mississippi
    21st Mississippi

Wofford's Brigade
  Brig. Gen. William Wofford

    3rd Georgia Battalion
      Sharpshooters
    16th Georgia
    18th Georgia
    24th Georgia
    Cobb's (Georgia) Legion
    Phillips' (Georgia) Legion

Artillery Battalion
  Col. Henry C. Cabell

    1st North Carolina Light Artillery, Battery A: Capt. Basil Manly
    Pulaski (Georgia) Artillery: Capt. John Fraser (mw)
    1st Richmond Howitzers: Capt. Edward McCarthy (w)
    Troup (Georgia) Artillery: Capt. Henry Carlton (w)

Pickett's Division
Maj. Gen. George Pickett

Garnett's Brigade
    Brig. Gen. Richard Garnett (k)
    Maj. Charles Peyton

    8th Virginia
    18th Virginia
    19th Virginia
    28th Virginia
    56th Virginia

Kemper's Brigade
    Brig. Gen. James Kemper (w)
    Col. Joseph Mayo Jr.

    1st Virginia
    3rd Virginia
    7th Virginia
    11th Virginia
    24th Virginia

Armistead's Brigade
    Brig. Gen. Lewis Armistead (mw)
    Col. William Aylett

    9th Virginia
    14th Virginia
    38th Virginia
    53rd Virginia
    57th Virginia

Artillery Battalion
    Maj. James Dearing

    Fauquier (Virginia) Artillery: Capt. Robert Stribling
    Hampden (Virginia) Artillery: Capt. William Caskie
    Richmond Fayette Artillery: Capt. Miles Macon
    Lynchburg (Virginia) Artillery: Capt. Joseph Blount

Hood's Division
Maj. Gen. John Bell Hood (w)
Brig. Gen. Evander Law

Law's Brigade
    Brig. Gen. Evander Law
    Col. James Sheffield

    4th Alabama
    15th Alabama
    44th Alabama
    47th Alabama
    48th Alabama

Robertson's Brigade
    Brig. Gen. Jerome Robertson

    3rd Arkansas
    1st Texas
    4th Texas
    5th Texas

G.T. Anderson's Brigade
  Brig. Gen. George T. Anderson (w)
  Lt. Col. William Luffman (w)

  7th Georgia
  8th Georgia
  9th Georgia
  11th Georgia
  59th Georgia

Benning's Brigade
  Brig. Gen. Henry Benning

  2nd Georgia
  15th Georgia
  17th Georgia
  20th Georgia

Artillery Battalion
  Maj. Mathis Henry

  Branch (North Carolina) Artillery: Capt. Alexander Latham
  German (South Carolina) Artillery: Capt. William Bachman
  Palmetto (South Carolina) Artillery: Capt. Hugh Garden
  Rowan (North Carolina) Artillery: Capt. James Reilly

First Corps Artillery Reserve
  Col. James Walton

  Alexander's Battalion
  Col. Edward P. Alexander

  Ashland (Virginia) Artillery: Capt. Pichegru Woolfolk Jr. (w)
  Bedford (Virginia) Artillery: Capt. Tyler Jordan
  Brooks (South Carolina) Artillery: Lt. S. Capers Gilbert
  Madison (Louisiana) Artillery: Capt. George Moody
  Virginia (Richmond) Battery: Capt. William W. Parker
  Virginia (Bath) Artillery: Capt. Osmund Taylor

Washington (Louisiana) Artillery
  Maj. Benjamin Eshelman

  1st Company: Capt. Charles Squire
  2nd Company: Capt. John B. Richardson
  3rd Company: Capt. Merritt Miller
  4th Company: Capt. Joseph Norcum (w)

SECOND CORPS
Lt. Gen. Richard Ewell

Early's Division
Maj. Gen. Jubal Early

Hays's Brigade	Smith's Brigade
Brig. Gen. Harry Hays	Brig. Gen. William Smith

5th Louisiana	31st Virginia
6th Louisiana	49th Virginia
7th Louisiana	52nd Virginia
8th Louisiana	
9th Louisiana	

Hoke's Brigade	Gordon's Brigade
Col. Isaac Avery (k)	Brig. Gen. John B. Gordon
Col. Archibald Godwin	

6th North Carolina	13th Georgia
21st North Carolina	26th Georgia
57th North Carolina	31st Georgia
	38th Georgia
	60th Georgia
	61st Georgia

Artillery Battalion
Lt. Col. Hilary Jones

Charlottesville (Virginia) Artillery: Capt. James Carrington
Courtney (Virginia) Artillery: Capt. William Tanner
Louisiana Guard Artillery: Capt. Charles Green
Staunton (Virginia) Artillery: Capt. Asher Garber

Rodes's Division
Maj. Gen. Robert Rodes

Daniel's Brigade	Iverson's Brigade
Brig. Gen. Junius Daniel	Brig. Gen. Alfred Iverson

2nd North Carolina Battalion	5th North Carolina
32nd North Carolina	12th North Carolina
43rd North Carolina	20th North Carolina
45th North Carolina	23rd North Carolina
53rd North Carolina	

Doles's Brigade
 Brig. Gen. George Doles

 4th Georgia
 12th Georgia
 21st Georgia
 44th Georgia

O'Neal's Brigade
 Col. Edward O'Neal

 3rd Alabama
 5th Alabama
 6th Alabama
 12th Alabama
 26th Alabama

Artillery Battalion
 Lt. Col. Thomas Carter

 Jeff Davis (Alabama) Artillery: Capt. William J. Reese
 King William (Virginia) Artillery: Capt. William Carter
 Morris (Virginia) Artillery Capt. Richard Page (w)
 Orange (Virginia) Artillery: Capt. Charles Fry

Johnson's Division
Maj. Gen. Edward Johnson

Steuart's Brigade
 Brig. Gen. George Steuart

 1st Maryland Battalion
 1st North Carolina
 3rd North Carolina
 10th Virginia
 23rd Virginia
 37th Virginia

Ramseur's Brigade
 Brig. Gen. Stephen Ramseur

 2nd North Carolina
 4th North Carolina
 14th North Carolina
 30th North Carolina

Nicholl's Brigade
 Col. Jesse Williams

 1st Louisiana
 2nd Louisiana
 10th Louisiana
 14th Louisiana
 15th Louisiana

Walker's (Stonewall) Brigade
  Brig. Gen. James Walker

2nd Virginia
4th Virginia
5th Virginia
17th Virginia
33rd Virginia

Jones's Brigade
  Brig. Gen. John M. Jones (w)
  Lt. Col. Robert Dungan

21st Virginia
25th Virginia
42nd Virginia
44th Virginia
48th Virginia
50th Virginia

Artillery Battalion
  Maj. James Latimer (mw)
  Capt. Charles Raine

  1st Maryland Battery: Capt. William Dement
  Alleghany (Virginia) Artillery: Capt. John Carpenter
  Chesapeake (Maryland) Artillery: Capt. William Brown (w)
  Lee (Virginia) Battery: Capt. Charles Raine

Second Corps Artillery Reserve
  Col. J. Thompson Brown

First Virginia Artillery
  Capt. Willis Dance

  2nd Richmond (Virginia) Howitzers: Capt. David Watson
  3rd Richmond (Virginia) Howitzers: Capt. Benjamin Smith Jr.
  Powhatan (Virginia) Artillery: Lt. John Cunningham
  Rockbridge (Virginia) Artillery: Capt. Archibald Graham
  Salem (Virginia) Artillery: Lt. Charles Griffin

Nelson's Battalion
  Lt. Col. William Nelson

  Amherst (Virginia) Battery: Capt. Thomas Kirkpatrick
  Fluvanna (Virginia) Artillery: Capt. John Massie
  Georgia Battery: Capt. John Milledge

THIRD CORPS
Lt. Gen. Ambrose P. Hill

Anderson's Division
Maj. Gen. Richard H. Anderson

Wilcox's Brigade
  Brig. Gen. Cadmus Wilcox

    8th Alabama
    9th Alabama
    10th Alabama
    11th Alabama
    14th Alabama

Mahone's Brigade
  Brig. Gen. William Mahone

    6th Virginia
    12th Virginia
    16th Virginia
    41st Virginia
    61st Virginia

Posey's Brigade
  Brig. Gen. Carnot Posey

    12th Mississippi
    16th Mississippi
    19th Mississippi
    48th Mississippi

Artillery Battalion
Sumter Battalion
  Maj. John Lane

    Company A: Capt. Hugh Ross
    Company B: Capt. George Patterson
    Company C: Capt. John Wingfield (w)

Wright's Brigade
  Brig. Gen. Ambrose Wright

    2nd Georgia Battalion
    3rd Georgia
    22nd Georgia
    48th Georgia

Perry's Brigade
  Col. David Lang

    2nd Florida
    5th Florida
    8th Florida

Heth's Division
Maj. Gen. Henry Heth (w)
Brig. Gen. J. Johnston Pettigrew (w)

First Brigade
    Brig. Gen. J. Johnston Pettigrew (w)
    Col. James Marshall (k)
    Maj. John T. Jones

    11th North Carolina
    26th North Carolina
    47th North Carolina
    52nd North Carolina

Second Brigade
    Col. John Brockenbrough

    22nd Virginia Battalion
    40th Virginia
    47th Virginia
    55th Virginia

Third Brigade
    Brig. Gen. James Archer (c)
    Col. Birkett D. Fry (w)
    Lt. Col. Samuel Shepard

    5th Alabama Battalion
    13th Alabama
    1st Tennessee (Provisional Army)
    7th Tennessee
    14th Tennessee

Fourth Brigade
    Brig. Gen. Joseph Davis

    2nd Mississippi
    11th Mississippi
    42nd Mississippi
    55th North Carolina

Artillery Battalion
    Lt. Col. John Garnett

    Donaldsville (Louisiana) Artillery: Capt. Victor Maurin
    Huger (Virginia) Artillery: Capt. Joseph Moore
    Lewis (Virginia) Artillery: Capt. John Lewis
    Norfolk (Virginia) Light Artillery Blues: Capt. Charles Grandy

Pender's Division
Maj. Gen. William Dorsey Pender (mw)
Brig. Gen. James Lane
Maj. Gen. Isaac R. Trimble (w)

First Brigade
    Col. Abner Perrin

Second Brigade
    Brig. Gen. James Lane
    Col. Clark Avery

1st South Carolina (Provisional Army)
1st South Carolina Rifles
12th South Carolina
13th South Carolina
14th South Carolina

7th North Carolina
18th North Carolina
28th North Carolina
33rd North Carolina
37th North Carolina

Third Brigade
    Brig. Gen. Edward Thomas

Fourth Brigade
    Brig. Gen. Alfred Scales (w)
    Lt. Col. G.T. Gordon
    Col. W. Lee J. Lowrance

14th Georgia
35th Georgia
45th Georgia
49th Georgia

13th North Carolina
16th North Carolina
22nd North Carolina
34th North Carolina
38th North Carolina

Artillery Battalion
    Maj. William Poague

    Albemarle (Virginia) Artillery: Capt. James Wyatt
    Charlotte (North Carolina) Artillery: Capt. Joseph Graham
    Madison (Mississippi) Light Artillery: Capt. George Ward
    Virginia (Warrington) Battery: Capt. James Brooke

Third Corps Artillery Reserve
Col. Reuben Lindsay Walker

McIntosh's Battalion
    Maj. D.G. McIntosh

    Danville (Virginia) Artillery: Capt. Sidney Rice
    Hardaway (Alabama) Artillery: Capt. William Hurt
    2nd Rockbridge (Virginia) Artillery: Lt. Samuel Wallace
    Virginia (Richmond) Battery: Capt. Marmaduke Johnson

Pegram's Battalion
  Maj. William Pegram

  Crenshaw (Virginia) Battery: Capt. William Crenshaw
  Fredericksburg (Virginia) Artillery: Capt. Edward Marye
  Letcher (Virginia) Artillery: Capt. Thomas Brander
  Pee Dee (South Carolina) Artillery: Capt. Ervin Brunson
  Purcell (Virginia) Artillery: Capt. Joseph McGraw

CAVALRY DIVISION
Maj. Gen. Jeb Stuart

Hampton's Brigade
  Brig. Gen. Wade Hampton (w)
  Col. Laurence Baker

  1st North Carolina Cavalry
  1st South Carolina Cavalry
  2nd South Carolina Cavalry
  Cobb's (Georgia) Legion Cavalry
  Jeff Davis (Mississippi) Legion Cavalry
  Phillips's (Georgia) Legion Cavalry

Fitzhugh Lee's Brigade
  Brig. Gen. W. Fitzhugh Lee

  1st Maryland Battalion Cavalry
  1st Virginia Cavalry
  2nd Virginia Cavalry
  3rd Virginia Cavalry
  4th Virginia Cavalry
  5th Virginia Cavalry

Jenkins's Brigade
  Brig. Gen. Albert Jenkins (w)
  Col. Milton Ferguson

  14th Virginia Cavalry
  16th Virginia Cavalry
  17th Virginia Cavalry
  34th Virginia Battalion Cavalry

W.H.F. Lee's Brigade
  Col. John Chambliss Jr.

  2nd North Carolina Cavalry
  9th Virginia Cavalry
  10th Virginia Cavalry
  13th Virginia Cavalry

Imboden's Brigade
  Brig. Gen. John Imboden

  18th Virginia Cavalry
  62nd Virginia Mounted Infantry
  Virginia Partisan Rangers
  Virginia (Staunton) Battery

Robertson's Brigade
  Brig. Gen. Beverly Robertson

  4th North Carolina Cavalry
  5th North Carolina Cavalry

Jones's Brigade
    Brig. Gen. William E. Jones

    6th Virginia Cavalry
    7th Virginia Cavalry
    11th Virginia Cavalry

Stuart Horse Artillery
    Maj. Robert Beckham

    Breathed's (Virginia) Battery: Capt. James Breathed
    Chew's (Virginia) Battery: Capt. R. Preston Chew
    Griffin's (Maryland) Battery: Capt. William Griffin
    Hart's (South Carolina) Battery: Capt. James Hart
    McGregor's (Virginia) Battery: Capt. William McGregor
    Moorman's (Virginia) Battery

Selected Bibliography

By no means exhaustive, this bibliography is simply a listing of those secondary sources most frequently consulted in the researching and writing of this book.

Adelman, Garry E. *The Myth of Little Round Top*. Gettysburg, PA: Thomas Publications, 2003.

Adelman, Garry E., and Timothy H. Smith. *Devil's Den: A History and Guide*. Gettysburg, PA: Thomas Publications, 1997.

Archer, John M. *Culp's Hill at Gettysburg: "The Mountain Trembled."* Gettysburg, PA: Ten Roads Publishing, 2011.

———. *"The Hour Was One of Horror": East Cemetery Hill at Gettysburg*. Gettysburg, PA: Thomas Publications, 2002.

Bennett, Gerald R. *Days of "Uncertainty and Dread": The Ordeal Endured by the Citizens of Gettysburg*. Littlestown, PA: Gerald Bennett, 1997.

Boritt, Gabor S. *The Gettysburg Gospel: The Lincoln Speech that Nobody Knows*. New York: Simon and Schuster, 2008.

Boritt, Gabor S., ed. *The Gettysburg Nobody Knows*. New York: Oxford University Press, 1997.

Brown, Kent Masterson. *Retreat from Gettysburg: Lee, Logistics, & the Pennsylvania Campaign*. Chapel Hill: University of North Carolina Press, 2005.

Busey, John W., and David Martin. *Regimental Strengths and Losses at Gettysburg*. Hightstown, NJ: Longstreet House, 1994.

Clark, Champ, et al. *Gettysburg: The Confederate High Tide*. Alexandria, VA: Time-Life Books, 1985.

Coco, Gregory A. *A Strange and Blighted Land: Gettysburg, the Aftermath of a Battle*. Gettysburg, PA: Thomas Publications, 1995.

Coddington, Edwin B. *The Gettysburg Campaign: A Study in Command*. New York: Scribners, 1968.

Conrad, W.P., and Ted Alexander. *When War Passed This Way*. A Greencastle Bicentennial Publication. Shippensburg, PA: Beidel Printing House, 1982.

Creighton, Margaret S. *The Colors of Courage: Gettysburg's Forgotten History: Immigrants, Women, and African-Americans in the Civil War's Defining Battle*. New York: Basic Books, 2005.

Desjardin, Thomas A. *These Honored Dead: How the Story of Gettysburg Shaped American Memory*. Cambridge, MA: Da Capo Press, 2003.

Dougherty, James. *Stone's Brigade and the Fight for McPherson's Ridge*. Conshohocken, PA: Combined Publishing, 2001.

Dowdey, Clifford. *Death of a Nation: The Story of Lee and His Men at Gettysburg*. New York: Alfred A. Knopf, 1958.

Frassanito, William A. *Gettysburg: A Journey in Time*. New York: Charles Scribner's Sons, 1975.

Gallagher, Gary W., ed. *The First Day at Gettysburg: Essays on Confederate and Union Leadership*. Kent, OH: Kent State University Press, 1992.

———. *The Second Day at Gettysburg: Essays on Confederate and Union Leadership*. Kent, OH: Kent State University Press, 1993.

———. *The Third Day at Gettysburg and Beyond*. Chapel Hill: University of North Carolina Press, 1994.

Georg, Kathleen R., and John W. Busey. *Nothing but Glory: Pickett's Division at Gettysburg*. Hightstown, NJ: Longstreet House, 1987.

Gottfried, Bradley M. *The Brigades of Gettysburg: The Union and Confederate Brigades at the Battle of Gettysburg*. Cambridge, MA: Da Capo Press, 2002.

———. *The Maps of Gettysburg: An Atlas of the Gettysburg Campaign, June 3–July 13, 1863*. New York: Savas Beatie, 2007.

Gragg, Rod. *Covered with Glory: The 26th North Carolina Infantry at the Battle of Gettysburg*. Chapel Hill: University of North Carolina Press, 2010.

Grimsley, Mark, and Brooks D. Simpson. *Gettysburg: A Battlefield Guide*. Lincoln: University of Nebraska Press, 1999.

Grunder, Charles, and Brandon H. Beck. *The Second Battle of Winchester: June 12–15, 1863*. Lynchburg, VA: H.E. Howard, 1989.

Harman, Troy D. *Lee's Real Plan at Gettysburg*. Mechanicsburg, PA: Stackpole Books, 2003.

Hassler, Warren W. *Crisis at the Crossroads*. Tuscaloosa: University of Alabama Press, 1970.

Herdegen, Lance J. *Those Damned Black Hats!: The Iron Brigade in the Gettysburg Campaign*. New York: Savas Beatie, 2010.

Hess, Earl J. *Pickett's Charge: The Last Attack at Gettysburg*. Chapel Hill: University of North Carolina Press, 2001.

Hessler, James A. *Sickles at Gettysburg: The Controversial Civil War General Who Committed Murder, Abandoned Little Round Top, and Declared Himself the Hero of Gettysburg*. New York: Savas Beatie, 2009.

Jorgensen, Jay. *Gettysburg's Bloody Wheatfield*. Shippensburg, PA: White Mane Books, 2002.

LaFantasie, Glenn W. *Twilight at Little Round Top: July 2, 1863—The Tide Turns at Gettysburg*. New York: John W. Wiley & Sons, 2005.

Leehan, Brian. *Pale Horse at Plum Run: The First Minnesota at Gettysburg*. St. Paul: Minnesota Historical Society, 2002.

Maier, Larry B. *Gateway to Gettysburg: The Second Battle of Winchester*. Shippensburg, PA: Burd Street Press, 2002.

Martin, David G. *Gettysburg, July 1*. Conshohocken, PA: Combined Books, 1996.

McPherson, James. *Hallowed Ground: A Walk at Gettysburg*. New York: Crown Publishers, 2003.

Mingus, Scott L. *Flames Beyond Gettysburg: The Confederate Expedition to the Susquehanna River, June 1863*. New York: Savas Beatie, 2011.

———. *The Louisiana Tigers in the Gettysburg Campaign: June–July 1863*. Baton Rouge: Louisiana State University Press, 2009.

Nesbitt, Mark. *Saber and Scapegoat: Jeb Stuart and the Gettysburg Controversy*. Mechanicsburg, PA: Stackpole Books, 1994.

O'Neill, Robert F., Jr. *The Cavalry Battles of Aldie, Middleburg and Upperville: June 10–27, 1863*. Lynchburg, VA: H.E. Howard, 1993.

Patterson, Gerard A. *Debris of Battle: The Wounded of Gettysburg*. Mechanicsburg, PA: Stackpole Books, 1997.

Penny, Morris, and J. Gary Laine. *Struggle for the Round Tops: Law's Alabama Brigade at the Battle of Gettysburg, July 2–3, 1863*. Shippensburg, PA: Burd Street Press, 1999.

Petruzzi, J. David, and Steve Stanley. *The Complete Gettysburg Guide: Walking and Driving Tours of the Battlefield, Town, Cemeteries, Field Hospital Sites and Other Topics of Historical Interest*. New York: Savas Beatie, 2009.

———. *The New Gettysburg Campaign Handbook*. New York: Savas Beatie, 2011.

Pfanz, Harry W. *Culp's Hill and Cemetery Hill*. Chapel Hill: University of North Carolina Press, 1993.

————. *Gettysburg: The First Day*. Chapel Hill: University of North Carolina Press, 2001.

————. *Gettysburg: The Second Day*. Chapel Hill: University of North Carolina Press, 1987.

Reardon, Carol. *Pickett's Charge in History and Memory*. Chapel Hill: University of North Carolina Press, 1997.

Rummel, George A. *Cavalry on the Roads to Gettysburg: Kilpatrick at Hanover and Hunterstown*. Shippensburg, PA: White Mane Publications, 2000.

Sauers, Richard. *Gettysburg: The Meade-Sickles Controversy*. Washington, D.C.: Brassey's Inc., 2003.

Schildt, John. *Roads to Gettysburg*. Parsons, WV: McClain Printing Company, 1978.

Sears, Stephen W. *Gettysburg*. Boston, MA: Houghton Mifflin, 2003.

Sheldon, George. *When the Smoke Cleared at Gettysburg*. Nashville, TN: Cumberland House, 2003.

Shue, Richard S. *Morning at Willoughby Run: The Opening Battle at Gettysburg: July 1, 1863*. Gettysburg, PA: Thomas Publications, 1998.

Stackpole, Edward J. *They Met at Gettysburg*. Harrisburg, PA: Stackpole Books, 1956.

Stewart, George R. *Pickett's Charge: A Microhistory of the Final Attack at Gettysburg, July 3, 1863*. Boston, MA: Houghton Mifflin, 1959.

Symonds, Craig. *American Heritage History of the Battle of Gettysburg*. New York: HarperCollins, 2001.

Tagg, Larry. *The Generals of Gettysburg: The Leaders of America's Greatest Battle*. Cambridge, MA: Da Capo Press, 2003.

Time-Life Books, ed. *Voices of the Civil War: Gettysburg*. Alexandria, VA: Time-Life, 1995.

Trudeau, Noah Andre. *Gettysburg: A Testing of Courage*. New York: HarperCollins, 2002.

Tucker, Glenn. *High Tide at Gettysburg: The Campaign in Pennsylvania*. Gettysburg, PA: Stan Clark Military Books, 1995.

Wert, Jeffry D. *Gettysburg: Day Three*. New York: Simon & Schuster, 2001.

Wheeler, Richard. *Gettysburg: Campaign of Endless Echoes*. New York: Plume, 1999.

Wills, Garry. *Lincoln at Gettysburg: The Words that Remade America*. New York: Simon & Schuster, 1992.

Wingert, Cooper H. *Almost Harrisburg: The Confederate Attempt on Pennsylvania's Capital*. Camp Hill, PA: C.H. Wingert, 2012.

Wittenberg, Eric. *The Battle of Brandy Station: North America's Largest Cavalry Battle*. Charleston, SC: The History Press, 2010.

————. *Gettysburg's Forgotten Cavalry Actions*. New York: Savas Beatie, 2012.

Wittenberg, Eric, and J. David Petruzzi. *Plenty of Blame to Go Around: Jeb Stuart's Controversial Ride to Gettysburg*. New York: Savas Beatie, 2006.

Wittenberg, Eric, et al. *One Continuous Fight: The Retreat from Gettysburg and the Pursuit of Lee's Army of Northern Virginia, July 4–14, 1863*. New York: Savas Beatie, 2008.

Woodworth, Steven E. *Beneath a Northern Sky: A Short History of the Gettysburg Campaign*. Wilmington, DE: SR Books, 2003.

Index

B

About the Author

John David Hoptak is an interpretative park ranger at both the Antietam National Battlefield and at Gettysburg National Military Park and is an instructor of American history, Civil War history and Mexican-American War history at American Military University. He is the author of several other books, including *The Battle of South Mountain* (published by The History Press in 2011), *Antietam: September 17, 1862* (2011), *Our Boys Did Nobly* (2009) and *First in Defense of the Union: The Civil War History of First Defenders* (2004), and he also hosts a Civil War–themed blog at www.48thpennsylvania.blogspot.com. He and his wife, Laura, reside near Gettysburg with their cats.

Visit us at
www.historypress.net